WELCOME!

We all see it. Our country is in chaos, but why?

Many of us have decided that we can no longer just sit here and watch. In fact, thousands of people each week are standing up to be part of the resistance. We recognize that the constant shadow of hopelessness and despair blanketing our country is the product of self-serving people in government and extremist pressure groups. We've had enough of the absurdity.

We no longer have a beneficial tension between the two dominant political parties in this country. The Democratic and Republican parties still exist but there is little difference between them at this point. The battles they stage are just that, staged! Few in power are willing to hold the others accountable for fear of severe backlash.

But here's the thing; at this moment we have never been more empowered to stand up to the self-serving ruling class and the chaos they are creating. Independent information outlets are very quickly overtaking the legacy news media in reach and impact. We now have reliable information sources that bravely speak truth to power instead of being the mouthpiece of the powerful. Built on this new foundation of reality and truth, online communities enable us to unite and elevate our voices like never before.

We now have the power to stand up and hold the ruling class accountable!

To resist the self-serving agenda of the ruling class, we have no choice but to unite around this objective and refuse to be divided.

This book is our field guide to uniting in peaceful, authentic resistance.

The aimless, joyless, self-indulgent, and those who prey on them will try to prevent you from reading this book.

Help us bring hope and insight to people near you!

Follow us on social media!

Post about the book! Gift the book!

Leave a compelling review!

DETHRONING THE RULING CLASS

REBUILDING COMMUNITY FROM THE RUBBLE OF TYRANNY

G.L. MCGARVIN

Dethroning the Ruling Class

Rebuilding Community from the Rubble of Tyranny

Copyright © 2024 by G.L. McGarvin All rights reserved.

No portion of this book may be reproduced in any form without written permission from the publisher or author, except as permitted by U.S. copyright law.

This publication is designed to provide accurate and authoritative information in regard to the subject matter covered. It is sold with the understanding that neither the author nor the publisher is engaged in rendering medical, legal or other professional services. While the publisher and author have used their best efforts in preparing this book, they make no representations or warranties with respect to the accuracy or completeness of the contents of this book and specifically disclaim any implied warranties of merchantability or fitness for a particular purpose. The advice and strategies contained herein may not be suitable for your situation. You should consult with a professional when appropriate.

Cover Images:iStockPhoto.com orders 2096554619, 2096554614. Images 1484245550, 1270067432, 598070534, 1346578615, 1127754969, 1285580163, 1485083286, 1227261223, 1141391842, 1480920713, 973285058

eBook ISBN: 979-8-9905110-9-5

Paperback ISBN: 979-8-9905110-8-8

GLMcGarvin.com

CONTENTS

Introduction vii

PART 1
THE AUTHENTIC RESISTANCE

1. Outcast, Irreverent, Joyful, Aspirational Individuals 3
2. Conservatism 2025 13
3. Come As You Are! 19
4. But I'm Not Racist, Sexist, or Homophobic? 25
5. Complying with Reality 37
6. Opportunity for All 43
7. Radically Generous 47
8. Engaged in Community 53
9. Partners in K–12 Education 67
10. Protecting Individual Rights 77
11. Holding Government Accountable 87
12. (In)Effective Use of Taxpayer Funds 99

Part 1 Recap 115

PART 2
SNAFU, RINSE, REPEAT

13. Carefully Orchestrated Chaos 119
14. Influential People Know the Game 127
15. Big Tech: Both Maestro and Tool 139
16. Censorship Incorporated 155
17. The Wealth Magnet of Public Office 175
18. Never Let a Crisis Go to Waste! 185
19. The Fed: Enabling Outrageous Spending and Unsustainable Debt 199

PART 3
INCITING CITIZEN ENGAGEMENT

20. You Are an Influencer! 215
21. Debating the…Challenged 223
22. Debating the Emotionally Invested 229

23. Debating the Financially Invested	235
24. The Kings of Astroturfing: Fake Grassroots Movements	241

PART 4
COURAGE TO SEE THE TRUTH

25. COVID Response – Epic Power Consolidation	253
26. Donald Trump Disruptor-in-Chief	277
27. The January 6 "Insurrection"	293
28. January 6 Scorched Earth Aftermath	313
29. Trump Indictments—Punishing the Resistance	329

PART 5
TOGETHER WE ARE THE SOLUTION

30. Overthrowing Absurdity With Reality	343
About the Author	351
Notes	353

INTRODUCTION

If the Democratic Party and the Republican Party have merged into some sort of uniparty, who can stand against them? If 96% of voters are aligned with one or the other, who can stand against them?

Have they really merged? Don't the Democrats represent the little guy while Republicans look out for the interests of big business? Well, they have promoted that narrative for decades. Is that no longer true? Was it ever true?

Over time, more and more of the battles between the parties have been fabricated to define and divvy up constituencies. These colorful matches, like Saturday night professional wrestling, give politicians on both sides the opportunity to build a fan base. The parties negotiated decades ago to decide which side of an issue each party takes and thus which voters and financial supporters they capture. Remember the ruling class mentioned earlier? Forget about shadowy conspiracy theories. We don't need to spend resources and credibility

INTRODUCTION

chasing ghosts. These things happen right out in the open for all to see.

Again, who can stand against them and hold them accountable? We the people can, but it will require exceptional levels of determination and focus. If we are going to take on this challenge, and millions of us have, we must unite on this singular mission and reject all attempts to divide us.

Fortunately, we are not building a resistance movement from the ground up today. There are groups that have been actively building the infrastructure of resistance for many years. While these groups disagree on some issues, they are united on this one. Many groups are active in this area but the two largest and most energized are generally identified as libertarians and conservatives.

The legacy media does their very best to diminish and dismiss these groups. According to them, libertarians are just potheads and conservatives are just Republicans in drab suits. Neither characterization is anywhere close to the truth. Both groups are vocally opposed to oppressive self-serving government of any form and of any party. Not only are conservatives decidedly not Republican, but they are very critical of the Republican Party when it fails to stand strong for accountable government. In this book we explore our common objectives mostly from a conservative perspective. However, you will not find much disagreement here, if any, with libertarians.

Despite the doom and gloom, this book will ultimately restore your hope and give you the opportunity to engage with a very effective and supportive community.

INTRODUCTION

Think about this; people don't actually decide to be conservative. They simply realize over time that many of their core beliefs seem to be consistent with the principles of natural rights of the individual and accountable government. For some that realization can trigger confusion, followed by intense investigation, followed by the calm accompanying understanding.

That sums up my experience fairly well. It has been a long journey up many rocky paths. For me, it was also a very costly journey at times. Most of us are intelligent enough to recognize the mistakes of others and take hold of a free lesson when we can. Me, I don't think I have ever learned a lesson that didn't cost me something. Tim McGraw's song, "Can't Tell Me Nothing," seemed to be my theme song at various times in my life. Maybe the same is true for you to some degree.

Through this journey I have found that there are actually benefits of having a hard head filled with far too many relentless "whys" that are not easily put to rest. I naturally developed a passion for digging beyond the surface of challenges to understand the reasons they exist. In many cases, I kept digging until I began to understand how we might address them in an effective and sustainable manner. The analytical problem-solving skills gained, along with the learned ability to effectively communicate problems and solutions, have also led me to success in the software industry.

In this book I have tried to apply those hard-won skills to my analysis of culture and politics, distilling the stifling chaos of both down to some essential truths. The vital skill in this effort has been the ability to quickly identify and filter out the staggering level of background noise. That is the fundamental

INTRODUCTION

challenge we all face in educating ourselves. The theatrics, the circus, the noise, or whatever you call it, make it extremely difficult to recognize the core issues and the why behind them. When we calm our minds and block out the interference, things start to become clear. The issues, the causes, and the solutions start to come into focus.

What does all of that have to do with the natural rights of the individual and accountable government? Keep reading. It'll come to you!

You may have grabbed this book because you are either considering the journey or are on the journey to understanding these principles. Or maybe you are preparing yourself to be a guide to others on the journey. You are in the right place.

Culture and politics seem to be in utter disarray. We as a country seem to be racing down an unsustainable path. Why are high-profile people gleefully encouraging this steady decline? Why do highly educated political leaders say things they cannot possibly believe? Why are problems getting worse even though government programs have been generously funded to solve them? Is it possible to pull up from this nosedive or is our country destined to slam to the ground in a spectacular final act of self-indulgence?

It is not too late and that is why I am writing this book. You and I have grappled with the same questions and some of them seem to be unanswerable. I assure you that they can be answered. I am writing this book as a field guide to help us navigate to many of those answers. Consensus is growing naturally in response to the chaos we are witnessing. I am writing this book to help us all quickly get past some of the struggle as we try to make sense of it all.

INTRODUCTION

We must never stop asking, "How does that make sense?" The answers are out there. You and I need to find them. You and I also need to help our fellow voyagers find them.

We don't need to convert anyone to believe in the principles of natural rights of the individual and accountable government. We just need to help them recognize the truth in their heart that they have been taught to ignore, distrust, or even despise.

That is our call to action and the entire point of this book.

Recognition is on the rise! After the turmoil the United States economy and culture have suffered in recent years, more and more people are realizing that we need to get back to the principles that once enabled this country and its people to thrive.

Search Facebook for #WalkAway and you will find a very active community of people who have walked away from the Democrat Party and the accelerating growth of government. There are many other groups of former big government advocates across social media and they are growing rapidly.

It is long past time to get back to creating opportunity and freedom for all, not just the privileged. It is clear to many of us that an out-of-control government, which encourages its subjects to be dysfunctional and dependent, or at least damaged and silent, will not result in a country or culture that we can proudly hand off to future generations.

Whether we accept it or not, we have been blessed to live in an environment where we can thrive beyond the wildest dreams of

INTRODUCTION

people in most other countries. It is our responsibility to not only protect but also improve that environment. It is our responsibility to ensure that future generations will have even greater opportunity and will be able to achieve things we could not have imagined.

In the words of Russell Kirk:

 Conservatives sense that modern people are dwarfs on the shoulders of giants, able to see farther than their ancestors only because of the great stature of those who have preceded us in time.

Please read that again. I don't think there is a more powerful reminder of who we are!

This resistance movement is growing at a rate that could not have been anticipated just a few years ago. What motivates so many to openly identify with these beliefs? There are as many reasons as there are people but if you look closely, you will see that there are some common components in their thought processes.

Some people arrive here after a careful analysis of the issues and challenges that our country faces. They study the different approaches promoted as solutions to these issues. Through this process they conclude that, in most cases, the solutions embraced by conservatives are based in logical reasoning, are designed to be long-term and sustainable, and are most likely to minimize the impact of unintended consequences.

Others begin to recognize their repressed leanings based on their instinctive reactions to what they see with their own two eyes. They find themselves muttering the same phrase every

INTRODUCTION

individual rights, accountable government, use of taxpayer funds, and many others.

The second half of the book is focused on actions we can take to encourage others to open up to these ideas and begin to recognize the damage being caused by other approaches and self-serving politicians. How can we do that? Can we adjust our communication style and even the words we use to improve our chances of being heard? Science tells us that yes, we can.

Unfortunately, we often energetically argue for our positions and against opposing positions as if we are in combat and there can be only one survivor. Too few of us are interested in actually understanding the issues well enough to persuade anyone. We only want to win the argument with a pithy comeback that leaves the other side in stunned silence.

When we take that approach, we only succeed in showing people that we are rude, vicious, and seem to be on a singularly focused mission to crush and destroy anyone foolish enough to disagree with us.

Is anyone persuaded by our angry clichéd retorts?

The point is that we must decide right now, today, if we want the cathartic release of bashing the other side or if we want to win new friends and influence people. I believe it is in the best interests of our country, now and for the long term, that we stop repelling onlookers with overly dramatic language and replace that with nontoxic thought-provoking conversations free of name-calling, talking points, clichés, memes, and conspiracy theories.

Name-calling, talking points, clichés, memes, and conspiracy theories . . . I think that accurately sums up the current state of

INTRODUCTION

dialogue on topics that are extremely important to us, our families, and the future of this country.

That is the number one takeaway from this book! We can win new friends and influence people if we want to. If we choose to. However, nothing hard is ever easy, or so the tavern philosopher told me in my youth. This will be difficult for many of us. The real work is in redefining how we prepare ourselves and how we conduct ourselves. Through that effort, together we will take a huge step forward in our knowledge, communications skills, and willingness to listen and understand.

My hope is that together, we will show the world the truth! Conservatives are the most community-minded people in the virtual room! Our approaches to our nation's challenges provide the greatest opportunity to enable everyone in the community to create the amazing life they deserve.

We win by being gracious, welcoming, cordial, genial, and affable as we assist others through their transition to embracing sustainable conservative principles.

 Your power to choose your direction of your life allows you to reinvent yourself, to change your future, and to powerfully influence the rest of creation.

STEPHEN COVEY

PART 1

THE AUTHENTIC RESISTANCE

1
OUTCAST, IRREVERENT, JOYFUL, ASPIRATIONAL INDIVIDUALS

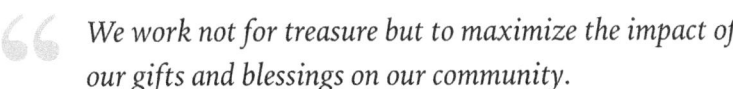 *We work not for treasure but to maximize the impact of our gifts and blessings on our community.*

This may be a startling revelation for some but the conservative community is a joyful community. We are a joyful people! Most of us don't skip through the day whistling a happy tune. Our joy is authentic and much deeper than fleeting gleefulness. It is the result of evidence-based beliefs and principles along with a very aspirational and hopeful approach to life.

Even when our circumstances are not great, our hopes and aspirations are. Even in those moments, we have an underlying confidence that our principles, self-discipline, and focused effort will enable us to achieve our best-possible outcome.

Most of us eventually learn that the person we become through this process is by far the most rewarding outcome of this journey to ourselves, our families, and our communities. The reward at the end of the rainbow is who you become, which is far more valuable than a pot of gold. You are the pot of gold!

Conservative principles are based on science. Shocking, right? It's true. Centuries of experiments and analysis on the behavior of individuals and groups have brought us conservatism. Scientists did not "invent" it. In fact, it wasn't invented at all. It was discovered and nurtured by incredibly brilliant people during the last 400 years or so.

This area of science is driven by the fundamental question:

> What is the most effective approach to encouraging individuals to become the best possible versions of themselves and, as a result, impact the world around them in unforeseeable and powerful ways?

The answer to that question is demonstrated daily in the United States and was crisply summarized as *"ordered liberty"* by historian Lee Edwards. Not chaos. Not anarchy. Not every man for himself. Not clinging to the past. Ordered liberty.

How do we achieve and maintain this ordered liberty? The answer varies depending on who you ask but always relates back to core principles. The conservative community in the United States is a very diverse group in every sense. It includes people of all religions and people who are not religious. It includes people of every race and all backgrounds, educational levels, and occupations. The community also includes people who hold a wide range of ideas on the role of government and how we as a nation can most effectively use our collective resources to the benefit of our country's inhabitants and the world.

In terms of how we prioritize social, political, and policy objectives, diversity thrives in the conservative community. You could say that conservatism in the United States is a broad spectrum of priorities that represent the evolution of a social philosophy that has been very effectively captured in and advanced by the founding documents of this country.

As implied, this spectrum of priorities includes those who actively disagree on what should be the primary focus of the community and the nation. That's OK. Rigorous and sometimes contentious debate is necessary for a people and a system to evolve.

Iron sharpens iron. Retreating to our corners to sulk for extended periods is not a tactic that promotes healthy evolution. But periodic and brief periods of sulking and isolated reflection can be productive.

This diversity is a power source that strengthens the community, which is bolstered by our numbers and in-depth understanding of our challenges. However, this diversity can also be an Achilles' heel that can be exploited to instigate and ferment division within the movement.

We must be persistently vigilant and always return to hugging it out when purveyors of division attempt to storm the gates of our community! Vigorous, respectful, and productive debate is the opposite of division. Those who are irreconcilably divided really have nothing to discuss. That is not who we are.

 Vigorous, respectful, and productive debate is the opposite of division.

The ancient proverb, "the enemy of my enemy is my friend," is somewhat pessimistic but we are living in the real world, and we are facing real enemies. We should hold tightly to this proverb, together actively navigate to common ground, recognize that low priority issues are not worth dividing over, and work to expand our friend base as much as possible.

Who is the enemy? The rich and powerful often work together to support each other as they pursue their objective to become more rich and more powerful. This includes people at the top of our society in terms of heritage, education, and opportunity.

To be clear, when we talk about the "rich and powerful", we are not referring to you or your neighbor who made a few million on crypto, AI, or other businesses. We are referring to incredibly wealthy business leaders in highly profitable industries, politicians, and government employees at the highest levels. It is essentially an informal virtual club that only the ultra-privileged are accepted into. There are no meetings. There is no initiation ceremony. There is no member list. I call them the wealthy ruling class, and they are essentially our version of monarchy.

The wealthy ruling class is a powerful and dangerous antagonist of the people, even the people who do not yet believe such a thing exists.

In what way are they dangerous? How are they hurting the country?

Those questions do not have simple or concise answers, but the answers will become clear as you read through the pages of this book.

Conservatives pose a problem for the wealthy ruling class. We believe that businesses, the government, and individuals should be held accountable for their mistakes and crimes. We believe that nobody should be allowed to operate above the law. The law should be applied equally to everyone. We believe that the government must be accountable to the people and exists for the people.

The only purpose of government is to maintain an environment where the people can thrive and achieve their full potential.

For the wealthy ruling class to achieve their objectives, they have no choice but to make government accountable to them and them alone. *We the people* take a back seat or, more accurately, are booted from the opportunity bus entirely.

 The essence of Government is power; and power, lodged as it must be in human hands, will ever be liable to abuse.

JAMES MADISON

That's where conservatives become a problem. We are not followers. We do not just go along with the crowd because it is the polite thing to do since everyone seems to agree with the direction. We are not swayed or silenced by the aggressive mobs who vocally celebrate the continuous deterioration of core values that have helped make this country and its people great for nearly three centuries.

We stand up and call out those who attempt to use government for their corrupt purposes of personal enrichment.

Knowing that the people of this country are strong, have a rich heritage of standing up for what is right, and will again stand in the face of the self-serving and the corrupt, the wealthy ruling class has no choice but to diminish us, to quench the fire in our souls, and squelch our voices. How can they possibly do that to many millions of people?

Their hope is that they can successfully degrade our past heritage, our present principles, and our future effectiveness by greatly diminishing our shared history, aspirations, purpose, and hope. If they can do that, they will render us anchorless, aimless, hopeless, and powerless to resist.

If we are unmoored like an abandoned ship adrift, untethered from our heritage, history, or a hopeful endeavor to improve our lives, we will be left with no energy or motivation to resist. The struggle to survive and find some sense of purpose will demand our full attention.

Resist what? Their sole objective is to become unaccountable by amassing enough wealth and power to ensure any resistance can be quietly extinguished before it is even noticed by the general public. Their power grows exponentially as they slowly drain our power and our ability to resist. Their power grows as *we the people* become dysfunctional, dependent, and divided.

For those who cannot be rendered dependent, they want you to be so damaged and ashamed, or so concerned with being seen as "tolerant," that you meekly hide within your labels, incapable of becoming part of the solution that leads others out of their dysfunction. If you are dependent on them, or rendered dysfunctional, or recovering but damaged, or are just too afraid to openly resist, they have you exactly where they want you.

Let's not argue about the day-to-day tactics of the ruling class. Instead let's focus on their strategy to eliminate the principles that empower us to be strong and independent. Those principles are family, faith, shared history, community, objective truth, reality, personal goals, and other aspirational, foundational ideals of our country. These ideals are contrary to their mission because they give us power by enabling us as individuals, and ultimately as a community, to become the very best versions of ourselves.

They fear that our strength may lead to their day of reckoning. Let's focus on their strategy and not become divided by their day-to-day tactics.

We know the enemy. It is not "the government." It is the people in control of our system and resources of government. The enemy of my enemy is my friend. The arguments used to separate us are less than trivial, merely dust, in light of this threat. More people are waking up to these facts every day, which means the conservative community, our friend base, is growing rapidly.

Who are our friends? Anyone and everyone of character and integrity who is outraged by the ruling class and the dramatic decline in hope and aspiration they are forcing onto our culture and communities.

So, what does this term *conservative* mean in this context? What are we trying to conserve? If we had to boil down the movement to a single defining principle it would be best summed up by John Adams, founding father and second president, who stated that we are "a nation of laws and not of men," which I interpret as:

Rule of Law: The government must follow the guidance of our founding documents, which dictate that power be decentralized, and that the policy and lawmaking process be very deliberate and measured to ensure a change is actually needed, the area affected is within the scope of the government, the change will benefit the citizens, the change will not place undue burden on others, intended outcomes can be achieved, unintended consequences are minimized, and the solution is the most cost-effective and viable approach to the problem.

Resulting laws and policies must be designed and applied fairly and equally to all.

Governing should be a deliberate and measured process. Not a continuous stream of knee-jerk reactions to the events of the day.

Look back over the actions of the government since the beginning of this century. You will see that at almost every opportunity the government created laws and policies that transferred power to government agencies and placed an unimaginable financial burden on future generations, our children and grandchildren.

Transferred power from where to government agencies? That power had to come from somewhere, right? Yes, it did, and it came from you and me. Every time their power is increased, our choices, rights, privacy, and financial opportunity are taken from us to fuel that increase in their power.

As conservatives, what are we trying to conserve? The status quo? Of course not. Change is continual and the rate of change increases daily.

Conservatives want to conserve the power of the people to hold government accountable for how we as a nation prepare for and respond to inevitable change.

We are trying to conserve deliberate and measured change to this nation of the people, by the people, for the people.

2

CONSERVATISM 2025

 The best form of government is that which is most likely to prevent the greatest sum of evil.

JAMES MONROE

Conservatism has a rich history in the United States. Most agree that the modern conservative movement in the United States was born around 1954, when William F. Buckley Jr. founded *National Review* magazine. Buckley himself was influenced by authors Whittaker Chambers, who published the book *Witness* in 1952, and Russell Kirk, who published the book *The Conservative Mind* in 1953.

If conservatism is based on the ideals of the nation's founding, doesn't it date back to 1776 or earlier? How could the modern conservative movement in the United States have been created in the 1950s? Very good question. I'm glad you asked.

The progressive movement in the United States started to take hold around 1890 with a mission to fundamentally change the nature of the nation. This is known as the Progressive Era. Progressives believed that the greater good of society could only be achieved if the government was given the authority to carefully control the nation's resources for the purpose of forcing change politically, economically, and behaviorally.

Progressives were convinced that if government controlled and managed the resources and energies of society, the roles of members, and the contributions of members, government could ensure that society progressed toward greatness.

For the progressive movement to bring about a government with the required level of power, that government would have to expand in size and scope far beyond what anyone could imagine in 1890.

The progressive movement on the surface seems to look good on paper. However, a reasonably objective person with a cursory knowledge of human nature and world history can easily see the flaws. Our ancestors lived under rulers with that level of control. They called it monarchy and tyranny.

The Progressive Era, 1890–1920, did help bring about needed reforms. However, the underlying beliefs and long-term objectives were viewed by many to be contrary to human nature and the natural rights that inspire individuals to achieve their best lives to the benefit of their families and communities.

It is in that environment of an accelerating decline into the tyranny of massive controlling government that the modern conservative movement was born.

The Constitution is not an instrument for the government to restrain the people; it is an instrument for the people to restrain the government—lest it come to dominate our lives and interests.

PATRICK HENRY

Conservatives in the United States understand that the country was founded on the principles as clearly documented in the Declaration of Independence, the Constitution, the Federalist Papers, and other instruments related to the founding. Not only do we have the general principles of conservatism from brilliant people like Chambers, Kirk, Buckley, and many others, we have the founding documents of this nation, which embody the foundation of those principles.

The conservative movement in the United States is very different from "conservative" movements in other countries. Keep that in mind as people try to conflate our movement with others past and present. They are entirely different.

Dishonest people try to represent conservatives as a loose collection of adamantly sovereign individuals who answer to no person and no government. That could not be further from the truth.

We are adamant in our belief that the connectedness of the local community is critical to the success of the individual and the nation. Success of the community is irrevocably dependent on the success of the individual members of that community.

Some of those same dishonest people attempt to associate the conservative movement with every death cult of the past 200 years, including the brutal oppression and mass genocide perpetrated by Hitler, Mao Zedong (Chairman Mao), Stalin, Lenin, Castro, Marxism, communism, socialism, and fascism.

What do all of these movements have in common? They used an existing crisis, or fabricated a crisis, to seize power by co-opting popular political sentiment of the day and promoting themselves as the only person who could save their country from a dismal future. Once in power, they quickly bestowed absolute power on themselves and used the power of the government to swiftly and viciously crush all suspected opposition.

With absolute control of all government resources and the ability to unilaterally create laws as they chose, leaders were free to construct a system where they alone would hold power for the rest of their lives. Being accountable to no one, they were able to use the power of the government to make themselves extremely wealthy.

Absolute control? Vicious? Unaccountable? Focused on using government to build personal wealth and power? These do not sound like conservative principles to me!

The historically repetitive scenario described above is exactly the opposite of conservatism and the reason conservatism is growing rapidly among the people!

The dishonest people strike again with inflammatory labels like "militia," "white nationalists," "Christian nationalists," "racists," "right-wing," "alt-right," "extremists," "fascists," and even "patriots."

The purpose of those labels is to evoke a mental image of a person who is uneducated, unhinged, and dangerous. If conservatives are seen as ignorant, dangerous, and almost less than human, there is no reason to hear their message or even allow the message to exist.

These labels also serve to frighten the uninformed into strict obedience lest they suffer the humiliation of being marked as a drooling ranting lunatic. However, those words have lost much of their sting recently after various liberal groups in the United States, with support of the Democratic Party, attempted to loot and burn much of the country in 2020. Tell me again who is unhinged and dangerous?

Their favorite degrading label to hang on conservatives is "fascist" because it is scary, and most people have no idea what the word actually means. A short definition of fascism is: oppressive, dictatorial control. Antifa (anti-fascists) certainly doesn't know the meaning of the word. If they did, they would realize that their movement is organized to oppose itself. Essentially Antifa is anti-Antifa, because Antifa uses brutal oppressive fascist tactics to attempt to crush anyone who disagrees with them.

Somehow fascism is supposed to be the opposite of socialism and therefore fascism must be the same thing as conservatism. Who is more likely to use vicious oppression to achieve their self-serving objectives? Clearly it is not conservatives.

Some try to complicate the discussion by asserting that conservatives in the United States are really just proponents of classical liberalism. It is the term "liberalism" that causes the confusion. The principles of classical liberalism bear no resemblance to the beliefs and behaviors of modern liberals in the United States.

The definition of classical liberalism reads nearly exactly word for word as the definition of libertarianism, which shares many core principles with conservatism. In fact, some conservatives have started calling themselves classical liberals in an attempt to distance themselves from recent shenanigans of the Republican Party. Conservative certainly does not equal Republican.

 The spirit of conservatism is entirely encapsulated in the words *ordered liberty*.

3

COME AS YOU ARE!

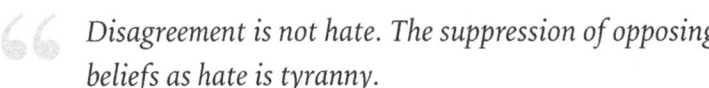 *Disagreement is not hate. The suppression of opposing beliefs as hate is tyranny.*

When I ask people if we could possibly take a different approach and have a better chance of persuading people to recognize the value of conservative views, they often respond with some form of "Screw them" or "They are not savable" or something to that effect.

Really? There is no hope? We are deadlocked as a polarized country and there is no chance of reconciliation?

Nonsense! That is simply not true. We are seeing in this country a massive revival of "do the right thing" mentality, and we are seeing more and more people stand up for self-discipline and accountability. Conservatives for many years have kept their views to themselves out of politeness, fear of being viewed as opinionated, fear of being attacked, or fear of offending someone.

Many of these people are now standing up and speaking out, often softly and politely. Some are going a bit further and becoming bravely assertive. They are not naive. They know there are risks. But they also take to heart the words of philosopher John Stuart Mill, who said in his inaugural address at the University of St. Andrews:

> *Let not anyone pacify his conscience by the delusion that he can do no harm if he takes no part and forms no opinion. Bad men need nothing more to compass their ends, than that good men should look on and do nothing.*

Think about that. The only thing required for the corrupt to succeed is for good people to make no attempt to stop them. Why do we do nothing? Again: politeness, fear of being viewed as opinionated, fear of being attacked, or fear of offending someone.

We frequently hear liberals call their followers to action with phrases like "Silence is violence" and "Silence is complicity." These are calls to viciously shout down or punish, by all available means, anyone foolish enough to voice a non-liberal opinion or fact. This tactic is very effective at squelching the opposition, especially gracious people who prefer to take a well-reasoned and informed approach to difficult discussions.

Educated and polite people rarely allow themselves to be dragged down into the gutters of pointless shouting matches. So, they remain silent. We need to learn how to match the activism of liberals, but maintain our principles, while countering their attempts to suppress dissent. They can be vicious, but we must commit to being heard.

For people who have seen enough to be outraged, the personal risk is far outweighed by the impact on the next several generations if we do not act.

The young are seeing the light as well. Young people who have been steeped in a culture that promotes self-indulgence, dysfunction, and hostility toward self-discipline and personal success, are turning away from that cult of despair in large numbers. They cannot ignore the fact that, while their lives spiral into pointless nothingness, successful people they encounter seem to be guided by a very different philosophy that leads them along a much more hopeful path to very different and enviable results.

The cult of despair is often the loudest voice in the virtual room and has a very aggressive recruiting machine. The young are drawn in by the edgy eloquent prose of the public educational system where they spend most of the first 18 years of their lives. From there, they are saturated in anything-goes messaging from the entertainment industry, and from celebrities and influencers, who vocally and viciously espouse the liberal cause of the day, driven by desperation for relevance, adoration, and clicks.

In many cases influencers eventually lead them to the artificial resistance movement. Artificial resistance movement? What else would you call a counterculture movement focused on supporting and protecting ruling class politicians and their corrupt agendas? They call themselves the resistance! Hilarity overshadowed by sadness.

Stop and look around at the influences that fill the hours and days of a young person's life. If they are not very diligent and intentional, their minds will be filled with messaging from the cult of despair nonstop, 24/7. And all of it is aggressively promoted and viciously defended by the most vocal, visible, and influential people in their world: educators and celebrities.

After being raised by the cult of despair into cynical and miserable adults, traditional news outlets provide them with community for daily care and feeding of their hopelessness.

Even after being bathed for many years, their formative years no less, in this hatred for anything resembling principles, faith, or tradition, they are recognizing the toll on them personally and on their peers. Some are standing up and openly rejecting the cult of despair. Most are keeping their views to themselves while they smile and nod, pretending to agree with their peers. They fear the mob backlash that is often unleashed on "misguided" souls who foolishly speak up against the "obvious truths" that have been reinforced in them continually their entire lives.

As they wake up and stand up, we owe these people love, support, and community. They will lose all three to some degree as they extricate themselves from the cult of despair. Their "tolerant" former brothers and sisters will be merciless.

We need to have their backs and stand with them. Suddenly they are released from the illusion of everything they had known to be real and true their entire lives. This can be freeing but it often brings intense anxiety as they struggle to find something to hold on to. We should accept them like family and provide a soft place for them to land and regroup as they work through this process of redefining their values.

We also need to stand for the truth in a sympathetic manner that encourages them and validates their fledgling feelings that there has to be a better way. That can mean a lot of different things depending on the situation. It will almost always require that we be patient, kind, tolerant, supportive, and willing to politely step away from or lose a battle here and there.

We must be willing to "not win this one" to protect the relationship with our new friend and nurture their long-term growth. We need to accept them and their baggage with open arms and a warm embrace. They will be looking in our eyes for any hint of disapproval, which they have encountered nearly daily in the past. If they detect disapproval, even mistakenly, that may only validate in their minds what they have been told for years about narrow-minded, judgmental, and even evil conservatives.

"Come as you are!" should be our heartfelt embrace.

4

BUT I'M NOT RACIST, SEXIST, OR HOMOPHOBIC?

> *Love cures people—both the ones who give it and the ones who receive it.*
>
> DR. KARL MENNINGER

Are you a conservative? If you are, think you might be, or are interested in understanding what that would look like, I am very happy for you! Being a conservative offers many benefits to you personally and results in very powerful far-reaching positive effects on your community.

Despite erroneous "conventional wisdom" to the contrary, conservatives in general are happier overall and in their family life, find their life to be more purposeful and meaningful, and are far more generous with their time and money than others. Studies supporting to these facts are explored broadly in an article in *American Affairs*,[1] a quarterly journal of public policy and political thought. While many of us intuitively recognize this in the daily interactions we observe, this article and the studies it examines provide quantified proof that our eyes and our biases are not deceiving us. The gap is real.

Not only are we living our best lives, but we are very generous and sacrificial in offering a hand to others as they pursue their best life as well.

Unfortunately, not everyone is happy to see us become successful individuals or to see the communities we are building based on conservative principles. Our detractors benefit from a divided culture dominated by self-indulgence, dysfunction, and hopelessness. The conservative movement is a threat to them. If they had one wish it would be for the conservative movement and its members to vanish.

To that end, they put tremendous effort into labeling the movement and its members with words that evoke mental images of an uneducated and ignorant, but also somehow an arrogant and powerful villain to be feared and destroyed at any cost. No means of destruction is out of bounds when battling the conservative beast! After that image is embedded in the minds of the impressionable, it is difficult, but not impossible, to fade that mental image with facts and reason.

> It's quite an image too: kind of a drooling, hapless cross between Freddy Krueger, Chucky, and Satan himself.

A wall of perceived hate has been carefully crafted by ultraliberals over many decades. The casual observer has no choice but to conclude that conservatives are hateful, greedy, evil people who think the old, sick, and poor should just die. We as conservatives, with the rhetoric we sometimes use, help perpetuate those lies. In part three of this book, we look into how we can avoid inflicting injury on ourselves and our movement with our words and behavior.

That wall of perceived hate is beginning to crumble, mainly because ultraliberals have become overconfident in the massive power that they wield and are now showing everyone who they really are. Their rhetoric of hopelessness and division, along with their recent massive overreach, is frightening to nearly all but the insiders.

These ultraliberals have very vocally aligned themselves with the vile pressure groups that use any means necessary to promote their objectives and suppress all opposition, including extortion, slander, threats of violence, actual violence, rioting, looting, arson, as well as false reports of crimes to local police, Child Protective Services, the Secret Service, the IRS, and others. As these groups are exposed as terroristic at the street level, and nothing more than wealth-building opportunities at the top level, everyone associated with them is exposed as self-serving and complicit in the fraud.

Who are these ultraliberals? Those who believe in liberal ideology primarily identify with the Democratic Party in US politics, while conservatives and others primarily identify with the Republican Party. The Democratic Party specifically caters to those who think the government should take care of everything so the people can go blissfully on their way. The Democratic Party is also a magnet for those who want to be viewed as "tolerant" above all else. The Democratic Party has also very effectively gathered up all people who believe they are oppressed. They have successfully defined new groups of oppressed people who believe the party will punish their oppressor.

> Fortunately for the country, many are waking up and realizing that the Democratic Party is that oppressor!

What do I mean by the phrase "conservatives and others"? There are groups that are closely aligned with conservative beliefs but differ on a few key points. Libertarians are the largest group in this category. In fact, you may now or in the future more closely align with libertarian ideas. If so, that's great. The foundational principles of conservatism and those of libertarianism are very closely aligned.

This wall of perceived hate created by ultraliberals is directed at all non-liberals. They broadly group all non-liberals under the banner of the Republican Party, even though many conservatives do not identify as Republican and most libertarians identify with the Libertarian Party. Republicans, conservatives, and libertarians are the enemy of liberal ideology. Liberals take broad swipes at the Republican Party, knowing that it is the most prominent symbol of all those who want to take down the cult of despair and its mission to destroy the character and ideals of our country.

Recently the ruling class and its groupies have been on an angst-filled campaign to warn the country that conservatives are the greatest threat our democracy has ever faced! Their rally cries are "Preserve our democracy!" "Guarantee our democracy for future generations!" "If the wrong person is elected…" and similar claims of imminent doom. In reality their only concern is protecting their power and conservatives represent the only real threat to their absolute control.

Their campaign of despair offers a solution to this conservative threat in the form of government policies that can make sure the people hear the "right messages" and the "right person" is elected. That thought should cost us all a little sleep tonight!

Below are a few of the mischaracterizations directed at all who oppose the liberal agenda. We need to be vigilant to dispel these slanderous statements and avoid reinforcing them with our own language and behavior:

The Taliban should be suing the GOP for trademark infringement.
—Dean Obeidallah, a frequent CNN columnist and MSNBC guest

Daily Reminder: Today's GOP is no longer a political party, it's a white nationalist, FASCIST movement that seeks to impose their EXTREME religious beliefs as the law of our land. It must be utterly defeated in order to save our Republic.
—Dean Obeidallah, a frequent CNN columnist and MSNBC guest

These folks are evil. They have allowed evil into their house with Donald Trump.
—Roland Martin, liberal internet news host

Should [Republicans] win, they will certainly attempt to end

democracy as we know it in their states. The effort will probably look like an updated version of Jim Crow.
—Ryan Cooper, MSNBC opinion columnist, three weeks before Election Day 2022.

But the extreme MAGA Republicans in Congress have chosen to go backwards—full of anger, violence, hate, and division.
—President Joe Biden

Romney wants to let the—he said in the first hundred days, he's going to let the big banks once again write their own rules, unchain Wall Street. They're going to put y'all back in chains.
—Vice President Joe Biden

And it's not surprising then they get bitter, they cling to guns or religion or antipathy toward people who aren't like them or anti-immigrant sentiment or anti-trade sentiment as a way to explain their frustrations.
—Senator Barack Obama

In contradistinction to the Republicans, Democrats don't believe kids ought to go to bed hungry at night.
—Howard Dean, the former head of the Democratic Party

I want to say a few words about what it means to be a Democrat. It's very simple: We have a conscience.
—Rep. Alan Grayson (D-FL)

…you could put half of Trump's supporters into what I call the basket of deplorables. Right? They're racist, sexist, homophobic, xenophobic, Islamophobic—you name it.

—Hillary Clinton

Conservatism is inherently anti-intellectual...Conservatism rests on the latter, primitive foundations which protected every form of barbarism for thousands of years, from tribal bigotry to patriarchy to slavery to autocracy.
Once you allow for the freedom of thought, you effectively end the tyrannical bullying that's the hallmark of any "conservative tradition."
—Benjamin Cain, Dialogue & Discourse

Last week, we went through a familiar ritual: Hand-wringing and alarm over Republican politicians denying scientific reality.
—Chris Mooney, Huffington Post

A pile of research has found that conservatives are more distrustful than liberals of scientific forms of knowledge and are prone to believe conspiracy theories about scientists.
—Jonathan Chait, New Yorker magazine

The GOP has proven to be an even "greater threat" to US democracy than Trump in 2021, experts warn.
—John Haltiwanger, Business Insider

Religion is fast growing incompatible with the emergence of a global, civil society.
—Sam Harris, "Science Must Destroy Religion," Huffington Post

It's Putinite fascism mixed with Talibanism. And it's what they hope to impose on us: unbreakable rule by far right Christian

ideologues, coal & oil polluters, heeled corporations & the super rich.
—Joy Reid, MSNBC host

Many hear statements like these and don't even question their legitimacy because the statements align with the perceptions they have developed. They have heard similar claims for years and have not challenged them in their own minds or even allowed themselves to be the least bit skeptical. I call it the "everyone knows" syndrome. Since everyone knows and we are all in agreement, there is no reason to question these statements of common knowledge.

That is the picture presented anyway.

Those of us who are conservative easily see through the lies because we research issues and inform ourselves. In the process we become aware of and work to close gaps in our knowledge, previously held misperceptions, and blind spots. We know that no person is perfect and therefore no group of people can be perfect. In our research into the challenges our country faces and our pursuit of realistic fact-based solutions, we intuitively recognize the overwhelming contrast that should be obvious to all objective observers when principled conservatism is stood up next to the cult of despair.

What role does the media play in perpetrating these lies? After all, they are just reporting the facts, right? Wrong. Without a complicit media, these lies would not be endlessly repeated and reposted. The ruling class demonstrates daily that they can say anything they want, and they will not be challenged by any "credible" news agency. Anyone foolish enough to pose uncomfortable questions on significant issues will be quickly "exposed" as dishonest or fringe.

According to a 2023 Gallup poll,[2] 39% of people in the United States have no confidence at all in mass media. In 1976 that number was 4%. Essentially 10 times as many people distrust the mass media now as compared to 1976. The media has earned every bit of that distrust.

The poll reveals that there is a sharp division between political parties. Among Democrats, 58% have a great deal or fair amount of trust in the mass media. That's down from 70% one year earlier! Only 11% of Republicans and 29% of independents trust mass media. This sharp decline in trust is likely due to their handling of the COVID debacle of 2020 and the unbalanced narrative related to the 2020 presidential election.

While 58% of Democrats trust the media, younger Democrats have far less trust in the mass media compared to older Democrats. Young Democrats probably represent the bulk of the dramatic decline from the record high of 76% in 2018, but many still trust the media and see no need to research issues on their own. After everything we have seen in the past few years, that is shocking!

Again, it is those who think the government should take care of everything so they can go blissfully on their way, living their best life knowing that the community requires no thought or effort from them. They read the headlines. They shared the memes. They voted Democrat. They shamed and harassed the noncompliant. They consider themselves to be informed, caring, and civic-minded. They have taken all required actions to fulfill the criteria for being a good liberal.

They sleep well knowing their obedience enables them to check off the good-liberal box. But are they good citizens? It boils down to a question of how self-aware we are as individuals. According to organizational psychologist Tasha Eurich, 95% of people believe that they are self-aware but only 15% of people actually are self-aware.

So, who is delusional and who is self-aware? That's a frightening question! If I believe that I am self-aware, statistically I have an 85% chance of being wrong! I think the safe bet is to believe that I am somewhat self-aware and have some knowledge of my own deficiencies but that I still have work to do. Maybe that's the right approach for most of us. Let's assume that we are not as self-aware as we think and continue to diligently do the work to be aware, informed, and sharp for the challenges ahead.

Many people seem to confuse self-awareness with a very superficial form of other-awareness. They believe that they are aware of the needs of others because they advocate, with a social media like or comment, for programs that purport to address those needs. Their occasional likes here and there on social media enable them to believe that they are enlightened and other-focused.

In reality, most are simply trying to boost their relevance and likability by just following the herd. Of course, the government should fix that problem! And that one…and that one…and the rest of the unending flood of challenges!

Their enlightened stance is that everyone should have a great day and it is the government's responsibility to make sure that happens!

Anyone who disagrees is obviously ignorant at best, evil at worst. That's how they see it. They are so confident in their moral superiority that any information to the contrary is considered an uninvited attack on their peace.

Did you catch that? You must be invited into the conversation and you will be expelled immediately for endangering their peace by uttering a word contrary to their views. Does that indicate a person is self-aware?

So, if conservatives are not racist, sexist, homophobic, science deniers, what are they? It'll come to you!

5

COMPLYING WITH REALITY

The conservative movement is growing rapidly today and there are many drivers behind that. Conservative pundits and organizations would probably like to take credit for the rapid expansion, at least in private.

No doubt many high-profile conservatives have taken significant personal risks to provide accurate news reporting, expose corruption, take legal action against that corruption, and offer a port of reason in a storm of chaos. Their presence, the information they provide, and the gathering places they have created for the conservative community are critical to the movement's ability to coalesce, organize, and synergize.

But the most impactful driver behind the current rapid expansion of the conservative movement is the aforementioned storm of chaos—that storm intentionally created and fed daily to ensure that it continues to intensify. Intentionally created by who? Why would anyone want society to be rendered inoperable under the weight of constant turmoil? How does that help anyone now or their children and grandchildren in the future?

If you are asking questions like that, you are already winning, even if you don't yet have the answers.

The simple phrase "It'll come to you" packs a lot of meaning. Actor Kenny Johnson played police officer Danny Voss in the ABC TV series *Secrets and Lies*. Voss used his knowledge of criminal behavior to help a family solve a very serious legal issue. They sometimes asked Voss questions that he knew they were not yet ready for him to answer. Maybe there were other dots they needed to discover before trying to connect those dots. Or maybe they needed to find the truth for themselves so they would believe it and own it. In those cases, he would tell them "It'll come to you."

At the time my wife and I watched the show, we had two daughters in college. They were and are awesome people but were not always interested in hearing any input from Mom and Dad. Imagine that! Kids not listening to their parents!

At that point in my life, Danny Voss spoke to me. I was captivated by the phrase for some reason. It is to me the most memorable part of the show. I realized later that the phrase helped me understand that some things cannot be taught. Sometimes people have to find the truth for themselves. As a parent, that realization was very meaningful to me. It did in fact come to me!

> Keep asking questions and doing your own research. It'll come to you!
> In the process, let's try to remember to very intentionally and graciously support others as they do the same.

More and more, the conservative movement is a collection of very different people that come together to defend and support a handful of core principles. Those core principles have helped make this the greatest country in the history of the world. Is it the greatest country in the history of the world? Maybe in the last 500 years? Although not without faults, if we settle on the narrow criteria of providing the greatest opportunity to the greatest number of people for creating a fulfilling life, this is the greatest country in the history of the world.

I strongly believe that to be true based on my own experience. If I can be enabled, or even allowed, to have this blessed life that I live every day, this must be the greatest country in the history of the world!

The point is that we in the conservative movement are often very different from each other and often do not agree on some pretty important and sensitive issues. Some of those issues are quite divisive. Maybe even irreconcilable.

But we have put those issues aside. We may debate them in other communities, but we refuse to be divided by our differences when the concerns and objectives we have in common are far more powerful and will impact many future generations, either positively or negatively.

The bigger picture is far too important. We will no longer allow profiteers and hustlers to seduce us into wasting our energies and resources on no-win disputes over personal views. Political operators continually throw blood in the virtual water in gleeful anticipation of a feeding frenzy. The battle achieves nothing but results in all participants being consumed or rendered inoperable, normally due to self-inflicted injury.

Think about the permanent loss of opportunity that you suffer if your credibility is consumed or rendered inoperable. How could that happen? Normally this is the result of a senseless self-inflicted injury incurred while disputing some point of lesser value in light of the bigger picture. Let's not allow that to happen!

Let's find and build on common ground. Some things, many things, are not worth fighting over. Some things that are worth fighting for should be deferred so we can focus on common ground. Let's stop taking ourselves out of the fight by making stupid comments while arguing about things that are way down the list of most important topics, or not on the list at all.

So, what are our common concerns and objectives?

I think Russell Kirk said it best in his essay *"Ten Conservative Principles"*:[1]

> *The attitude we call conservatism is sustained by a body of sentiments, rather than by a system of ideological dogmata. It is almost true that a conservative may be defined as a person who thinks himself such. The conservative movement or body of opinion can accommodate a considerable diversity of views on a good many subjects, there being no Test Act or Thirty-Nine Articles of the conservative creed.*
>
> *In essence, the conservative person is simply one who finds the permanent things more pleasing than Chaos and Old Night. (Yet conservatives know, with Burke, that healthy "change is the means of our preservation.") A people's historic continuity of experience, says the conservative,*

offers a guide to policy far better than the abstract designs of coffee-house philosophers.

Russell Kirk's 1953 book, *The Conservative Mind*, has been a very influential guide within the conservative movement. The phrase "Chaos and Old Night" in the quote above is likely a nod to the chasm between heaven and hell in *Paradise Lost*, the seventeenth-century epic poem written by John Milton. The "Burke" he mentions is Edmund Burke, an eighteenth-century statesman, economist, and philosopher, who Russell Kirk studied.

The Kirk Center is also the home of the Edmund Burke Society of America, which works to ensure his thoughts continue to be the subject of vigorous discussion and debate.

Research the people and writings mentioned above and throughout this book. Not now! You're busy right now. Highlight items to research later.

In familiar terms of the current time, the following chapters highlight the conservative characteristics where the majority of us can find common ground.

6

OPPORTUNITY FOR ALL

> *The capacity for hope is the most significant fact of life. It provides human beings with a sense of destination and the energy to get started.*
>
> NORMAN COUSINS

We do recognize, as Russell Kirk said, that we are dwarfs on the shoulders of giants. We feel a great responsibility to elevate and prepare our shoulders for the spectacular launch of the generations that follow.

We are all incredibly blessed to live in this time of abundant resources and opportunity handed down to us by those who came before us. We believe that everyone should have the opportunity to create the life that they desire. That obviously means different things to different people.

Some are fighting daily battles to break generational cycles that have held their families in poverty for decades. They want more than anything the opportunity to develop skills needed to launch a career and become a highly valued and well-compensated employee. Those skills might be learned on the job, through technical school, college courses, or other methods. They are making the commitment and putting in the time and effort required to make that happen. They are doing everything they can to become indispensable and reap the long-term rewards for their families.

Others are blessed to be born into families that provide broad shoulders for them to stand on as they set off on their journey to become who they will be. Many people so blessed will achieve their full potential in every way and be very generous with their time and resources. They can provide the hand up that others desperately need to escape their very difficult conditions.

How is opportunity made available to more people every year in the United States? Or maybe the question should be, is opportunity made available to more people every year in the United States? The answer to that question is a solid *yes*! Let's discuss what that looks like.

In the United States more than 3.5 million students per year have graduated from high school in recent years. About 200,000 more students leave high school without a diploma every year. This dropout rate of approximately 6% in recent years is a dramatic improvement over the 15% dropout rate we saw in the seventies. Progress!

In 2020, about 43% of high school graduates immediately enrolled in four-year institutions and another 20% immediately enrolled in two-year institutions.[1] That's a total of 63%! Amazing!

In recent years more than 16 million students attended college per semester, with over 4 million of those students attending two-year colleges. Another 4 million attended technical schools to gain valuable skills from auto mechanics to radiology and just about everything in between.[2]

Companies in the United States provide millions of hours of training per year to their employees. In fact, the e-learning industry that provides much of that training has grown 900% since the year 2000.[3]

Massive Open Online Courses (MOOCs) have exploded in terms of the millions of hours of training offered and consumed, much of it at no cost or very low cost. MOOCs offer subject-focused plans and degree programs from accounting to zoology, and everything in between. Harvard, Stanford, Oxford, and many other highly regarded universities offer MOOC-based degree programs.

We clearly aspire to do more and be more! As the individual digs in to increase their potential and opportunity, their families and communities reap the rewards. The resulting technical skills, problem-solving skills, self-awareness, leadership, and generosity provide a huge boost to the common good!

What about those who were born with barriers or born into situations that limit their ability to achieve the same results? It is true that many people face challenges that are no fault of their own. I believe that the same principles hold for them as well.

With the resources and services available in the United States, most have the opportunity to reach their full potential. However, it is often difficult for some to leverage those resources due to their location or mobility issues. Their families may also be unaware of the resources or be unable to assist in accessing them. That's where we, the community, have an opportunity to assist generously. Later chapters on radical generosity and community engagement go into detail on how we as conservatives can step up to help people overcome their circumstances.

Blessed far beyond what I deserve with opportunity, struggle, failure, grace, and forgiveness, my only reasonable response is to leverage those blessings to help spread hope to generations that are desperate for it.

> "Opportunity for all" is the foundation upon which the remaining characteristics are built.

7

RADICALLY GENEROUS

> The essence of conservatism is the individual. The rights of the individual are indispensable to the responsibilities of the individual.

Many of us recognize how blessed we are and are very generous in sharing those blessings with others in need. People in the United States donated $484.85 billion to charity in 2021. This reflects a 4% increase from 2020. This giving is directed to religious organizations (27%), education (14%), human services (13%), grant-making foundations (13%), and public-society benefits (11%).

Despite uncertainty about further spread of COVID, 86% of affluent households maintained or increased their giving during the pandemic.[1]

We are just as generous with our time. An estimated 30% of US adults, 77.9 million, volunteered in 2019, contributing an estimated 5.8 billion hours, valued at approximately $147 billion.[2]

As active members of our community, and very blessed members in many cases, we are fully engaged in supporting people in need and initiatives that are beneficial to our community. If we are ever tempted to say, "Someone ought to do something," we look in the mirror and see that "someone" looking back at us. We spend less time demanding that something be done and more time actually doing something to help solve the problem.

This chapter on generosity follows the topic of opportunity for all because there is a necessary and powerful feedback loop between the two. Those who have achieved generously support those still trying to achieve. The cycle continues as long as the economy continues to grow and continues to provide the opportunities that we are preparing ourselves to take on.[3]

My Rule of 70 states:

> If everyone achieves 70% of their potential, no one will go without the things they need.

OK, I made up the 70% figure. But it illustrates the concept and is probably fairly close. Think about it. Think of 70% as the average target for individual achievement. Some will achieve more, and some will achieve less than 70% of their potential. If the vast majority are within 15% of that target in either direction, I believe that nearly everyone will have more than they need and will feel very blessed.

A very small percentage of people who have achieved 70% of their potential, and often much more, will still not be able to support themselves or care for themselves. To them this can be a demoralizing and dehumanizing struggle. Their drive for dignity motivates them to fight hard and achieve far more than others thought possible. We should always celebrate them and their achievements. They have worked harder and achieved more of their potential than most of us. Fortunately, if enough of us hit the 70% mark, we will have the resources needed to generously assist those in need.

If the rest of us average 70%, that's OK. We will be able to support ourselves, our families, and our communities. It also leaves plenty of room for me-time, missteps, missed opportunities, and learning experiences. It also allows for the occasional failure that may come when you push yourself to new levels that you're pretty sure are just beyond, or maybe way beyond, your current abilities. That's OK. How else will you learn what you are capable of?

Nobody ever achieved their potential by having it handed to them. Quite the contrary. Potential cannot even be seen on the distant horizon without a prolonged and sometimes risk-unaware overconfident push to develop and reveal the person you suspect may be hiding behind your fears and perceived limitations.

Strength does not come from reading about climbing that mountain. It comes from realizing you are about halfway up the mountain and you're pretty sure you're gonna die! It's a proverbial mountain, of course, and you're gonna make it! You are in way over your head, but you did the work before you started climbing and you're gonna do the work along the way to make sure you safely reach the top, with minimal scrapes and bruises.

Everyone around you will benefit from your example and generosity.

Throughout this book I use the terms *common good* and *community* quite a bit. If someone were to lightly scan the text, they could see these terms again and again without understanding the context. They might jump to the conclusion that I am quoting communist philosophy!

Let's be clear. It is undeniable that the community benefits when individual members are successful. A vital and natural feedback loop is created where success of many enables success of many more. That is how the community establishes common good. Marxists, communists, and socialists use the term very differently. They believe the individual must be subordinate to the common good and the individual must serve the common good as directed. The exact opposite of the conservative view of the common good.

You did not start life asking how you could become a valuable asset to your community. None of us did. You started out just trying to understand yourself, the world around you, and where you fit in that bizarre world. As you mature into an effective human being, you seize opportunities to build a good life for yourself. During that process you focus on yourself, your needs, your next steps, and what you hoped to achieve. Throughout this process, existing systems and resources provide the materials and tools for building your life.

Over time as you mature into a functional adult, you start to see new opportunities. You begin to recognize that the skills and resources you have accumulated enable you to contribute to your community in very meaningful ways. You begin to feel the tug of individual responsibilities.

Your individual rights enable you to use your time and resources to become the best possible version of yourself. You are empowered to achieve a level of success that is beneficial to you and everyone around you. Individual rights are the cornerstone of individual responsibilities. Effective and aspirational individuals who exercise their rights and embrace their responsibilities are the one vital ingredient of a thriving community.

In a flourishing community, each generation harnesses their individual rights and responsibilities to build the systems and resources needed by the next generation. The launchpad created for the next generation enables them to become the best possible version of themselves.As long as rights, responsibilities, and resources can be secured by each generation, the cycle continues.

The cycle begins to break down when people no longer have dominion over their time, money, choices, and voices. In that scenario aspirations are crushed and the passion to become more is replaced with the safety of conformity and complacency. Each successive generation descends further and further towards merely surviving. Take a minute and think about recent events that indicate we are slowly losing power over our time, money, choices, and voices.

When the rights of the individual begin to decline, the community suffers immediately, and each successive generation suffers more than the previous. The ability to fulfill the natural longing for self-actualization continually decays from generation to generation.

8

ENGAGED IN COMMUNITY

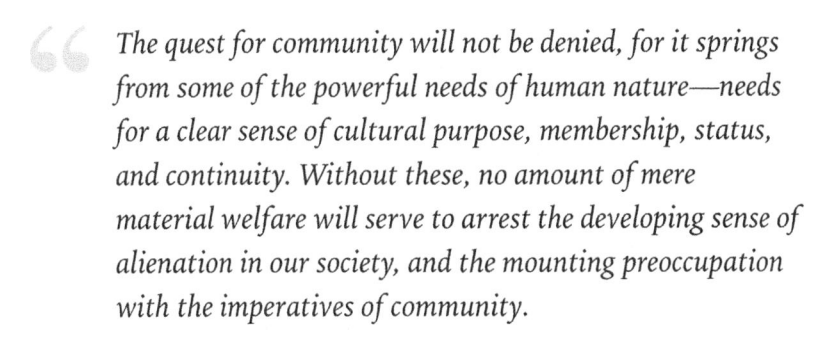

> *The quest for community will not be denied, for it springs from some of the powerful needs of human nature—needs for a clear sense of cultural purpose, membership, status, and continuity. Without these, no amount of mere material welfare will serve to arrest the developing sense of alienation in our society, and the mounting preoccupation with the imperatives of community.*
>
> ROBERT NISBET

The local community has always provided the incubator, spark, and fuel for positive sustainable progress in this country. The local community is where individuals find the support, experience, inspiration, and opportunity to set out on courageous journeys.

Powered by community-fostered aspirations to do more, and be more, individuals find the place they add value, and achieve success in that place. Through this process they become who they will be. They band together with others and achieve more as a group than they could individually. Their success, their talent, their leadership, and their resources provide the incubator, spark, and fuel for the next generation.

Read the quote from Robert Nisbet at the top of the chapter again. Unpack it. Absorb it. It has meaning far deeper than first appears.

Conservatives believe that the needs of people can be met best through local initiatives instead of distant government bureaucrats that are thousands of miles and generations of experience away from the challenges. Some challenges must be met by the local community. Others can be met at the state level. Issues of national importance can be dealt with at the federal level.

There is a business leadership principle that states: The effectiveness of the solution declines as the distance increases between the problem and the solution creator.

> In other words, the people on the ground closest to the problem are in the best position to create a solution to the problem.

The mayor of your town is probably not planning to negotiate global oil supply concerns with OPEC or try to bring an end to Russian incursions into sovereign nations. The governor of your state will not be wading into those waters either.

There are an enormous number of issues that are tended to by state and local government. Most are related to economic development, safety and security of residents, and protecting civil and property rights of residents. I have generalized the massive responsibilities of state and local government to a few very broad categories, but I am not trying to oversimplify their role in our communities. Think of anything they do and, one way or another, it probably aligns with these categories.

It is important to recognize that, before the Declaration of Independence was penned, no government had ever stated that it derived its legitimacy, its powers, based on *"the consent of the governed."*

Think about that for a minute. The US government was the first in history to submit that they were appointed by, and therefore accountable to, the will of the people. All other governments in history appointed themselves through the exercise of force. The kings and rulers declared themselves to be accountable only to themselves, and in some cases the god who had granted them the divine right to sit on the throne.

The first in history!

The preamble to the Constitution of the United States provides the following:

> *We the people of the United States, in Order to form a more perfect Union, establish justice, insure domestic Tranquility, provide for the common defense, promote the general Welfare, and secure the Blessings of Liberty to ourselves and our Posterity, do ordain and establish this Constitution for the United States of America.*

Additional details are provided in Article I of the Constitution of the United States.[1] It is a very quick and enlightening read. Grab a copy when you get a chance.

So, what then are the responsibilities of this new government of, by, and for the people?

The Constitution places a limited number of concerns within the care of the federal government. This limited list is referred to as the enumerated powers of government. They include powers specifically called out as delegated to the federal government (Article I, Sections 8 and 9) and specific areas where the Constitution prevents state governments from acting (Article I, Section 10).

All other powers are delegated to the states and protected by the Constitution from federal meddling.

However, if conflict arises between the various governing entities, the federal government is granted an automatic win, at least initially, by the supremacy clause of the Constitution.

At a high-level the federal government is empowered to:

- Provide for common defense of the United States
- Protect the general welfare of the United States
- Regulate commerce with foreign nations and among the states and with the Native tribes
- Establish uniform rule of naturalization
- Establish uniform bankruptcy laws
- Coin money, regulate the value thereof and of foreign currency
- Punish the counterfeiting of US money
- Establish post offices and post roads
- Promote the progress of science and useful arts through patent and copyright protection
- Constitute tribunals inferior to the Supreme Court
- Fight piracy on the high seas

- Declare and execute war

Obviously in 1787 they could not have foreseen the complexities of life and governing decades or centuries into the future. Even then they realized that the lines between federal powers and state powers would be impossible to define in advance of the exercise of actually governing. The Supreme Court was given the responsibility to resolve those disagreements as they came to light.

So, what does any of that have to do with community? Everything! When distant bureaucrats create laws that limit the options available to the local community for meeting their local needs, the community becomes weakened.

> The problems that exist in our communities can best be solved by those closest to the problem, not nameless, faceless bureaucrats thousands of miles away.

When the members of the local community band together to help members in need, the community is strengthened in very powerful and long-lasting ways. Members are motivated to bring their skills and resources to the mission. Members work together to leverage the strengths of each to accomplish more as a group than any one person could. The bonds created through this type of comradery are often lifelong.

When governments step in and prevent this type of community-based problem-solving or replace it with solutions created by people far too distant from the problem, the community is damaged. The bureaucrat's distance and detachment are reflected in the solution they force upon us and in its long-term unintended consequences. The strength of the community is drained slowly over time through this repetitive cycle of "federal assistance."

As the federal government takes more control of local concerns, the traditional community-based institutions of civil society suffer and decline. Churches, Little League, volunteer organizations, and other face-to-face social networks are diminished or vanish entirely. These foundational components of community provide members the opportunity to develop and fulfill the most rewarding aspects of who they are as spouses, parents, children, friends, and leaders.

The support of a strong community enables its members to become the best versions of themselves, and then, as contributing members, to support other members in their growth journey. Think of it as a stable and reliable social infrastructure that empowers its members to thrive.

How strong are our communities today? Many recent studies and reports go into detail on the overall decline in mental health in the United States. Loneliness, disconnectedness, depression, anxiety, thoughts of suicide, and actual suicide attempts have increased nearly every year in recent decades. Teenagers and young adults are suffering the most.

The COVID pandemic, along with the hysteria and extended lockdowns, caused a dramatic decline in mental health in a very short period, but the downward trend had been present for decades. According to the CDC, 37% of students at public and private high schools reported that their mental health was not good most or all of the time during the pandemic.[2] That is an enormous number!

Clearly, the deterioration of family and community has contributed to declines in health and effectiveness of members, especially the most vulnerable.

The Joint Economic Committee of the US Congress initiated an effort in 2017 to study the strength of communities throughout the United States. The initiative is known as the Social Capital Project.[3] Their research confirms what many are witnessing before their very eyes. Communities in the United States are growing weaker.

What is social capital? In Robert Putnam's article, "The Prosperous Community" (1993), he defines social capital:

> *features of social organization, such as networks, norms, and trust, that facilitate coordination and cooperation for mutual benefit*

Robert Putnam further explored the idea of social capital in his bestselling book *Bowling Alone,* in which he defines social capital similarly as:

> *connections among individuals—social networks and the norms of reciprocity and trustworthiness that arise from them*

The Social Capital Project uses the term *associational life* to refer to:

> *the web of social relationships through which we pursue joint endeavors—namely, our families, our communities, our workplaces, and our religious congregations. These institutions are critical to forming our character and capacities, providing us with meaning and purpose, and for addressing the many challenges we face.*

Pause for a moment and read again the words of Robert Putnam and then the definition of associational life. Take some time to dissect them and internalize the depth of meaning woven into those statements.

The Social Capital Project investigates the evolving nature, quality, and importance of our associational life. Their goal is to create a better understanding of why the health of our associational life feels so compromised. Some of their findings are outlined below.

Families in the United States look very different than they did a few decades ago. Men and women are having fewer children and more of those children are born to people who are not married. A majority of children in the United States now live with just one parent at some point. The number of children living with one or neither parent has increased dramatically, from 12% in 1970 to 31% in 2016. During this time frame, births to single mothers increased from 11% to 40%.

Robert Putnam refers to religious communities as "the single most important repository of social capital in America." Unfortunately, people are spending less time in religious communities. Church attendance has dropped sharply since the 1970s. In the early 1970s, 98% of adults had been raised in a religion, and just 5% reported no religious preference.

Today, however, the share of adults who report having been raised in a religion is down to 91%, and adults who report no religious preference is up to 22%. That's roughly 30 million adults who were not raised in a religious home and 73 million adults who report no religious preference.

The sharp drop in church attendance corresponds to a sharp decline in connectedness in our communities. This is devastating to the quality of life of their members.

The Social Capital Project found that those with financial means are able to gather in wealthy neighborhoods, where there is no common heritage to bind them. People are mobile and tend to gravitate to areas based on the amenities found there, leaving behind the neighborhoods they grew up in and the people with shared heritage. As a result, for many in the United States, they live among their neighbors but do not necessarily live "with their neighbors." These people are impacted very significantly by isolation from local institutions that give meaning and purpose to the human soul.

What is the root cause of the decline of community strength in the United States?

The Social Capital Project research indicates that much of the blame for the decline of communities lies at the feet of government, which has encroached into areas of community life that had been left to the vital institutions of civil society. During this time when local communities have been in decline, the reach and power of the federal government has been growing at a rate that is both apparent and alarming.

The trends in government and civil society are related. They have a correlated reinforcing effect on each other. When government grows, civil society contracts. When the muscles of government grow, the muscles of community-based organizations atrophy. Inevitably, as support services provided by the community decline due to atrophy, the government attempts to fill the resulting services void. The repetitive cycle continues based on this correlated reinforcing effect.

An American Enterprise Institute survey found that one-third of Americans personally know someone who has not gotten married because they would no longer qualify for government assistance payments. That is startling! A significant number of people are forgoing the most important and personally enriching human relationship a person can have because it would cost them their relationship with a faceless government! That is incredibly sad.

Clearly government assistance programs are encouraging people to make decisions that are not in their best interest long-term. They discourage marriage, career planning, upward mobility, and the personal fulfillment that those essential elements of life bring.

Government programs have created a situation where people agree to be held captive in their isolation and despair.

Government programs compete with civic organizations that provide social services. This forces many civic organizations out of areas of their missions that are vital to those they serve, creating a separation between those who served and those in need whom they served. The government essentially robs these civic organizations, and to some extent their members, of purpose. The groups wither, leaving a void in the server, the served, and the gathering places, thus weakening the community further. People are robbed of a sense of purpose! If people have no purpose, what is left for them?

And the cycle repeats. "The government expands again, fueled by the dead timber of a devastated civil society," as Senator Mike Lee vividly states.

We as individuals generally do not yet seem to recognize the deep trauma being inflicted on society by the rapid loss of vital networks, norms, and trust that facilitate coordination and cooperation for mutual benefit. We don't yet acknowledge the damage caused by the loss of natural and necessary connections among individuals—social networks and the norms of reciprocity and trustworthiness that arise from them.

It is a slow drain devastating community-based institutions of civil society, and the entire community. We haven't noticed because we live in isolation. When we do decide we are ready to reengage with our community, we will likely be shocked at what we find.

In his presentation to the American Enterprise Institute on localism and social capital, Senator Mike Lee illustrates the impact on our country of community contraction correlated to the government solutions. He makes a very compelling argument. You can find it on American Enterprise Institute website or on YouTube.[4]

Robert Nesbitt wrote:

> *Mutilate the roots of society and tradition, and the result must inevitably be the isolation of a generation from its heritage, the isolation of individuals from their fellow men, and the creation of the sprawling, faceless masses.*

We are clearly seeing the isolation of a generation from its heritage as Mr. Nesbitt warned. So, where does that leave the individual? The entire generation or individuals? What does he mean by "sprawling, faceless masses"? Mass movements like political parties and protest movements?

These faceless mass movements can sometimes provide benefits similar to those offered by actual location-based communities; things like perceived identity, a sense of purpose, and a sense of belonging. However, attending marches, signing petitions, and posting vigorously on social media do not provide anyone with the most valuable benefits of community. Those benefits can only be achieved through the process of working with others on the basis of iron-sharpens-iron, face-to-face, digging the ditches together.

I think Robert Putnam sums it up:

> *From the point of view of social connectedness, the Environmental Defense Fund and a bowling league are just not in the same category.*

It should be no surprise that mental health professionals report the United States is experiencing an epidemic of loneliness. Surgeon General Dr. Vivek Murthy sounds the alarm by stating, *"Our epidemic of loneliness and isolation has been an underappreciated public health crisis that has harmed individual and societal health."*[5]

You may have seen on social media the loneliness remedies posted that encourage us to chat with someone in line at the store. It's a nice sentiment but the challenges go much deeper and the solutions will be much more fundamental. Building community by building an actual community together will be a key part of the solution.

In the words of Mike Pence:

"The time has come for conservatives to retake the helm of this movement and renew our commitment to fiscal discipline and to what we know to be true about the nature of government:

- *Conservatives know that government that governs least governs best.*
- *Conservatives know that as government expands, freedom contracts.*
- *Conservatives know that government should never do for a man what he can and should do for himself."*[6]

In the words of Ronald Reagan: *"Millions of individuals making their own decisions in the marketplace will always allocate resources better than any centralized government planning process."*

In his 1955 column announcing the *National Review's* mission statement, William F. Buckley, Jr. listed several defining conservative doctrines. Among them: *"It is the job of centralized government (in peacetime) to protect its citizens' lives, liberty and property. All other activities of government tend to diminish freedom and hamper progress. The growth of government (the dominant social feature of this century) must be fought relentlessly. In this great social conflict of the era, we are, without reservations, on the libertarian side."*[7]

We must bring back to the local level the responsibility for deciding the identity of our local community and the task of implementing that vision together, investing time, energy, and resources with our neighbors.

> *About a third of my cases are suffering from no clinically definable neurosis, but from the senselessness and emptiness of their lives. This can be defined as the general neurosis of our times.*
>
> CARL JUNG

Engagement in a mission-focused local community is often the cure. We can start to rebuild the cultural purpose of community by working together to build an actual community.

9

PARTNERS IN K–12 EDUCATION

> *You will be hollow. We shall squeeze you empty, and then we shall fill you with ourselves.*
>
> GEORGE ORWELL, *1984*

Conservatives believe that the schools their children attend should be primarily academically focused, with a balanced approach to extracurricular activities like sports and clubs. The focus should be on enabling our children to eventually compete in the global economy. Other activities are important to balanced child development but should not be allowed to take the focus away from the primary objective.

We eagerly partner with the school system in that mission. Our first responsibility as parents is to make sure our children are prepared, polite, and well-behaved. Our next responsibility is to make sure our children do the work that is expected of them to the best of their ability. Getting the work done is not enough. It must be done as well as they are capable.

As partners in our children's education, we maintain a calm and subtle alertness for any issues that may be developing, whether academic or behavioral. We work with teachers and school administrators in a constructive and polite manner toward the common goal.

We live in a very diverse country consisting of people from many different national origins and religions. We believe that K–12 education should avoid singling out any student or dividing students based on their differences in terms of heritage or religion.

We believe that we are one nation. Together we are brothers and sisters working together to continually improve our community. There is no room for division in our mission. Division provides no benefit to the community. Who does benefit from division? We need to understand that so that we can recognize their attempts to divide and protect our communities by intelligently exposing and addressing those attempts. Who benefits from divisiveness? It'll come to you!

Many believe that we are one nation under God. Many believe that we are one nation under a different God or a different concept of the same God. Many believe that we are one nation and there is no God.

That is all fine. We can discuss religion anywhere and anytime, but we must not let agents of chaos divide us on that basis. You may think my religion is silly. You may even think it is heretical or evil. That's fine. It is my religion. I guarantee you that I am woefully ignorant of your religion. I apologize for that, but I have been hyper-focused for many years on overcoming my own challenges, and someday becoming a useful member of my community. That often-difficult work has left me with little time to explore what exists on other horizons, including other religions.

To be honest, I'm one of those Americans who has little knowledge of other cultures. I have not done an in-depth study of other countries, religions, languages, or cultures. However, that does not mean that I am unaware of other cultures or disrespectful toward them. I do well to have a reasonable understanding of my own country! When I travel to other countries for business, I try to research their culture before I arrive and take in as much history and context as possible while there.

In the software industry I work with people in many different countries weekly. These aspects of my career have helped me become more aware of other cultures. I still would not claim to have an in-depth understanding of those countries.

Sometimes we can start to believe that we are educated about other cultures based on what we have seen in movies, TV, and news media. That's a little frightening. Would you rather be uninformed or misinformed? I try to wrap such information in a heavy layer of skepticism until I have done my own research.

So, what steps can we take to reduce division among such a diverse people? It's obvious, right? Let's say it out loud here just for the sake of conversation. We can start by showing respect and being intentionally welcoming to others who initially seem different. We can also be especially understanding when others do or say things that are contrary to our customs or beliefs. We can avoid the appearance of attempting to force our beliefs, customs, and traditions on others. We can be intentional about showing respect and being welcoming. Did I already say that?

This is not new to any of us. Most of us can probably think back on missed opportunities but we do this every day.

If we really want them to know that we are humans and view them as a vital part of our community, we can show an interest in who they are, their beliefs, customs, and traditions. That can be tricky because some cultures are very private about such things. We need to take care not to make anyone feel uncomfortable with our curiosity.

In light of this diversity, how should the topic of prayer in school be handled?

As members of the conservative movement, we may need to separate or compartmentalize the various aspects of who we are as individuals. I think each person has to ask themselves if they want to be part of a world-changing big tent conservative awakening or if they only want to hang out with people who look, behave, and think just like them.

Me? I'm a "big tent, let's change the world together" conservative. The mission is too critical, and the window is closing too quickly to be anything else. That does not mean that I am stepping away from my religion or putting it aside. On the contrary! I am actually following the tenets of my religion. I don't think public schools in the United States should force students to repeat prayers or statements of faith that may not be consistent with the student's own religion. Private schools built on shared religion should have the right to observe practices and ceremonies consistent with that religion.

Let's discuss some of the sensitive topics covered in school and how they are presented. As partners in the education of our children, we attempt to be aware of the information that is given to our children at school. This can be difficult and time-consuming. It takes more effort and persistence than ever before but we know it must be done.

Schools are being infiltrated by "generous" organizations that provide educational material that promote their messages and agendas. We have to be on the lookout for these disingenuous organizations and the harmful information they try to implant in the minds of our children. In this area, the following issues have been hot topics recently:

Critical Race Theory (CRT):

Every parent should do their own research on this topic, be able to recognize CRT in all its forms, and make their own decisions. The indisputable outcome of promoting this ideology is division. Critical race theory promotes the fallacy that everyone in the United States is either oppressor or oppressed, depending on their race, gender, or sexual orientation. Children in school are taught by critical race theory that their role as oppressor or oppressed is predetermined at birth.

According to its promoters, critical race theory is the only perspective that enables us to view the world accurately. The social construct of race was created by and is still enforced by the powerful (white men) and predetermines each person's opportunity in life and role in community.

It is not enough to agree that racism should be eliminated. You must agree with all aspects of critical race theory, or you are labeled racist and part of the problem.

Critical race theory is taught in public schools, universities, in the workplace, in the military, and many government agencies. This prevents any effective discussion of racism, encourages victimhood, and divides those who were once so close to being united. The divisions created also keep us distracted from other vitally important issues that affect all students.

The 1619 Project:

For decades, public universities have taught students that the United States is an irreparably racist nation that must be reset or rebooted to root out that evil. The 1619 Project now brings those teachings to tens of thousands of middle school and high school students in all 50 states.

The unmistakable message is that you must hold in contempt everything in this nation's past and present, from its founders and founding documents to the economic engine that made it what it is today. It teaches that the only reasonable response for those now enlightened with the truth is to fight to destroy the oppressor, defined as anyone with anything, and promote the oppressed to power.

The 1619 Project is closely related to CRT and has many failures including: (1) it is factually inaccurate in many areas, (2) it prevents any effective discussion of racism, (3) it encourages victimhood, and (4) it divides those who were once so close to being united. The divisions created also keep us distracted from other vitally important issues that affect all students. Sound familiar?

Sex Education:

Some school districts have begun to present sexual topics to children in the first or second grade, sometimes even kindergarten (Chicago Public Schools). Most parents believe that a child under nine or ten years old should not in any way be encouraged to start thinking about sex. However, many parents feel they are forced to discuss the topic with their children at a young age to present the loving and relational aspects of sex before they are taught in school about sex from a self-indulgent perspective.

In some cases, schools use material that encourages children to start experimenting with sexual activity of nearly every imaginable variety and to start questioning their sexual identity. As a parent you have rights regarding the sex education curriculum your child is exposed to. Ask your school to provide you with the timing and content of their sex education program. Submit a request in writing to the superintendent of your child's school.

There are many resources available to parents who want to make sure their children are taught about sex with an emphasis on loving and committed relationships. You have the right to opt your child out from school-sponsored sex education and use resources available to provide a healthy education to your child.

Transgenderism has become an epidemic social contagion in the last few years. Public schools have been a conduit for its rapid spread by embracing and encouraging it. Our children are increasingly disconnected and vulnerable largely due to the pervasive identity crisis nurtured by social media and public schools. Many are searching for solutions to difficult personal challenges and need engaged adults and professionals to help them work through the issues. However, the culture and some schools often prevent accurate diagnosis by enthusiastically promoting gender dysphoria as the probable cause of the child's struggles.

A child struggling to fit in is more likely to accept the identity thrust upon them by their peers and the culture. Gender dysphoria is an actual condition recognized by mental health professionals. However, before it swept through our schools as the latest way for kids to avoid other less trendy labels, authentic cases were extremely rare.

If your young child's school exposes children to the topic of transgenderism in any way, directly or indirectly, you have the right to unite with other concerned parents and possibly take legal action against the school system and its board. Explicit books, drag shows, and other displays exposing children to sexual material should be considered adult content that is not appropriate for children.

Common Core:

The Common Core State Standard has been controversial from the beginning for a variety of reasons. Many are concerned that core competencies of logical analysis and reasoning are replaced with a focus on rote repetitive skills.

Some are concerned that Common Core removes works of literature that are vital to developing a proper understanding of those works, their context, and the value of art to our culture. Others believe that, based on the enumerated powers of the federal government in the Constitution, defining educational standards should clearly be the responsibility of each state without intrusion from the federal government.

The Common Core State Standard initiative is led by the National Governors Association and the Council of Chief State School Officers. It seeks to establish a set of clear, consistent educational standards for K–12 students in English language arts and mathematics.

After implementation began in 2010, Common Core Standards were initially adopted by 46 states but in many cases not actually implemented completely. Common Core has been repealed in at least 12 states. At least five other states have ended support of it. For more insight into the topic, research the Parental Rights in Education bill passed in Florida in 2022, which repealed and replaced Common Core.[1]

Ironically, the vocal promoters of CRT and the 1619 Project are also leaders in the artificial resistance movement that enables the wealthy ruling class to maintain power. With that in mind, read the descriptions above again and try to figure out how that makes sense.

As parents we need to be fully aware of what our children are being taught and what topics they are being exposed to. It's not easy. It takes time and effort to work closely with teachers and the school system on these matters. Is it worth the effort? Is it worth the risk of taking side-eye glances from teachers and other parents?

When it comes to protecting the emotional health of our children and protecting their future as wholesome adults making wise aspirational life choices, there should be no limit to the effort we are willing to expend or the personal risk we are willing to take.

Leadership is not always running up ahead of the mob in the same direction and yelling, "Let's go!" Leadership sometimes means standing in the path between the mob and the regrettable mistake they are about to make.

> *Power is in tearing human minds to pieces and putting them together again in new shapes of your own choosing.*
>
> GEORGE ORWELL, *1984*

10

PROTECTING INDIVIDUAL RIGHTS

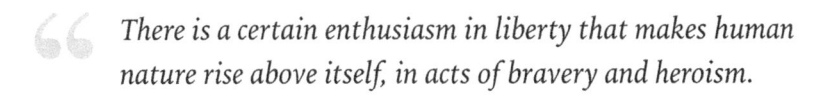

> *There is a certain enthusiasm in liberty that makes human nature rise above itself, in acts of bravery and heroism.*
>
> ALEXANDER HAMILTON

Individual rights can sometimes be difficult to adequately define. Clearly, we cannot all just do what we please. If we did, the rights of some would certainly be diminished by the overreach of others.

It is a difficult line to draw. Pick any topic related to the well-being of the community. One could argue that any action taken on behalf of the community that requires that the individual involuntarily contribute time, effort, or resources is a violation of that individual's right to provide for himself and his family. It essentially violates the individual's right to use their resources to pursue self-actualization.

The concept of self-actualization is described by Abraham Maslow in his 1943 book *A Theory of Human Motivation* as "the desire to become more and more what one is, to become everything that one is capable of becoming."

But no man is an island. If he were, it would be a very sad island. Community is a vital part of self-actualization. The order, support, and resources provided by the community and its members enable those same members and their families to prosper, grow, and become everything they are capable of being.

Again, it is a difficult line to draw.

Conservatives willingly and gladly support their community generously. So, then what is the problem?

It can start to become a problem when the community, a group of members working together in a cooperative manner, begins to transition into power struggles, where there is a constituency of available votes that must be won in order to achieve and maintain power. Those votes must be thoughtfully cast to ensure that people trusted with that power are truly focused on service to the community and not their own self-interests. In their leadership they must strike that delicate balance to build and sustain community without placing unreasonable burden on the individual members.

Even when those in power lead and manage community affairs with integrity, on every issue there will be community members in full agreement, others in partial agreement, and a small number who completely disagree with actions proposed or taken. That is just how community works, if there is more than one member. Yes, there is always more than one member. The voices in your head don't count.

As the community grows, it becomes more difficult to hold accountable the elected officials, appointees, and employees. It may be at risk of devolving away from members who work together for the greater good to a handful of powerful authoritarians, their minions, and the small number of community members who stand to benefit from the decisions eventually made.

Members of the community can find themselves in a situation where a small minority is making far-reaching decisions that require all members to participate in some way. The most obvious participation requirement placed on members is that of providing funding in the form of taxes.

Participation may mean that some are required to sell their property for new developments, as when eminent domain is used. Others may be required to deal with new facilities that will be built nearby, which could reduce the value of their property or reduce the peace and joy they experience in their homes.

You can begin to see in our sample community how the rights of the individual can be at risk. The vast majority of us have never experienced a significant encroachment of our rights. We have never had to fight city hall, the public school system, or any other authority to protect our family's well-being or our property. Does that mean we don't need to be concerned with protecting the rights of the individual? No! It is persistent concern and vigilance that keeps authority in check to some degree and we cannot lose sight of that.

In the words of Ayn Rand in the book "Textbook of Americanism", 1946:

> *Man holds these rights, not from the Collective nor for the Collective, but against the Collective—as a barrier which the Collective cannot cross...these rights are man's protection against all other men.*
>
> *Since Man has inalienable individual rights, this means that the same rights are held, individually, by every man, by all men, at all times. Therefore, the rights of one man cannot and must not violate the rights of another.*[1]

Again, your rights are not granted by the community and they do not exist for the benefit of the community. They are your protection against the community.

The collective, or community, does have the mission to act on behalf of and for the benefit of the majority of its members, within the scope of its authority. However, it should not do so at the cost of the rights of the minority of its members.

What are your rights? They are completely and entirely stated in one sentence in the Declaration of Independence:

> *...that all men are created equal, that they are endowed by their Creator with certain unalienable Rights, that among these are Life, Liberty and the pursuit of Happiness. That to secure these rights, Governments are instituted among Men, deriving their just powers from the consent of the governed...*[2]

That literally covers every aspect of your rights. "Life, Liberty and the pursuit of Happiness" covers it all! Think through every possible scenario where you know you have rights, or you think you probably have rights, even if you cannot put a finger on words describing a specific right. In every case, your right to "liberty" or "the pursuit of happiness" encapsulates your rights in that area. I didn't mention the right to life only because there is no ambiguity on that one.

Also note that a primary purpose and role of government is to secure those rights for its people. The significance and power of that historic statement should not be overlooked! The US government was the first in history to submit that they were appointed by and therefore accountable to the will of the people for the purpose of protecting the rights of the people. All other governments in history appointed themselves through the exercise of force. The Declaration of Independence also clearly states that those rights are granted by God, not by man or any government.

The Declaration of Independence is not law and does not define our system of government. However, it does clearly describe the intent and nature of the system of government that the founders were determined to implement once independence had been secured. The Declaration of Independence issued in July of 1776 was essentially a declaration of war. It listed a long list of grievances against the king and asserted that the colonies were no longer associated with or under the rule of Great Britain.

After several years of war, the British finally agreed to recognize the independence of the United States in September 1783. It took four more years for the founders of our nation to create and sign the US Constitution in September 1787. At that time the Constitution did not contain or reflect the sentiments of the Declaration of Independence.

Were the founders backing away from their previous statements that all men are created equal and have inalienable rights granted by God? Were they reneging on their grandiose claims that "Governments are instituted among Men, deriving their just powers from the consent of the governed" and following the norm of creating a monarchy or dictatorship? No, not at all.

The Constitution is administrative in nature. It defines elected offices of the federal government, their roles and responsibilities, and limitations on the power of that government. As we covered earlier, the Constitution places a limited number of concerns within the care of the federal government. Everything else is the responsibility of state and local governments. It is designed to be a government of the people to the extent possible. So, when do they get back to protecting the rights of the individual?

The first 10 amendments to the Constitution, adopted in June of 1790, are known as the Bill of Rights[3] and list some of the rights of individuals that shall not be infringed. The rights included were primarily selected based on experience, based on egregious violations that the authors had witnessed.

Some argued at the time that the amendments were not needed. They were concerned that the Bill of Rights could be interpreted as the government granting rights and only those called out. Amendments IX and X were added to address those concerns. With that it was clear that the Bill of Rights made no attempt to be comprehensive. It does provide the context for developing an understanding of our individual rights, those listed and those implied.

Please take some time to carefully read the Declaration of Independence, the Constitution, and the Bill of Rights. In the process, think through the implications and context of each document. Recognize that these documents define a federal government that is limited in scope and designed to protect the rights of the people, protect the nation's borders, and enable economic prosperity. While you are at it, compare the intent of those documents with the size and scope of the federal government today. There is little resemblance between the founding documents and our current state.

Again, Ayn Rand adds clarity to the debate: "The rights of one man cannot and must not violate the rights of another."

That is especially true when those in control of government take actions to the benefit of a few that clearly violate the rights of the many.

We sometimes don't recognize a specific right until someone tries to take it from us. Did you know you had a right to incandescent light bulbs before they were banned? Did you realize that your doctor had the right to disagree with the Centers for Decease Control (CDC) and provide advice and health care services to you based on your specific needs instead of the mandates of the CDC?

Did you realize you have the right to have a gas stove in your house? Gas powered lawn equipment? Charcoal grill? Depending on your address, some of those rights are already history or are scheduled for elimination.

Keep in mind that we do not all have to agree on exactly where that line is drawn. I'll say it again and again: I'm a "big tent, let's change the world together" conservative. The mission is too critical and the window is closing too quickly to be anything else. We must find common ground and refuse to be divided over the rest.

Laws are created nearly every day that some of us may consider a violation of our rights. When conservatives find that the law violates individual rights, they work to change that law.

Generally, conservatives think that the best protection for individual rights is proactive participation in community matters. Most of us are probably thinking right now some form of "Oh great! All I need is one more thing to do!" That's true. Most of us have very busy lives. But involvement in community and local government does not have to be difficult or time-consuming.

Most of us can spare a couple hours per month. We should consider using that time to support groups and organizations that share our concerns and are very effective in defending the rights of the individual. It is important to do the research and make sure the mission and tactics of the group are consistent with your views. However, we need to be careful to avoid the trap of letting perfect become the enemy of good.

There is no perfect group of people. Intellectual honesty and accountability of leadership must be held to a high standard, though, in the order of selection criteria—especially financial accountability!

> Make the most effective use of your limited time and resources by supporting credible, mission-focused organizations.

Those of us with concerns at the local or state level can find like-minded people nearby who share our concerns. Often that group is a local chapter of a larger organization.

In rare cases, legal action may be required to protect the rights of the individual. There are nonprofits that specialize in providing legal assistance and taking legal action against organizations and government entities that have violated the rights of individuals or groups of people. Again, do the homework needed to locate credible, mission-focused organizations.

Activism and legal action are not the only recourse. We also need to support with our time, energy, and resources the campaigns of political candidates that share our values. We should also support conservative get-out-the-vote (GOTV) initiatives to inform and encourage voters on conservative concerns. This is a vital aspect of the conservative movement. Every mature conservative should be vigorously engaged in these efforts.

In extremely rare cases, there may be so much distance between the beliefs of the individual and the mission of the community that the individual may find it necessary to leave that community entirely. Conservatives are known for never walking away from a fight, but we are smart enough to recognize that our limited energy and resources should be focused on the savable.

Hundreds of thousands of people leave California, New York, and other states to escape heavy-handed government and cultures devastated by an anything-goes mentality and a complete lack of reality-based guiding principles. A survey released in June 2023 by Strategies 360 revealed that 40% of people living in California would like to move out of the state. According to the US Census Bureau, California lost more residents than any other state in 2022. That's what is meant by the phrase "voting with your feet!"

But again, no man is an island. A functional community is vital to the success of individuals and families. Reasonable sacrifices and accommodations are required for that community to prosper. Honest people can come together and agree on what is reasonable.

> *In the main, it will be found that a power over a man's support [salary] is a power over his will.*
>
> ALEXANDER HAMILTON

11

HOLDING GOVERNMENT ACCOUNTABLE

> *When the people find that they can vote themselves money, that will herald the end of the republic.*
>
> BENJAMIN FRANKLIN

The principle of accountable government seems to bring more people to the conservative movement than any other. It is the most difficult issue facing the people of the United States today because of the massive size of government and the protections those in control of government have created for themselves.

> *Our Constitution was made only for a moral and religious people. It is wholly inadequate to the government of any other.*
>
> JOHN ADAMS

Our "government" is inherently accountable when executed as designed. Unfortunately, we have strayed so far from that design that its thumbprint is barely discernible today. It is the individuals within our government that are out of control, not our government. I believe we should make a clear distinction between our system of government and the people in control of that system.

> *If Congress can employ money indefinitely, for the general welfare, and are the sole and supreme judges of the general welfare, they may take the care of religion into their own hands; they may appoint teachers in every state, county, and parish, and pay them out of the public treasury; they may take into their own hands the education of children, the establishing in like manner schools throughout the union; they may assume the provision of the poor... Were the power of Congress to be established in the latitude contended for, it would subvert the very foundations, and transmute the very nature of the limited government established by the people of America.*
>
> JAMES MADISON

James Madison made that statement in 1792. Read his statement again and think about what he must have believed about the need to maintain limits on government in order to protect the rights of citizens. James Madison was instrumental in creating the Bill of Rights while in the US House of Representatives and later became the fourth president of the United States.

As you read his statement again very carefully, he seems to be answering the question we frequently ask ourselves today, "How did we get in this mess?" instead of offering a warning on the consequences of unrestrained federal government. How different would our country be today if we had taken his warning seriously and we had fully engaged in the political process to resist the ambitions of the wealthy ruling class?

How do those ambitions manifest? Are their strategies and tactics detectable or carefully hidden from view? We cover this in more detail later but this seems like an appropriate place to point out that the government's response to COVID resulted in the largest and fasted transfer of wealth in our nation's history, possibly in world history! In just two years during the crisis 573 new billionaires were created.

Oxfam International (Oxfam.org) reported those figures in a May 23, 2022, report. They also reported that the wealth of those billionaires rose more in the first 24 months of the crisis than in the previous 23 years combined. Read that again! That is a shocking rate of wealth transfer! Words fail me. I have no idea how to convey just how devastating that is to the rest of us. Perhaps hyper-inflation and crushing interest rates will drive the point home!

At the time of the report, 2,668 billionaires owned $12.7 trillion in wealth. That is a very small number of people in control of a staggering level of wealth that exceeds that of more than 100 countries combined. Only the top 10 wealthiest countries in the world have more wealth than these 2,668 individuals.

The holders of $12.7 trillion in wealth can make elected officials, legacy media, and social media platforms in the United States fabulously wealthy and still have $12.7 trillion. The return on that investment would quickly push them toward the $15 trillion goal and beyond.

Conservatives believe that government cannot be held accountable unless it is substantially reduced in size and scope. The number of departments, unelected bureaucrats, and employees breached the threshold of "out of control" many years ago. The people in control of these government agencies have a vested interest in continued expansion of their size and influence, as if they were running private businesses.

But they are not private businesses. The growth of government agencies does not deliver financial returns to shareholders. In fact, the growth of government agencies does the exact opposite. In a very meaningful and powerful way, the massive size of government and its continued growth undermines the interests and rights of the people it is supposed to protect.

This can apply to government at all levels—from local mayors, commissioners, and schools to the federal level.

We should heed the warning of Plato and avoid the tendency to take the easy path of surrendering to apathy, or the feeling of being overwhelmed, toward public affairs, lest we be ruled by evil.

> *The price of apathy towards public affairs is to be ruled by evil men.*
>
> PLATO

If people were actually aware of the extent of the problem, and that it continues to grow unimpeded at an alarming rate, they would be outraged and would be compelled to take action. They would become fully engaged citizens and hold those in control of the government to an entirely new level of accountability.

The Declaration of Independence, the Constitution, and the Bill of Rights together are a brilliantly defined instrument that makes clear that the rights of people are granted by God and clarifies the limited powers of the federal government. It really is astounding that nearly 250 years ago the people of that time could create a system of government that lives on centuries later.

They were statesmen and students of human nature. The colonies had been governing for over 170 years before the Constitution was created. The challenges faced during that time provided a base of experiences, failures, and lessons learned. The founding documents were not created in a vacuum based on abstract theory. They were created based on incredibly valuable hard-earned knowledge along with some very informative bumps and bruises.

By the time the Constitution was being written, many of the colonies were already creating their own constitutions. Long before the Constitution was written, the original intent of the federal government was to provide for the common defense and ensure that states deal with each other fairly. This was spelled out in the Articles of Confederation adopted in 1781.

The state governments, as defined in their own state constitutions, were supposed to be the centers of democracy and the exercise of government of the people, by the people, for the people. The intent was for the federal government to be uninvolved in the daily lives of the citizens of the states. In that design, the federal government was an arbitrator where representatives of each state went to advocate for the interests of their state. State governments were to be the seat of representative government.

However, the Articles of Confederation were replaced by the Constitution in 1787, giving the federal government more power and authority. It was a relatively small "however," however, in comparison to the massive federal government we have today, one that reaches into seemingly every aspect of our lives. The Constitution also placed limits on the federal government. Those limits have long since been forgotten by the people in control of our government and that was made possible by voters who continually vote for the person that seems like a nice guy.

> If it were easier, or even possible, to locate the truth, would we do the research and vote more wisely?

We don't have to continue living in the dark, unaware of the behavior of those in government. Resources are available that expose their actions. Those resources enable us to fully grasp the magnitude of the problem and empower us to help others do the same.

One of those resources is OpenTheBooks.com, an organization that analyzes federal and state government actions and reports on government waste and overreach.[1] The meticulous data gathering and analysis work they do is incredibly time-consuming. In a single year OpenTheBooks filed 55,000 Freedom of Information Act (FOIA) requests with state and federal governments. These legal requests provide them access to revelations hidden behind the nearly impenetrable walls that allow the inept and corrupt in government to operate with impunity.

The tag line for OpenTheBooks is "Every Dime. Online. In Real Time." You can keep up with their investigations by joining their email list and following them on social media.

Other resources are available to help us be informed citizens. Before he passed away in 2020, Senator Tom Coburn[2] created the annual *Wastebook* report, exposing the most outrageous government waste. Senator Rand Paul has since taken the baton with help from government watchdog White Coat Waste Project (WCWP). The annual report is now called the *Festivus Report*,[3] a reference to the made-up holiday introduced in a 1997 episode of the *Seinfeld* comedy TV show. The 2023 report provides details of over $900 billion in government waste, including:

- $659 billion in interest on the federal debt
- $200 billion in pandemic relief funds paid out to fraudsters
- $38 million paid out to dead people
- $236 billion in other improper payments
- $170 million in military equipment destroyed by being left out in the elements
- $33.2 million to operate Dr. Fauci's Monkey Island in South Carolina
- $6 million to boost Egyptian tourism ($100 million total in previous years)
- $2.7 million to study cats on a treadmill in Russia

Take advantage of these valuable information sources so that you can be an informed and engaged citizen. The more we know, the more engaged we will be in holding accountable the people within our government!

Even the casual observer is now paying attention to the actions of our elected officials and their minions. The deeply self-indulgent may still live in the smoky haze of their mother's basement but nearly everyone else is taking notice. It is clear to us that those trusted with responsibility within our government are often not acting in the best interests of the people.

When a very large percentage of intelligent citizens see the actions of the government and often ask, "How could that possibly make any sense to anyone?" it is clear that the people in control of our government no longer feel the need to hide their ambitions because they have no fear of being held accountable.

How have they become so brazen? How could they not? It was inevitable. They have quietly operated with impunity and zero consequences for so long that they no longer bother putting effort into trying to hide who they really are or what they are doing. They often say the right words but no longer feel the need to even pretend to believe those words as they say them. You can see it in their faces.

This is the politician's equivalent of "Hold my beer and watch this!" and they can barely contain their own laughter long enough to get the words out. All along their co-conspirators can be seen glancing around the room grinning nervously almost in disbelief that the people are buying this nonsense and they are getting away with it again. We all know the look. "Really? No pushback? Really?" followed by obvious glee in their hearts and on their faces.

In his book *Murphy's Law Book Two*, Arthur Bloch unintentionally created the phrase that politicians hope will dominate the thoughts of citizens as they watch their government in action:

> *Never attribute to malice that which is adequately explained by stupidity.*

Are the people in control of our government just stupid instead of self-serving? They have advanced college degrees and many years of experience. Can they really just be stupid? No, their actions are not the result of stupidity! The damage their actions cause to our economy, businesses, communities, and people in need is entirely predictable. The casual observer, if they are paying any attention at all, could easily foresee the unintended consequences. This is not the result of stupidity!

Has the government grown to the point there is no turning back? No, I don't think so. Other representative governments have been significantly reformed in recent years. We can reform our government too.

It will not be easy. The ruling class is entrenched and extremely well supported by the legacy media and Big Tech. Dominant technology companies have implemented a cone of silence they enforce using content promotion algorithms, banning, shadow-banning, and deplatforming.

In addition to these highly effective misinformation machines, approximately 50% of adults in the United States rely on the government for all or part of their income. 50%! That's a staggering number that warrants scrutiny, so let's step through it.

As shown in the table below, 50% of adults in the United States rely on the government for all or part of their income.

Category	Adult Recipients (millions)
Federal employees, not military[4]	2.87
Federal contract workers and military[5]	6.30
Federal government retirees, including military[6][7]	4.00
State and local employees[4]	19.23
State and local government retirees[8]	11.50
Retirees receiving Social Security, excluding spouse and dependents[9]	48.23
Subtract those receiving both forms of retirement[9]	-8.00
People receiving Social Security due to a disability, excluding spouse and dependents[10]	8.38
Adults on federal social safety net programs[11]	35.00
Adults on state and local social safety net programs	Unknown
Total of known recipients	127.51

Figure 11.1 Adults in the United States Receiving Income from Government

Endnotes: [4] [5] [6] [7] [8] [9] [10] [11]

That's over 127 million who receive all or part of their income from the government! The adult population of the United States is about 250 million people. [12]

The math works out to 50.8% of the adult population relying on the government for all or part of their income. That's 50.8%! Again, this does not include the number of adults receiving assistance from state governments.

For perspective, the largest private employer, Walmart, has only about 1.5 million workers.

All of these people entered into a contract with the government. The "people" are not the problem. They followed the program and received what was promised to them. However, when over 50% of the country fears that their income could be reduced by any attempt to hold the government accountable or to reform it, that is a steep hill for *we the people* to climb if we hope to achieve any level of reform.

Now consider the businesses, nonprofit organizations, and other entities that receive grants and funding from the government. Then there are the businesses that sell products and services to the government. Think about that internal conflict for a minute. You are a business owner or salesperson selling to the government. You always want your customers to be successful and to continue to grow, right? Your success depends on their success. But your customer is the government, and you are a conservative. You are a conservative and you want your customer, the government, to continue to expand? Wow! That's a tough spot!

We are clearly up against a massive fortress that protects the people in control of our government. The size of government, the number of businesses and people that receive income from government, the overwhelming support provided by dominant media outlets, social media platforms using algorithms to promote or remove content, and the vicious mobs that destroy anyone foolishly stepping out of line with the messaging together is a lot to overcome.

In the face of that massive monolith it is difficult to build community around the truth of holding those in our government accountable, or one would think. But is it really? OK, yes, it is. However, while it does make it more difficult to build community, it also has the inevitable unintended consequence of forcing people from diverse backgrounds and interests to come together and bond over the common mission of government reform for the survival of our country.

But, I deceived you. It is not a monolith we are up against. It is just people. People can be persuaded. People are being persuaded! Thousands of people each week join the conservative movement. Our momentum is building and we will turn this around before it is too late!

> It is the individuals within our government that are out of control, not our government. Together we can hold them accountable.

12

(IN)EFFECTIVE USE OF TAXPAYER FUNDS

> *Public business, my son, must always be done by somebody. It will be done by somebody or other. If wise men decline it, others will not; if honest men refuse it, others will not.*
>
> — JOHN ADAMS

How the government spends taxpayer money is probably a top two or three concern for conservatives. Conservatives are very generous people, but they are also passionate about utilizing resources as effectively as possible to actually solve problems and promote economic opportunity. Unfortunately, too many government programs are ineffective at best and counterproductive at worst due to unintended consequences. Often those unintended consequences have devastating effects that far outweigh the supposed benefits that were sold hard by the politicians and insiders who actually benefit from the programs.

We can think of a failure in government as any situation where the benefits of the government intervention are outweighed by the costs of that intervention, including the ongoing costs of unintended consequences. As involved citizens, we are not measuring program intentions. We are measuring program outcomes. I seem to recall a hit country song by Randy Travis about a road to hell being paved with good intentions. The intentions always sound legitimate, even loving and caring. The product delivered often falls far short of the sales pitch and costs dramatically more than advertised.

Look closely at history. Many of the largest government interventions were ushered in to address the unintended consequences of previous government interventions.

When it comes to government programs and spending, many people are again asking, "How could that possibly make any sense to anyone?" There is an endless supply of examples where government action brought very costly consequences that were no surprise to many. Let's look at a few.

In 1977, Congress passed legislation known as the Community Reinvestment Act (CRA), which encouraged financial institutions to meet the lending needs of their communities, including low- and moderate-income neighborhoods. By the mid-1990s regulators stepped up their monitoring of CRA loans made by lenders and started aggressively penalizing those lenders if they were not making enough CRA qualifying loans.

Lenders began to relax loan qualification requirements on credit scores, income stability, and loan to value ratios to deliver significantly more CRA high-risk loans and avoid regulator scrutiny. In many cases, the amount the borrower needed for a down payment was drastically reduced or even eliminated.

While the details of the CRA law dictated some of this behavior, regulators creating their own guidelines within the context of CRA drove much of it as well.

In the end, the United States had a major economic meltdown—the housing bubble burst in 2008, causing the 2008 financial crisis, the beginning of the Great Recession. Home foreclosures rose by 225% from 2006 to 2009. Unemployment reached 10% as 8.7 million US jobs were lost. As the stock market plunged, US households lost about $19 trillion in net worth.[1] The net worth of many families was reduced in 2008 by 39% back down to their 1992 levels; essentially, they lost 16 years of savings.

Who could have seen that coming? Just about anyone with an objective pulse.

Another example of devastating unintended consequences can be seen in the 1990 luxury tax law that added an extra 10% tax on the purchase of luxury items like expensive boats. Yacht sales plummeted 77% in the US and many companies went out of business.[2] According to a July 16, 1993, *Washington Post* article, in the first year and half the additional tax on yachts brought in about $12.6 million in tax dollars. The tax revenue generated was minuscule even in 1990. The tax "contributed to the general devastation of the American boating industry—as well as the jewelers, furriers and private-plane manufacturers that were also targets of the excise tax that was part of the 1990 budget deal." Their attempt to tax the rich had very painful effects on workers in those industries, as usual.

Again, who could have seen that coming? Again, anyone.

Yet another example is the 2002 tariff imposed on steel imported from other countries. The goal was to protect the steel industry in the United States from cheap steel from countries with favorable currency exchange rates and lower costs due to their less burdensome labor laws, safety regulations, and environmental regulations. The impact of the tariff was devastating for US companies that used steel to manufacture products and those manufacturers could no longer compete globally. The tariff was removed in 2003 primarily because it was causing a net loss in US jobs. If it had continued, it is estimated that eight jobs would have been lost in industries using steel for every steel-producing job saved.

Politicians desperately trying to elevate themselves to the role of champion of the oppressed are interested in headlines, not outcomes.

The most visible and controversial example of government-induced disaster is the "war on terror" that was launched after the September 11, 2001, attack on New York City and Washington DC. There was little debate over who attacked US civilians or whether or not the US should respond. However, most believe the response was badly mishandled by the US government.

As of today the United States has been fighting this war on terror in Iraq and Afghanistan for over 22 years, has cost US taxpayers over $8 trillion, and has taken the lives of nearly 16,000 US military personnel and contractors. Far more have suffered life-changing physical and psychological injuries in battle.

After those horrible costs, both countries are once again ruled by corrupt authoritarians who seem to answer to nobody. The people still suffer the brutality of self-serving government officials from top to bottom. Iraq is somewhat better off now but still ranks in the bottom 25% in terms of democracy, corruption, economic opportunity, human rights, infrastructure, health care, and education.

Today about 2,500 US troops are still present in Iraq, down from over 170,000 at the peak of conflict. In Afghanistan, the US evacuated remaining personnel over a poorly organized seventeen-day operation in August 2021. Military experts described it as a completely incoherent nightmare of chaos. There is nearly unanimous agreement that this was Joe Biden's most devastating foreign policy debacle of many, dating back to the Vietnam war. Many people were killed or injured by advancing Taliban forces who exploited the opportunity to seize the country and take complete control while the evacuation was in progress. Hundreds of US citizens were left in Afghanistan by our government.

An estimated $20 billion in weapons and equipment was abandoned to the Taliban. The Pentagon reported that just over $7 billion of that equipment was left fully operational. Those weapons are now being used to attack Israel, India, and US personnel in the region. The people of our armed forces have suffered terribly from this poorly planned and managed war on terror.

This is just one of hundreds of examples of devastating unintended consequences spanning decades and lifetimes when politicians focus on self-serving agendas and choose to ignore actual experts.

In these examples politicians made choices that had disastrous unintended consequences. Those of us living in the real world, outside the gilded palaces of the ruling class, paid the price for those terribly misguided decisions. In every case experts offered dramatically more effective solutions but were ignored, either out of arrogance or the desire to make bold headlines and secure their political legacies.

For politicians, their careers are the entire point of everything they do publicly. The daily focus of most politicians is on doing everything possible to make sure they win that next election. They often surround themselves with victim groups and attempt to elevate themselves to the role of savior of those people. If they can't find a vocal victim group to align with and exploit, they will create one. Unfortunately, this far too often means that many of the actions taken by the government are designed to pacify or gain favor with a very small but very vocal segment. This enables the politician to project the image of a caring person focused on the well-being of the people.

The latest victim group exploited by politicians is criminals. Yes, criminals. Instead of focusing on maintaining an environment where *we the people* can thrive, many politicians have decided to focus on promoting criminals as a victim group. Politicians in many cities and states have made highly publicized attempts to save these poor defenseless criminals from their victimhood. Zero bail and defund the police initiatives are their most visible efforts. New York, San Francisco, Los Angeles, and Chicago are among the cities run by liberals for decades that have aggressively promoted soft-on-crime programs and have suffered detrimental consequences as a result.

How does this relate to the ineffective use of taxpayer-provided funding?

It's pretty simple. Taxpayers agreed to fund effective government that would maintain an environment that fosters economic progress and safety. When the government failed horribly in that mission, politicians requested far more funding to solve the problems they themselves created.

Let's look at the impact of reclassifying criminals as victims.

In New York, crime was up 38% from January 2021 to January 2022.[3] In February 2022 local NBC affiliate WNBC in New York reported the spike in crime but made no mention of the law passed in 2020 that greatly reduced the number of crimes that require a cash bail be paid and also reduced the amount of bail that must be paid for those that still required cash bail. The story also failed to mention that, on his first day on the job in January 2022, new district attorney Alvin Bragg issued the infamous Day One Memo, listing many crimes that would no longer be prosecuted by his office.[4]

Bragg also instituted new pretrial discovery rules on prosecutors that dramatically increased their workload and significantly increased the opportunity for convictions to be overturned on a technicality.

According to a local newspaper, the *New York Post*, felony conviction rates dropped from 68% to 51% and misdemeanor conviction rates dropped from 53% to 28%. Cases downgraded from felony to misdemeanor increased to 52% from 39%.[5] No bail, reduced bail, dramatically fewer convictions on significantly reduced charges resulting in a 38% increase in crime...who is naive enough to be surprised by that? What "public servant" is so focused on their success that they would allow it to happen to the people they are supposed to represent?[6]

San Francisco is probably the most tragic example of how a beautiful city can quickly be destroyed by politicians focused on showing people how much they care about those poor, unfortunate criminals. If you visited the city years ago you probably know how captivating it was with the bay, ocean, wharf area, Golden Gate Bridge, rolling streets, cable cars, and many other unique features. A November 2021 article by Lee Ohanian paints a very bleak picture of current conditions in San Francisco with a single sentence:

> *To put this in perspective, Compton, California, the infamous home of drug gang turf wars, and which today remains more dangerous than 90% of all US cities, is almost twice as safe as San Francisco.*[7]

The article goes on to say, "San Francisco's unacceptable crime track record is implicitly a choice that the city has made, which is all the more surprising when the city spends about $14,000 per San Franciscan per year on government services, about 40% higher than New York city's profligate budget."

San Francisco District Attorney Chesa Boudin won election in 2019 largely on a platform that was overtly soft on crime. He was clear that, if he were elected as DA, many "quality of life" crimes would no longer be prosecuted in a show of support for the city's disenfranchised groups. Once elected, he kept that promise and also implemented a no-cash-bail policy under which those arrested are immediately released unless they pose a "serious public safety risk."

The impact of these crime-friendly policies was more rapid than even his harshest critics could have anticipated. Crime rates quickly skyrocketed in most categories. Thefts from vehicles citywide more than doubled between May 2020 and May 2021. However, the Central Station reported a 750% increase in thefts from vehicles.[8] Retail store theft and group smash-and-grab robberies have risen dramatically since the DA announced that such crimes would not be pursued by his office.

According to the California Department of Justice's Criminal Justice Statistics Center, San Francisco has the highest property crime rate in the state. The crime rate rose by 16.9% in 2021 alone.[9]

Drug sales are now conducted in the open. People use those drugs right there on the sidewalks by the hundreds because they have no place else more private to get high. As you walk through San Francisco, passed-out addicts, hypodermic needles, urine, feces, and blood are always in view.

City policies on drug use and homelessness enable and encourage people to live in debilitating dysfunction by providing a decriminalized drug environment, free needles, medical supervision of drug consumption, and at least the promise of housing, which very few are able to obtain. These policies create a magnetic force drawing in more addicts and more homeless. Together they sound like a great plan for keeping people "comfortable" until they finally kill themselves by overdose or other means. However, the approach is obviously not an actual solution to the problems consuming these desperate people.

San Francisco is in free fall as people and businesses move out as quickly as they can. Walgreens has closed at least 10 stores in the city. Whole Foods, Nordstrom, Amazon Go, Banana Republic, the Container Store, Crate & Barrel, and many other retailers have closed some or all of their stores in the city. Most have cited organized retail theft and employee safety as their primary reasons for leaving. The owner of San Francisco Centre in downtown is turning it over to lenders and walking away after recent retail store departures left it 45% vacant.

Union Square, another retail center that was once a bustling center of activity, is now nearly 50% vacant. At the end of 2023, San Francisco reached an all-time record with a commercial vacancy rate of 36%.

Business Insider reported in June 2023 that the owner of the flagship Hilton San Francisco Union Square and the nearby Parc 55 hotel decided to hand the properties over to creditors and cease payments on a $725 million loan.[10]

A survey by the San Francisco Chamber of Commerce in 2021 revealed that 40% of the city's residents plan to move out of the city. The respondents were very clear on their reasons, as 80% are concerned about worsening crime, 70% are concerned about declining quality of life, and 88% are concerned about worsening homelessness.[11] In 2023, California had a net loss of residents of nearly 750,000, while the homeless population grew by 6%.

Many other large cities run by liberal politicians are in similar free fall for nearly identical reasons. The Los Angeles Homeless Services Authority released data in June 2023 showing that homelessness increased 10% in the city of Los Angeles from the previous year. A 10% increase in a single year! Los Angeles has the largest homeless population of any city in the United States.

A study recently released by the University of California, San Francisco, reveals that 30% of the homeless population and half of the unsheltered population in the United States live in California. California has more homeless than any other state and more than the next five highest states combined.[12]

So, how could this have happened? How could these once beautiful cities decimate themselves so quickly? Their city leaders are highly educated and remind us often that they are the smartest people in the room. How is it possible that they could be foolish enough to implement policies that anyone can see are guaranteed to deliver these outcomes? It seems unimaginable but here we are.

The politicians did the math and believed that they could get elected on criminal justice reform and soft-on-crime platforms. They are not stupid people and had to understand that a very high political price would eventually be paid by someone for these policies. They likely placed their bets that they would move up the ladder to the next office before that day of reckoning arrived. They were gambling that someone else would be in that seat and be forced to pay their debt. Once elected, they had no choice but to continue to at least pretend to fully believe in the campaign slogans that won the election.

And the people of these cities voted for them. And in some cases, voted for them again. Maybe those politicians really are the smartest people in the room? They somehow successfully convinced the majority of the voters to help them destroy their cities.

Those on the liberal side of the political spectrum make outlandish claims that conservatives will eliminate all social programs if they gain power. Based on how conservatives are portrayed, the casual observer has no choice but to conclude that conservatives are hateful, greedy, evil people who think the old, sick, and poor should just die. The more ridiculous the attacks on conservatives are, the more likely it is those casual observers will start to question the integrity of the attacker and the legitimacy of their claims.

No thinking person wants to eliminate valuable safety net programs that help people get back on their feet. However, conservatives do want to root out fraud, waste, and abuse in all government programs as much as possible. Conservatives also advocate for programs that are carefully designed to address actual needs, provide effective long-term solutions, and minimize unintended consequences like those described above.

> A well restrained government will break the cycle by creating fewer ineffective interventions and fewer unintended consequences that require additional government interventions.

Again, how does this relate to the ineffective use of taxpayer-provided funding? The issue is that there is a constant cycle of interventions spawning more interventions. In terms of use of taxpayer funding, the math is pretty simple. Let's take 2022 for example. The federal government took in tax revenue of $5.0 trillion, which is 19.6% of gross domestic product (GDP). For 2022 US GDP was $25.46 trillion.[13] That means the federal government consumed 19.6% of the total monetary value of all the finished goods and services produced. However, the federal budget for 2022 was $6.5 trillion, which is 25.5% of GDP.

So, the difference between federal government tax income and actual expenses is $1.5 trillion. The federal government spent 30% more than it took in. Where did the extra $1.5 trillion, or 30% come from? They spent it, so it had to be real money from somewhere, didn't it?

The delta, known as deficit spending, is covered by deficit financing, where the federal government borrows money by selling US Treasury bonds, bills, and other securities.

Those annual budget deficits add up year after year and are known as the national debt. The national debt is the accumulation of this borrowing along with associated interest owed to those who purchased the debt securities.

> Why do we care about government debt? Isn't it just board game money? They would like us to think so!

According to a *Peter G. Peterson Foundation* monthly survey in March 2022, 83% of voters say their concern about the debt has increased in recent years. That is up from 78% just one month earlier. Clearly the majority of Americans are concerned about out-of-control spending of taxpayer money.

Again, for 2022 the deficit was $1.5 trillion. For reference, during COVID lockdowns, the 2021 deficit was $2.8 trillion, and the 2020 deficit was $3.1 trillion. To put it into perspective, that is equivalent to a family earning $100,000 over three years but spending $150,000 in those years.

How long do you think you would get away with spending 50% more than you earn?

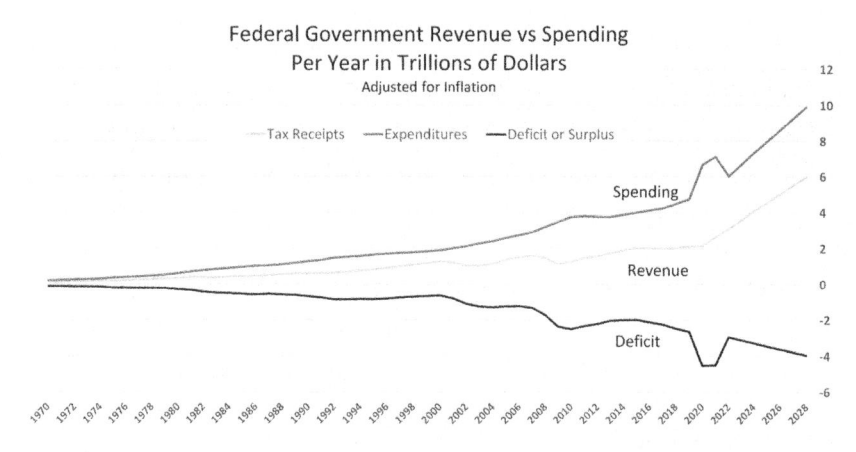

Figure 12.1 Federal Government Revenue vs Spending per Year in Trillions Adjusted for Inflation

14 15

That deficit spending adds up year after year. In December 2023, the accumulated national debt was $33.96 trillion, which is 122% of GDP.[16]

Your share of that is $101,000. That's real dollars, not board game dollars!

Comparing revenue, expenditures, deficit, and debt to GDP is useful because it enables us to evaluate those metrics as a percentage of the economic production that they rely on and consume. It also enables comparisons between countries.

So, when it comes to the ratio relative to GDP, what is good and what is bad? In terms of accumulated debt-to-GDP ratio, a study by the World Bank found that countries whose debt-to-

GDP ratios exceed 77% experience significant slowdowns in economic growth.[17] Economic growth as in your job, your business, your family's financial stability.

The US ratio today is 122%, or 158% *of the warning level* according to the World Bank. Our nation is not only deep in the red but has also far exceeded the level of debt deemed reasonable for sustained viability.

Let me repeat that: the US federal debt is 122% of US GDP! 158% *of the warning level* from the World Bank!

For reference, 2008 debt was $12.6 trillion, or 68% of GDP. It has more than doubled since then![18]

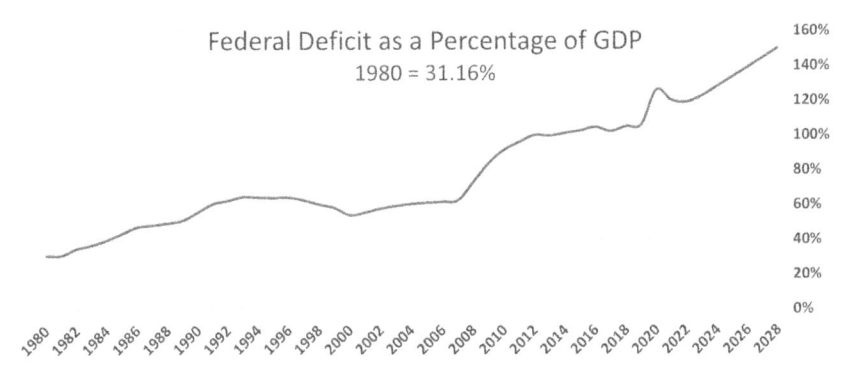

Figure 12.2 Federal Debt as Percent of Gross Domestic Product

Based on the World Bank warnings and continued lack of restraint on government spending, it is clear that our children will not have the margin needed to live their best lives. Their lives will be dominated by a culture of dysfunction, the weight of a government behemoth, and the burden of trillions of dollars wasted decades earlier on ineffective programs.

How will our children be impacted by the burden of trillions of dollars wasted on ineffective programs, decades before they had a voice?

PART 1 RECAP

So far, we have discussed some of the primary issues that cause people to recognize their conservative leanings. Conservatives are often very different from each other and often do not agree on some pretty important and sensitive issues. However, the bigger picture is far too important, and we refuse to be divided by our differences. We recognize that our common concerns and objectives will impact nearly every aspect of the lives of many future generations.

Some, but not all, of those common concerns have been covered in this section. Each of us could expand this list to include issues that we see as our primary concerns. All are welcome. The conversation has just begun.

So, after reading up to this point, are you a conservative? Are you all in for:

- Opportunity for all?
- Generosity?

- Local community?
- Effective education K–12?
- Individual rights?
- Accountable government?
- Appropriate use of taxpayer funds?

Yes! Could a more effective philosophy of community and government exist?

It is time for us to band together in civility and use our talents and resources to amplify our voice to encourage others to join us. By living out our values we can push back on the endless flow of misinformation about who we are and what we are trying to accomplish.

> We are determined to throw off lies about who we are and show people we are gracious, welcoming, cordial, genial, and affable but dedicated to preserving hope and opportunity for all.
>
> *A well-instructed people alone can be permanently a free people.*
>
> JAMES MADISON

PART 2
SNAFU, RINSE, REPEAT

13

CAREFULLY ORCHESTRATED CHAOS

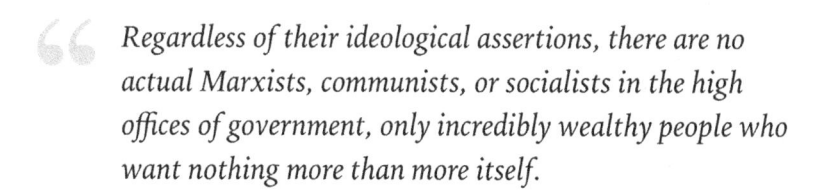

> *Regardless of their ideological assertions, there are no actual Marxists, communists, or socialists in the high offices of government, only incredibly wealthy people who want nothing more than more itself.*

Do our elected representatives really represent our interests or are they just using wealth and power to accumulate more wealth and power?

How did government spending get so out of control?

Why do we sit back and allow elected officials to mismanage taxpayer money and the US economy?

Where does it end?

What economic opportunity consequences will we as a country eventually have to face?

If you're asking questions like these, it'll come to you! I promise!

Governments grow because the people in control of government agencies have a deep desire for more wealth and more power. Most people who are driven to reach the top echelons of government, and often business too, are not like you and me. They are motivated, no, they are compulsively driven by an intense desire to reach the top and wield as much power as possible. They will never have enough of that power. It is who they are, and nothing will change that, short of a visit or vision from the divine.

What power and why? Power comes to them in the form of the ability to hire and fire people, the ability to fund massive projects, the ability to control how that funding is allocated, and the ability to make far-reaching policy decisions that effectively choose winners and losers. More importantly, as they work their way up the ladder, the budgets they control increase to levels most of us cannot even imagine.

With the control of massive budgets comes power, which they use to carefully navigate their way to more money and more power, and the cycle repeats endlessly.

The key to amassing more power now and even more power in the future is "the narrative," which encourages compliance among the people and enshrines the politicians as selfless, altruistic, humble servants who are only trying to save our country. In reality, those presenting themselves as public servants often view themselves as our far superior benevolent masters. The rest of us are just lowly, ignorant followers who don't understand what is best for us.

If you watch closely, you will catch a glimpse of who they really are and what they really think of the rest of us on those rare occasions when their mask momentarily slips in public. Research narcissistic personality disorder and you will start to see those who would be kings in an entirely new light.

> *I fear that in every elected office, members will obtain an influence by noise, not sense. By meanness, not greatness. By ignorance, not learning. By contracted hearts, not large souls... There must be decency and respect.*
>
> JOHN ADAMS

So, what is this narrative we speak of? In general, on a day-to-day basis, powerful insiders present a consistent message that is often accepted by the general population as conventional wisdom. Politicians and their handlers are at the top of the hierarchy because they ultimately determine what the narrative will be and the most effective methods for winning public opinion over to their side.

Clearly, many politicians are not intelligent enough to design and execute ingenious messaging strategies so multifaceted and far-reaching. Some are, but most are not. However, their sponsors, handlers, and staff are incredibly brilliant, well-connected political operatives. In many cases, those people are the brains behind the initiatives a political figurehead promotes and appears to be leading.

Powerful people outside of government are a key aspect of the messaging strategy. High-profile business owners and executives have become some of the most vocal and visible influencers of public opinion in recent years. They are "obviously" the smartest people in the virtual room based on the lofty position and massive wealth they have achieved. Everyone seems to accept that premise anyway.

Jeff Bezos, Bill Gates, Mark Zuckerberg, and Elon Musk are good examples but there are many others from billionaires to ordinary multimillionaires. Their elevated and amplified platform often enables them to immediately affect public opinion with just a few words or a brief statement. Media outlets, bloggers, and podcasters seize on their statements and repeat them relentlessly for days until there is another, more compelling statement or story to cover. The story and related memes are posted, reposted, and shared on social media millions of times.

As their followers loudly parrot them, they become more visible and more influential. You'd have to be a complete moron to disagree with the obvious truths that permeate the collective consciousness through this repetition, or maybe just an independent thinker to a degree that others cannot comprehend.

> Who are these influential people, and how do they use their influence?

This group of highly visible influencers of public opinion also includes the entertainment industry, sports entertainment, and traditional news media.

In terms of the number of people they reach and the repetitive reinforcement of the narrative, the impact of this group is far greater than that of politicians. The overall narrative and specific talking points are determined in the political realm through collusion among politicians, big business, and wealthy elites, but it is the businesses that disseminate the message in a carefully orchestrated manner. If they do their job effectively, the narrative will win enough hearts and ensure sufficient compliance to move the agenda forward. The narrative is viewed by the gullible masses as conventional wisdom, enabling politicians to meet their career and wealth objectives.

If you are visualizing a NASA-style control center full of evil masterminds crafting narratives and supporting messaging, that's not really how it works. Most of the messaging is on autopilot as long as things are going as expected. Everyone already knows what the issues are, what the approved position is on each issue, and the guidelines for creating messaging in support of the approved position.

Under normal circumstances there is little discussion between political operatives and their minions disseminating the messaging. If something out of the ordinary happens, everyone knows whose lead to follow. A political leader makes public statements and everyone falls in behind them. However, when events begin to unfold that present significant risk to public confidence in the ruling class, the wagons are circled and steps are taken to ensure everyone is on the same page. We will cover real world examples of this in later chapters.

Conservatives naturally find themselves in opposition to those seeking to enrich themselves by promoting false narratives and crisis after crisis, whether it is people in government, businesses, celebrities, pressure groups, or whoever. History shows that many movements "vital to our future" were primarily vehicles for those at the top to build wealth and power through lies and distortions. Remember BLM? Antifa?

Inflation Reduction Act? Climate change? All classic examples of initiatives designed and executed to make a few people extremely wealthy.

Being in opposition to "obvious truths" and "trusted science" often paints conservatives into a corner in some ways. Self-serving wealth-building initiatives like those mentioned demand complete compliance. You can't just agree in principle. You must agree with every sentence they utter, every point of their doctrine, or you are part of the problem. In the case of Antifa, you can't just agree that fascism is bad. You must agree that anyone who disagrees with them is a fascist and should be punished.

For those of us who have been around awhile and have seen it all at least once, it is easy to spot a disingenuous organization with an altruistic name and mission statement. The leaders of these groups are eventually exposed through their excessively self-serving behavior, where suddenly these poor disenfranchised rebels have multimillion-dollar homes and multiple homes. Until it unravels, anyone raising doubts is labeled a Neanderthal, a science denier, or a hater.

The group Black Lives Matter (BLM) is a typical example of a nonprofit enriching the founders instead of lifting up the less fortunate, as vividly described in their fundraising letters. BLM publicly claims to pursue justice and equality for all, and aggressively fundraises millions of dollars in the name of that cause. But is that really their core mission, and how are they using the funds generously provided by donors?

In 2020 the BlackLivesMatter.com website page titled "What We Believe" stated that one of the foundation's key aims is to "disrupt the Western-prescribed nuclear family structure."

Disrupt the family? It appears that the very social institution most effective at enabling opportunity, community, and self-actualization is the enemy of BLM. How does destroying that incredibly uplifting institution help the individual trying to build a better life? It doesn't. Their mission is division and chaos, not protecting the rights or enhancing the lives of marginalized people.

Have the millions raised by BLM been used to pursue justice and equality for all, destroy the family, or enrich the founders? BLM cofounder Patrisse Cullors has clearly profited from the "nonprofit." Between 2016 and 2021, she accumulated $3.2 million in real estate assets.[1]

That is a lot of wealth gained over a short period of time for someone who claims to be a trained Marxist aggressively promoting the end of privately owned property. She seems to view herself as a privileged member of the Marxist elite instead of a lowly Marxist citizen living under its rules. Most self-proclaimed Marxists do. At least her Marxist goal of destroying the family makes sense now.

There is a question that I want you to ask yourself every time you see a highly educated person promoting ideas that are not consistent with the reality of human behavior or obviously will not lead to a sustainable and fulfilling existence for future generations—for example, initiatives that encourage criminal behavior, reward people for avoiding self-discipline, reward people for continually making poor decisions, or continually send taxpayer money to other countries instead of using those resources to solve problems right here at home.

Remember that the people promoting these ideas hold advanced degrees in law, engineering, medicine, business, and other fields. They are supposed to be the smartest people on the planet, but they often promote ideas that defy logic. In many cases their assertions seem to indicate that they don't possess even the most basic understanding of human behavior or have the ability to recognize potential unintended consequences that are intuitively obvious to the rest of us.

Every time you see this insanity repeated, ask yourself and those around you: How can this highly educated person possibly believe the words they are saying? The answer is clear: they don't believe the words they are saying but, as long as you do, that's all that matters.

Remember that! They don't believe the words they are saying but, as long as you do, that's all that matters.

> *The man who speaks to you of sacrifice, speaks of slaves and masters. And intends to be the master.*
>
> AYN RAND

Members of the elite and their groupies believe that they will be the administrators of the utopia they promote and will not be subjected to the restrictions and financial burdens placed on the rest of us.

14

INFLUENTIAL PEOPLE KNOW THE GAME

> *The ruling class believes itself to be generous because they allow the compliant to exist.*

Who are these influential people and why are they aligned with a disastrous liberal agenda?

Considering how large and diverse the group "influential people" is, it seems like a complicated question with an unknowable answer, but it is really very simple. There are four main reasons businesses and individuals aggressively promote the approved narrative: they want to be viewed as relevant, they are parroting the indoctrination they received throughout their years of education, they personally gain wealth and stature, or they are trying to avoid being destroyed by the machine as others have been for "misusing" their influence.

We would all like to think that everyone is basically like us. They are honest, kind, supportive of others in need, have a strong work ethic, and just want to do the right thing for their family and community. Unfortunately, politicians and business executives are often not like us at all. However, they often try to convince us that they are just average joes trying to do the right thing. If they can convince us of that, we will check the "OK guy" box in our minds and not pay much attention to what they are actually doing.

But again, politicians and business executives are often not like us at all.

Large businesses are run by influential people who have a lot to gain and a lot to lose. If they navigate the political waters successfully, they can gain substantially from their loyalty to powerful politicians. Their businesses can benefit through favorable legislation and regulatory changes. They can also reap rewards in the form of government grants and contracts. In some cases, lucrative political careers can be launched when business executives are appointed to prestigious high-level government positions.

> The federal government is larger than the top 31 largest US companies combined!

Every large business in the United States recognizes that the federal government is by far their largest potential customer. Based on spending for the year 2022,[1] the federal government is larger than the top 31 largest US companies combined! *Combined!*

Salespeople refer to the US government as the "Fortune 1" of *Fortune* magazine's Fortune 500 due to its size and their desire to make the largest customer in the country their highest priority. Note that autocorrect tried to change that to "their heist priority." Seems like it is trying to tell us something. Maybe just that my typing skills are dismal.

Business executives and other high-profile individuals have other motivations for supporting the narrative, or at least not openly resisting it. These same high-profile influential people are painfully aware that the US government, and the people who control its resources and enforcement agencies, can be a very dangerous adversary. What government enforcement agencies? The IRS, FBI, CIA, EPA, FTC, FDA, NIH, Homeland Security, Immigration Services, ATF, DEA, and others. Again, we'd all like to think that everyone is basically like us, but they are not.

> *The essence of Government is power; and power, lodged as it must be in human hands, will ever be liable to abuse.*
>
> JAMES MADISON

These agencies, in the hands of self-serving authoritarians, can be, and have been, used to destroy individuals and businesses. There is a very good reason we hear the term *lawfare* more and more these days. It refers to the misapplication or selective application of laws to delegitimize or punish opposition. The use of lawfare tactics has exploded over the past few years. We will cover some of the most egregious examples in later chapters. In the words of one whistleblower within the FBI, the current state of the FBI is "cancerous" as the bureau has "let itself become enveloped in this politicization and weaponization."[2]

For high-profile people, the revenue potential of a favorable public image along with the desire to be relevant and liked can be powerful drivers. It is easy to see how this applies to entertainers, sports figures, and media personalities whose fortunes rise and fall in dramatic fashion based on their popularity. But the same applies to high-profile business owners and executives. They too owe their fortunes to their public image and popularity to some extent.

Business executives understand that the growth of the business and their personal fortunes are largely dependent on public image. They put tremendous effort into making the company appear more likable in the public view. That means generating as much positive press as possible by promoting their products, services, executives, and the company as good members of the community. Companies spend a large percentage of their advertising budgets trying to sell people on the virtues of the company instead of the value of their products.

On the other hand, one misstep can be devastating to public image, company revenue, and the personal fortunes of executives. A single off-message comment and influencers across all media will brutally make an example of them as a dire warning to others. They will be painted as ignorant, misogynist, racist, evil, planet-hating, oppressive, and supportive of fascist ideas. Influencers may call for a boycott. Government enforcement agencies may even start taking a closer look at them. Getting out of step with approved messaging can be a disaster for them, and they often have teams of people focused on making sure that does not happen.

For people in entertainment, sports, and news media, their ability to amass wealth is directly tied to, almost exclusively tied to, how well-liked they are by some significant segment of the public. If they are loved, they can sign lucrative deals to appear in a variety of venues and are rewarded with millions of dollars for their mere presence. They can also land incredibly rewarding sponsorship deals to promote products on social media, TV, radio, and through public appearances.

In many cases their earning potential is directly tied to their Q Score, which is recognized as the standard method for measuring consumer appeal of performers, characters, brands, and brand ambassadors. Many of their statements and behaviors are carefully crafted specifically to drive up their Q Score and earnings. The more outlandishly and aggressively they support some approved cause the more positive press they will receive, driving up their score. Really! See for yourself at QScores.com.

Their public statements and posts are often repackaged reflections of where they think the culture is currently focused. If they have accurately read the room and can execute their virtue-signaling strategy effectively and flamboyantly, they will go viral, be loved, and possibly be exalted as a hero of one oppressed group or another.

The more people love them, the more followers they have, the more money they make. Many live in fear of that one ill-advised statement that brings it all crashing down.

There are hundreds of examples of celebrities who have successfully leveraged their high-profile public image to generate enormous wealth outside of entertainment and sports.

Kylie Jenner in her early twenties can make more than $1 million per promotional post. Similar for Kim Kardashian.

George Clooney sold his tequila company for $1 billion.

Jessica Alba created the Honest Company, which is valued at about $700 million.

Kate Hudson's Fabletics fashion brand saw $500 million in revenue in 2021.

Beyoncé and husband Jay-Z have many business ventures and a net worth of about $1.8 billion.

Rihanna, the second wealthiest female entertainer, has a net worth of about $1.7 billion created largely from her beauty and lingerie brands.

Oprah Winfrey is the wealthiest female entertainer with a net worth of about $2.6 billion created by her many business ventures.

Great! They are fabulously successful! Why should I care?

We shouldn't care. We should be inspired and admire them for their success, unless they insincerely use their enormous influence to enthusiastically support corrupt causes and corrupt people in power.

So, what happens if a darling of culture and media loses their mind and says something off message? There are hundreds of examples of people who knowingly or unknowingly behaved in a manner contrary to the narrative and suffered greatly for their transgression.

With the dizzying schedules of many high-profile people, they are at risk of making a mistake or misstatement. Nonstop, night and day, public appearances can be a minefield of potential mistakes exacerbated by a god-complex and spotlight fatigue. One minor misstatement or misstep can bring an avalanche of negative attention that can quickly extinguish their likability and render them an outcast. They will be canceled and will lose potentially hundreds of millions of dollars.

There are many recent examples. John Gibson was fired from his position as president of Tripwire Interactive for posting a conservative tweet.[3] Actor Gina Carano was fired from her leading role in Disney and Lucasfilm's *The Mandalorian* after criticizing the fact that political disagreement is often viewed as hate instead of simply disagreement. She was essentially canceled for criticizing the cancel culture.

Mike Lindell, CEO of My Pillow, still has his job but his company has been thrashed in the media. His products were dropped by many retailers, costing the company $100 million in sales.[4] His crime was supporting Donald Trump. Goya Foods was boycotted after the CEO made positive statements about Donald Trump.[5]

Winston Marshall, banjoist in the musical group Mumford and Sons, felt he had to leave the group after he triggered a cancel uproar by making positive comments about a journalist who exposed the lies of the extreme fascist group Antifa.[6]

For some, their earning potential has been permanently reduced by an intolerant angry mob controlled by the executive suites of business and politics.

There are hundreds of examples of entertainers, sports figures, and media personalities who have gone to great lengths to make sure everyone knows they are kind and lovable because they support the narrative. The saddest examples are the fading stars' desperate attempts to recapture their relevance. As careers decline and desperation begins to take hold, some become sad caricatures of their former selves as they publicly flail about trying to recapture their allure with ridiculous antics and nonsensical statements. It always ends in humiliation and is just sad to watch.

These fading stars are effectively attempting to save their image by grabbing on to the coattails of the current enlightened narrative, whatever that may be at the time. Madonna's ongoing antics, major plastic surgery, and very revealing pictures posted at age 64. Lena Dunham, Alyssa Milano, Michael Rapaport, Chelsea Handler, George Takei, and many others who continually say the most ridiculous things, trying to prove they are worthy of love from the masses.

Disingenuous virtue-signaling is very easy to spot. Just look for the conviction or lack of conviction on their faces. High-profile people have learned that, if they repeat the right message, it will be accepted and amplified automatically. They no longer feel the need to pretend they believe the words they say. You can see it on their faces. It is both sad and a relief to see great actors deliver lines in such an unconvincing manner. It's a relief because even the casual observer can see that they are not emotionally connected to what they are saying and don't actually believe their own words.

So, are they driven by the desire to be liked or by the fear of being crushed by the mob? The answer is probably both, at all times. One or the other motivator is probably dominant at any given time, depending on where they are in their career ascent or descent.

Regardless of which motivator is dominant, it is clear that those who wholeheartedly buy into and continuously promote the narrative of liberal ideology are more likely to be embraced and foisted up as heroes and leaders in their fields.

What about the people who are employed by these very powerful promoters of liberal ideology? If they plan to keep their jobs, they had better openly hold up the same ideology or keep a very low profile. You will not find many conservatives in the entertainment industry, the legacy news media, or academia. For decades, hiring and advancement processes in those industries have been controlled by people highly motivated to reward or punish candidates based on their political views.

Most people seeking positions in those industries are either already in the industry or have been following it long enough to be aware of the political and cultural views that dominate the industry. They know how they must behave to have a shot at success.

Those in the industry believe that they don't have political views but rather an enlightened understanding of human existence. They don't have opinions. They have perspective and insight into the facts. Anyone holding opposing views is simply ignorant and unfit for the industry. They feel completely justified in their discrimination and bigotry.

Employees who work in companies or industries that lean toward liberal ideology or benefit significantly from government programs understand that is an undeniable and unchangeable fact and they behave accordingly. Most would like to be promoted out of the proverbial mailroom. They understand that their political views and actions are often as important, or more important, than their work ethic and their ability to perform the job they seek higher up in the company. This unwritten standard of behavior is engrained in employees from the beginning and reinforced in them through systems of rewards and punishments that play out in front of them daily. By the time they reach positions of leadership in the company, they are fully indoctrinated and well prepared to be active and vocal promoters of this corporate culture.

Whether you work in an environment that promotes and rewards liberal views or conservative views, or an environment that is completely neutral, the best approach is to avoid discussing politics or hot-button topics with coworkers at work and even outside of work. If you lean toward conservative views, it is unlikely that expressing those views at work will bring any benefit to you personally. The odds are clearly not in your favor.

If you want to influence at work, be a good leader by being the best employee, coworker, team member, and mentor you can possibly be. Your kindness, work ethic, positive attitude, and the way you always win, even when you lose, will have a bigger impact on those around you than a heated debate over the stifling effect of out-of-control government. Your leadership and influence will evolve and take hold naturally.

At some point you will have the opportunity to politely ask people thought-provoking questions to encourage others to analyze more deeply a topic they have raised or a position they have taken. Socratic questioning can be a very powerful tool for leading people to discover answers for themselves.

> Influence by being the best spouse, parent, employee, coworker, team member, and mentor you can possibly be.

15

BIG TECH: BOTH MAESTRO AND TOOL

> *The Party told you to reject the evidence of your eyes and ears. It was their final, most essential command.*
>
> GEORGE ORWELL, *1984*

Do we choose the information and sources we consume, or is it fed to us almost undetected?

The Big Tech effect on the pervasiveness of the narrative is indispensable to the ruling class. Big Tech has a captive audience and algorithms that make sure they see, by default, information that convincingly reinforces the narrative and those people and organizations that most effectively promote it. Their captive audience finds it very difficult to locate any credible contrary information and are often left with the impression that only ignorant extremists seem to disagree with what all the smart people in the room are saying.

I know that sounds outrageous but when you consider the overwhelmingly dominant presence of liberal ideology and the influential reach of Big Tech, I think it is a completely reasonable statement.

But let's back up a bit and define Big Tech. According to *Wikipedia*:

> *Big Tech, also known as the Tech Giants, refers to the most dominant companies in the information technology industry, most notably the five largest American tech companies: Alphabet (Google), Amazon, Apple, Meta, and Microsoft. These companies are referred to as the Big Five.*
>
> *The Big Five are dominant players in their respective areas of technology: artificial intelligence, e-commerce, online advertising, consumer electronics, cloud computing, computer software, media streaming, smart home, self-driving cars, and social networking.*[1]

Big Tech may only officially refer to the five companies mentioned, but 15 or 20 others can be lumped in based on their vast audiences and their ability to influence public opinion using algorithms to promote content they agree with and suppress content they do not agree with.

In the next chapter, "Censorship Incorporated," we delve into how people in government use their power of coercion to convince Big Tech and the media to do their dirty censorship work. We also expose the reality behind recently created rating services that provide "brand safety" by informing companies where it is safe to spend their advertising dollars to promote their brands. Compliant news, information, and media sources are "safe" and are thus generously rewarded as their share of global advertising spend continues to grow. The rest should be avoided, essentially defunded, by advertisers, according to these new brand safety rating services.

In this chapter we won't spend much time discussing members of the legacy news media. CNN, Fox News, MSNBC, CNBC, BBC, Newsmax, ABC, NBC, CBS, *Wall Street Journal*, *New York Times*, *USA Today*, and the others are content creators and providers. That content is distributed by Big Tech, which amplifies or suppresses as needed to support the dominant ideological narrative of the day.

The overwhelmingly unbalanced nature of the amplified content is important, but it is the persistent presentation of "the aligned" messaging by Big Tech that misleads the audience into assuming that all the smart people agree with the message. Everyone else is a drooling moron. The content creators who enthusiastically stay on message are rewarded with much greater visibility and revenue. Big Tech doesn't define the narrative, but they do ensure that supporting information is easy to find and detractors are nearly invisible.

> There is no longer any doubt that the default sources of information are carefully curated.

These tech companies are predominantly liberal from top to bottom. Their founders, board members, executives, and employees are heavily weighted toward liberal ideology. How do we know that? Well, even though it is intuitively obvious to those who have followed these companies even a little, let's explore the evidence.

One single case demonstrates the subversive capabilities of Big Tech, their liberal leanings, and the inevitable authoritarian consequence of concentrated power. Leading up to the 2020 presidential election between Joe Biden and Donald Trump, the Hunter Biden laptop story broke and briefly appeared to torpedo Joe Biden's presidential ambitions.

Hunter Biden had dropped a laptop off at a Delaware repair shop in April 2019 and did not return to pay for the repairs and pick up the computer. The FBI seized the computer in December of that same year after the shop owner notified them of potentially sensitive data on the computer. The shop owner also made a copy of the hard drive and provided it to Robert Costello, an attorney for former NYC mayor Rudy Giuliani. In September 2020, a copy of the hard drive was provided to the *New York Post* newspaper.[2]

On that hard drive was clear evidence that Hunter Biden was selling access to political power—his father, the Big Guy, the vice president of the United States. He was also being paid $50,000 per month to be on the Burisma board of directors, even though he had no technical or business experience relevant to the company. Strong evidence was found of influence peddling, money laundering, and inappropriate ties to high-level officials in the Chinese Communist Party. Numerous photos and videos of Hunter Biden participating in drug use, sex acts, and other destructive behavior were present on the hard drive as well. The Biden family was incredibly embarrassed, and the campaign went into panic mode.

Remember, this story broke just weeks before the 2020 presidential election between Trump and Biden. Joe Biden's career was essentially over if the truth became widely known.

But don't worry, that would not happen. Big Tech went into overdrive to protect their friends in politics. The story was suppressed by Google, Facebook, and Twitter. After the *New York Post* broke the story and would not retract, their Twitter account was shut down.[3]

Algorithms on the dominant platforms were tweaked to prevent users from even being aware of the story. Left-wing sites posted articles with headlines that read, "Russian State Media Is Desperately Trying to Keep the Hunter Biden Story Alive." When asked why the story of the laptop was not being covered, news sites responded that it wasn't a real story. Legacy media outlets flooded the zone with stories referring to the *Post's* article as "dubious," "in doubt," and "disinformation" in unison, almost as if reading from the same script.[4]

Over two years later, many of those same news organizations admitted that the information on the Hunter Biden laptop was real and extremely incriminating. Remember, up to that point, anyone foolish enough to promote the laptop story as legitimate was publicly lambasted for promoting Russian disinformation, and was banned from dominant social media platforms, or secretly suppressed or "shadow-banned" by those platforms.

On October 19, 2020, a few weeks before the election, 51 former government intelligence officials released a signed letter indicating the data dump from the laptop could be disinformation created by the Russians.[5] However, they also stated in the letter they had no evidence of that and had no opinion on whether or not any of the information was accurate. Those signing the letter included former Defense Secretary Leon Panetta, former Director of National Intelligence James

Clapper, former CIA director John Brennan, and many other high-profile intelligence officials.

Many of the signers appeared on news services promoting the idea that this was likely created by the Russians. This gave liberal outlets the support and cover they needed to scream nonstop that the entire story was fake.

Many of those intelligence officials have stated since then that they knew much of the information was very likely authentic evidence of crimes perpetrated by the Biden family. Their excuse now is that they only said the story could be fake, not that it was fake. "Weasel words!" is the term our grandparents used to call out thinly veiled lies.

Why would 51 former government intelligence officials sully themselves to protect the Biden family from the consequences of their disgusting criminal behavior? Why would they provide the cover needed to enable a corrupt man to be elected president of the United States? It seems unimaginable beyond the pages of a political intrigue novel. Keep asking those questions and searching for the answers. It'll come to you!

In this unimaginable case there is a clear answer to the why question. The letter was created at the request of Biden campaign advisors Anthony Blinken and Andrew Bates. Blinken later became Biden's secretary of state after the election. Bates later became Biden's deputy press secretary after the election. Blinken and Bates worked with Michael Morell to create the letter and encourage former intelligence officials to sign on in support. Morell, former CIA acting director in the Obama administration, became a front-runner for CIA director appointment after the election. According to Morell, the original draft of the letter was written by Marc Polymeropoulos, a retired CIA officer.[6]

The good old boys' network in this case fears no boundaries. None! At least one of the letter signers admitted that an active CIA employee informed him that the letter was being created and encouraged him to sign it. All those named above have admitted that their intention was to suppress the scandals revealed by the laptop, given Biden a strong talking point for the upcoming televised debate, and ultimately help Biden win the election.

Three days after the letter was released, during the final presidential debate on October 22, Trump referred to "the laptop from hell" prompting Biden to respond with the following statement:[7]

> Look, there are 50 former national intelligence folks who said that what this, [President Trump's] accusing me of is a Russian plan. They have said that this has all the characteristics—four—five former heads of the CIA, both parties, say what he's saying is a bunch of garbage. Nobody believes it except him and his good friend Rudy Giuliani.

The US House of Representatives created the Subcommittee on the Weaponization of the Federal Government to investigate the letter and other cases where government resources are used to suppress opposition. The investigation is not yet complete because the CIA and the Biden administration have refused to provide documents requested by the committee.

Did the cover-up of this scandal impact voters' perceptions of the candidates?

Did the dishonest actions of these intelligence officials, Big Tech, and the media impact the outcome of the 2020 presidential election? The data shows that they absolutely did. The Media Research Center had 1,750 Biden voters polled after the election. About 55% of those polled were not aware of the scandals revealed by Hunter Biden's laptop. About 9.5% of them stated that they would *not* have voted for Joe Biden if they had known.[8]

That same poll revealed that 35.4% were not aware of credible sexual assault allegations against Joe Biden. About 8.9% of them would *not* have voted for Joe Biden if they had known.

In another poll conducted in August 2022 by Technometrica Institute of Policy and Politics (TIPP), 71% stated that it is somewhat likely or very likely that Trump would have won the election if voters had known about the scandals revealed by the laptop.[9]

If the polling is accurate, it is clear Big Tech and the media did in fact determine the outcome of that election.

The actual historical events described above are the manifestation of the "by any means necessary" doctrine, which is unapologetically followed by many liberal organizations. It means exactly what it says. While you and I are bound by our own beliefs in common decency and honesty, those who despise the inspiring people and institutions of effective civil society have no boundaries. The laws and the norms of functional community mean nothing to them. They are dedicated to gathering up more power by diminishing our heritage, future opportunity, and will to resist by using any means necessary.

Those same people clearly understand that the "by any means necessary" doctrine can most effectively be executed from within the intelligence and law enforcement agencies of the federal government. Watch closely. Keep asking questions and searching for the answers.

The document dump known as the Twitter Files offers us another case study in how Big Tech and government collude to control information. After Elon Musk acquired Twitter in 2022, he began gathering and releasing internal documents and emails that prove Twitter was actively promoting information and suppressing other information and specific users.

An enormous amount of evidence, known as the Twitter Files, has been released in many installments. Investigative reporter Matt Taibbi has dug through much of the data and has found extensive ongoing communications between Twitter and government officials that should be alarming to everyone. While looking into dialogues related to the banning of Donald Trump in 2021, Matt Taibbi uncovered communications from government agencies requesting thousands of accounts be suspended. These requests came from the FBI, CIA, NSA, Pentagon, State Department, Department of the Treasury and others. Employees were directed to suspend or ban the users without delay and without discussion.

For Twitter accounts of many high-profile influencers, to avoid triggering backlash by suspending them, Twitter allowed the accounts to remain active but shadow-banned them using tags that enforced *visibility filtering*, a term used by Twitter employees to refer to making people invisible on the platform. Many high-profile conservatives were tagged with "Search Blacklist" and "Do Not Amplify."

Many users suspected that they were being shadow-banned because responses to and retweets of their tweets dropped substantially. Their tweets became invisible to most and did not appear in search results. Jack Dorsey, cofounder of Twitter, confidently delivered this lie many times: "We don't shadow ban, and we certainly don't shadow ban based on political viewpoints."

You can see extensive evidence of political coercion on social media platforms for yourself. A summary of each Twitter Files release can be found on a website managed by Matt Taibbi (https://taibbi.substack.com).[10]

Taibbi released the Twitter Files Part 1 on December 2, 2022. The IRS opened a case related to Taibbi's 2018 tax return on December 24, 2022. Note that was a Saturday and was Christmas Eve. Their dedication to getting his tax refund to him is certainly commendable!

On March 9, 2023, Taibbi testified before the US House of Representatives Subcommittee on the Weaponization of the Federal Government. On that same day, an IRS agent showed up at his house. The message was clear: You and everyone you love can and will, if necessary, be destroyed.

The scandals revealed in each release of the Twitter Files only saw the light of day because Elon Musk acquired Twitter and made sure the information was released to the public. Since then, Musk has become an extremely high-profile example of the ruling class using lawfare to punish those who refuse to play along.

After decades of being fawned over by political elites and celebrities, suddenly they have their sights set on making an example of Musk. In November of 2022 President Joe Biden stated that Musk's business dealings were "worthy of being looked at" and joked "there's lots of ways" in response to questions on what the statement meant.

> If lawfare can be used to bring down the wealthiest man on the planet, the rest of us should probably sit down and shut up! At least that is the message they hope we take from it.

Musk is now being sued by the DOJ for not hiring enough refugees and asylum seekers to SpaceX, a national security sensitive company. SpaceX uses its rockets and technology to launch payloads into space for the Defense Department and NASA. It is impossible to perform reliable background checks on people who have fled countries that are imploding. Musk responded on the social media platform X that the company cannot legally hire certain people due to International Traffic in Arms Regulations. Other federal agencies are now very interested in Musk's business dealings as well.

Big Tech has much bigger ambitions than making friends in high places and determining an election or two. Dr. Michael Rectenwald is a former professor at New York University and author of *The Google Archipelago: The Digital Gulag and the Simulation of Freedom*. Dr. Rectenwald provides alarming insights based on his study of Big Tech companies and the history of past business titans in the United States. According to him, Big

Tech companies control the flow of news, information, scientific data, and opinions on the dominant internet platforms.

Big Tech companies are using that power to aggressively move toward an authoritarian socialist system that is a key part of the political and policy landscape. Big Tech companies have adopted leftist ideology and are deeply engaged in what he calls "corporate leftism," which in mission and practice is similar to the totalitarianism of the communist regime in China. Totalitarianism. Absolute control of politics, policy, law enforcement, information, goods, services, and the individual's ability to thrive or even survive.

"Big Digital consists of a bunch of left-leaning authoritarians," Dr. Rectenwald states. He contends that the public square has become irrelevant because it has been effectively replaced by the digital square. This gives digital authoritarians more power to remove or exclude people from debate or remove their digital platform and presence entirely. They essentially render opposition leaders invisible and silent.

The public will have to be very resourceful and persistent to find well-articulated positions that conflict with those promoted by Big Tech. "Their objectives are the effective political death and financial and social ruination of their political opponents," Dr. Rectenwald states in the book.

Financial and social ruination of their political opponents! Deeply troubling!

> Is the public square irrelevant? Are we left with only a heavily curated digital square?

This is a very interesting and complex topic. For more information, pick up a copy of Dr. Rectenwald's book or see interviews with Dr. Rectenwald published in *The Epoch Times*.[11]

Big Tech companies are not the first to believe that a massive monopolistic global corporation could create a socialist utopia. Over 100 years ago, the founder of Gillette, King Camp Gillette, wrote two books promoting the idea that a "World Corporation" is the best instrument for building a socialist society.

Henry Ford and other business giants in history have had similar ambitions and failed in their attempts to implement their vision of utopia. These utopian visionaries always seem to ignore the fact that the objects that must be manipulated into submission are actually human beings, not ants, droids, or robots. All such attempts fail in spectacular certitude because the science of human behavior will not be denied!

Other evidence of liberal leanings in Big Tech is found in the July 2020 CNBC piece entitled "The Most Liberal and Conservative Tech Companies, Ranked by Employees' Political Donations,"[12] where they provide information on employee contributions to political campaigns for the 17 US tech companies valued at $100 billion or more. The article relies on data from the Center for Responsive Politics' OpenSecrets website.

Below is a ranking of those companies, including the Big Tech Five, from most liberal to most conservative.

Company	Democratic Donations	% Dem	Republican Donations	% Repub
Netflix	$340,485	98%	$7,124	2%
Nvidia	$154,466	93%	$11,673	7%
Adobe	$401,937	93%	$28,137	7%
IBM	$1,496,234	90%	$163,804	10%
Salesforce	$457,119	89%	$59,181	11%
Alphabet (Google)	$5,437,048	88%	$766,920	12%
Microsoft	$3,969,072	85%	$690,953	15%
Apple	$1,243,825	84%	$228,653	16%
PayPal	$145,483	84%	$27,529	16%
Cisco	$798,586	80%	$204,400	20%
Amazon	$2,677,112	77%	$783,349	23%
Facebook	$1,634,153	77%	$480,133	23%
Intel	$790,769	68%	$372,667	32%
Broadcom	$326,616	68%	$154,058	32%
Oracle	$785,882	67%	$380,240	33%
Texas Instruments	$123,543	60%	$82,571	40%
Qualcomm	$289,336	50%	$284,119	50%

Figure 15.1 Political Campaign Contributions by Employees per Party

Considering that more and more people every day live online, get their news online, and consciously or unconsciously absorb ideology online, it would be difficult to overstate the influence Big Tech has on personal views, public opinion, and the distribution of political power. The most alarming claim I could articulate on that point would pale in comparison to the depth and breadth of reality. Let's never forget their traitorous objectives:

DETHRONING THE RULING CLASS

> *Their objectives are the effective political death and financial and social ruination of their political opponents.*
>
> DR. MICHAEL RECTENWALD, THE GOOGLE ARCHIPELAGO: THE DIGITAL GULAG AND THE SIMULATION OF FREEDOM

16

CENSORSHIP INCORPORATED

> *And if all others accepted the lie which the Party imposed —if all records told the same tale—then the lie passed into history and became truth. "Who controls the past" ran the Party slogan, "controls the future: who controls the present controls the past."*
>
> GEORGE ORWELL, *1984*

Legacy media, Big Tech, and the people in control of our government have learned hard lessons in recent years and are working together to make their job of protecting the public from the truth much easier. They have lost credibility through their missteps attempting to control the narrative on Hunter Biden, COVID, climate change, Russiagate, and many other events impacting the country.

In the last six years the act of censorship has been mechanized and weaponized through a series of alliances between government agencies and a handful of companies founded by former intelligence officials. Together they are the censorship-industrial complex.

When we speak of the current state of censorship in this country, we are not talking about limiting the speech of a few individuals by publicly calling them morons. The censorship-industrial complex is far more impactful than a person here and there not being heard. We are talking about the complete elimination of all but one side of every story relevant politically or culturally!

Think about that! If an issue is important to the future of your country, one side is embraced as the gold standard of facts and reason while every utterance to the contrary is systematically and even proactively rendered invisible!

> How does the systematic purging of dissenting facts and opinions shape public perceptions on important issues?

To be clear, this is not about a search engine returning results prioritized with a bias or excluding results based on ideology. While those things are the norm today and are totally unacceptable in a free and open society, censorship has grown up to become something far more effective in its deception. The censorship-industrial complex is making dissenting content invisible entirely until the sources comply or die a slow starvation death. No views for you and no soup for you!

The most effective remedy to dissent is to brutally punish those advocating for that dissent. Few can withstand the destruction of the reputation and income they need to support their families. Even fewer will stand up for their beliefs after witnessing the obliteration of those who spoke up before them.

Please believe me when I say that I know how crazy that sounds. The common perception is that it cannot possibly be true. That blissful optimism is exactly what enables it to continue to hide in plain sight. You see the headlines and you automatically dismiss it as just another rambling crackpot because that just could not possibly happen in this country. Please sit down. I have some very sad news for you.

This is not a conspiracy theory. These facts are not hidden. They are out in the open for all to see, if we will only look! This is the reality that we live today. The Department of Justice (DOJ), Department of Homeland Security (DHS), Cybersecurity and Infrastructure Security Agency (CISA), FBI, and other enforcement offices within the government are the most egregious perpetrators.

If that doesn't motivate people to fully engage in holding accountable the people in control of our government, then nothing ever will!

Think about the origins and charter of the Department of Homeland Security for just a minute. From the DHS website: "The Department of Homeland Security was formed in the wake of the terrorist attacks of September 11, 2001, as part of a determined national effort to safeguard the United States against terrorism." But somehow that mission has morphed into monitoring US citizens and suppressing messaging that DHS decides is disinformation? Yes, to our shock it has!

In November 2018 a new cyber security agency was created within DHS. The mission of the Cybersecurity and

Infrastructure Security Agency (CISA) was initially cybersecurity and critical infrastructure security. Their job was to protect the "homeland" from threats to cybersecurity and critical infrastructure from computer hackers, be they nation-states or terrorist organizations.

Spoiler alert! Follow along here because the "critical infrastructure" component of their mission is eventually leveraged to give them unprecedented power to covertly monitor people and businesses in the United States.

Over the past 30 years I have held many roles in the software and computing industry. I see firsthand the relentless and devastating nature of the cybersecurity threat from bad actors. There is no doubt that our government must have the most advanced cybersecurity defense capabilities available. There are many bad actors in the world that have nothing but free time and deep-seated resentment for our country. It is an enormous undertaking to protect vital systems from these hackers. Our cybersecurity experts must get it right 100% of the time. The hackers only need to get it right once and it costs them nothing to keep trying 24/7.

Obviously, we need CISA to coordinate across many government agencies to protect our country, businesses, and citizens from these cybersecurity threats. However, the "critical infrastructure" component is vaguely defined and has provided the nebulous gray area needed for CISA to continually expand their mission scope. At this point their role as protector of critical infrastructure seems to include just about anything needed for the government and businesses to operate day to day. There is little left of our society and lives at this point that is outside of CISA's authority.

The Critical Infrastructure Information Act of 2002 provided the definition of critical infrastructure. It was further clarified in 2013 Presidential Policy Directive PPD-21 as "assets, networks, and systems—that are vital to public confidence and the Nation's safety, prosperity, and well-being."

In 2017, just after the election of President Obama, the DHS designated "election infrastructure" as critical infrastructure. That memo also lists 16 other areas considered critical infrastructure.[1] By labeling election infrastructure, and nearly everything else, as "critical infrastructure," CISA has been able to surveil and censor US citizens online through direct CISA action and through their proxies outside of government.

Many high-profile people were labeled as threats to election infrastructure and systematically suppressed because they raised questions about the 2020 election.

In November 2021, the director of CISA, Jen Easterly, made this incredibly alarming statement indicating that the government should be more active in protecting citizens from wrong thinking:

> *One could argue we're in the business of critical infrastructure, and the most critical infrastructure is our cognitive infrastructure, so building that resilience to misinformation and disinformation, I think, is incredibly important.*[2]

Who within CISA decides what is misinformation and disinformation? Frightening!

As revealed in later lawsuits and congressional investigations, CISA created the MDM Subcommittee to create synergy between CISA, Big Tech, and academia with the objective of protecting critical infrastructure from misinformation, disinformation, and malinformation (MDM). In July 2022, just after the DHS Disinformation Governance Board fiasco, covered later in this chapter, CISA began moving their surveillance and censorship activities to outside entities and began trying to cover their tracks.[3]

Once again, the cover-up proves knowledge of the crime! It is often said that the cover-up is worse than the crime. However, when it comes to targeting US citizens for what they think and say, no cover-up could be worse than that crime.

The collusion between DHS, CISA, Big Tech, high-profile academic institutions, and private companies to control the narrative on all media, not just social media, is the most outrageous scandal in the history of this country! In fact, their coercion tactics have been so effective that most people in the United States have no idea that it even happened and is still going on today. Did you know about it? If so, you are one of the few. It is an incredibly tangled web of conspiracy. As disturbing as it is, please take time to read through some of the information sources listed at end of this chapter.

Again, I know how crazy this sounds! Unfortunately, it is true. Don't take my word for it. In fact, don't take my word for anything. Every page of this book contains names, places, dates, and other details that are essentially breadcrumbs that you can use to research every topic for yourself. Please do.

In this case, take the word of Judge Terry A. Doughty in the US District Court of Western Louisiana. On July 4, 2023, Judge Doughty issued a preliminary injunction and temporary restraining order blocking federal agencies from interacting with the social media platforms on suspected misinformation. Judge Doughty issued this ruling in response to a request from the plaintiffs in the lawsuit filed against President Biden and a very long list of other defendants.[4] This suit, known as *State of Missouri v. Joseph R. Biden Jr.*[5] was filed by the state of Missouri, the state of Louisiana, and five citizens who contend in the suit:

> *Plaintiffs allege that Defendants, through public pressure campaigns, private meetings, and other forms of direct communication, regarding what Defendants described as "disinformation," "misinformation," and "malinformation," have colluded with and/or coerced social-media platforms to suppress disfavored speakers, viewpoints, and content on social-media platforms. Plaintiffs also allege that the suppression constitutes government action, and that it is a violation of Plaintiffs' freedom of speech under the First Amendment to the United States Constitution.*

The suit contains specific details of nearly 160 allegations of ongoing collusion and coercion tactics applied to social media platforms both directly and through private companies acting on behalf of government officials. The plaintiffs argue that their constitutional civil rights were violated and that they and their followers sustained actual harm when their voices were silenced by platforms that removed their posts, algorithmically shadow-banned them, and in some cases suspended or banned their accounts.

Those being sued, the 45 defendants, are listed by government entity in the following defendant categories:

- White House Defendants

- Surgeon General Defendants
- CDC Defendants
- NIAID Defendants
- FBI Defendants
- CISA Defendants (including DHS)
- State Department Defendants

The real harm to individuals detailed in the suit is easy to see. The states' claims of harm against the federal government are probably less obvious. The states of Missouri and Louisiana as plaintiffs in the suit make a very compelling argument that actions of the federal government infringed on the rights of the states and their ability to serve their citizens. The federal government restricted the states' ability to communicate freely with citizens by suppressing the citizens' ability to communicate freely on social media. The states argue that their ability to represent the interests of their citizens was impeded and thus the states and citizens were harmed. They contend that they were further harmed when the federal government subverted their ability to protect the constitutional rights of their citizens and protect their sovereign state constitutions.

The suit is ongoing, and Judge Doughty issued the July 4, 2023 ruling to provide immediate protection to the plaintiffs from further harm, stating:

> *The Plaintiffs have presented substantial evidence in support of their claims that they were the victims of a far-reaching and widespread censorship campaign. This court finds that they are likely to succeed on the merits of their First Amendment free speech claim against the Defendants.*

Hang on. Let's pause and take in the magnitude of the judge's statement. He is a government employee damning the actions of his government. That is impactful! He is not willing to just shrug it off as another day in government. He made that clear with the phrases "far-reaching and widespread censorship campaign" and "are likely to succeed on the merits" to be sure.

> The key takeaway point here is that the government can be held accountable if we have the courage and discipline to stand up to their overreach. If we stay seated, they will keep reaching until the only thing left is obedience.

The Biden administration appealed the judge's ruling. Even though the censorship-industrial complex is somewhat in autopilot mode in the hands of nongovernment entities, the Biden administration just cannot take the risk of relinquishing control entirely. They are appealing to ensure that they can still directly apply pressure where needed to maintain messaging compliance. Isn't appealing the ruling effectively admitting they are guilty? Yes! But the risk to their public image is minimal.

Most people in the United States have no inkling of their crimes, of the lawsuits, of the restraining order, or their appeal of that restraining order. If the entire country is unaware, then the risk of anyone noticing an implicit admission of guilt is extremely low. We are working very hard to overcome this type of blissful naiveté!

Unfortunately, a three-judge panel sided with the Biden administration and blocked Judge Doughty's preliminary injunction and temporary restraining order.[6] Biden's team argued that "The Government faces irreparable harm with each day the injunction remains in effect." The lawsuit continues.

On July 28, 2023, state attorneys general from 21 states filed an amicus brief asking the courts to side with the Biden administration. You would think the rats would abandon a ship that is taking on water so quickly, but not these people! We should probably memorize their names in case they show up on a ballot someday, and they will. Why would these highly educated people attach themselves to this odorous pile? It'll come to you!

With the lawsuits and congressional investigations, you might think this censorship issue has been dealt with and is no longer a threat to our civil rights. Unfortunately, the coercion beast has been unleashed and is in the hands of power-hungry business executives who will do anything and everything to gain favor with those in control of our government.

This battle rages on at the hands of nonprofit organizations such as the Center for Internet Security (CIS) and the Election Integrity Partnership (EIP).[7] In the words of EIP founder Alex Stamos, their role is to "try to fill the gap of the things that the government could not do themselves" because, in his words, the government "lacked both kinda the funding and the legal authorizations."

In transparent language, these organizations perform tasks for the government that the government is by law prohibited from performing. These organizations are often founded by and their ranks packed with former officials from DHS, CISA, and other government entities.

People are still being destroyed by our government or its agents in business for what they think or say. Reputations, careers, personal finances, and safety are all still counted as the cost when high-profile people refuse to submit to parroting the approved narrative.

Remember that the Media Research Center had 1,750 Biden voters polled after the 2020 election. About 55% of those polled were not aware of the scandals revealed by Hunter Biden's laptop. About 9.5% of them stated that they would *not* have voted for Joe Biden if they had known. An entire nation of people was egregiously harmed by a single instance of censorship.

> Remember that the people in government have enthusiastic groupies who are well compensated for their acts of loyalty.

Let's look at a few of the well-funded organizations launched in the past few years with the common goal of protecting people from misinformation, disinformation, and malinformation (MDM). They all present themselves as guardians of democracy and have very noble sounding mission statements, at least that's what the first few pages of Google results tell us.

The most highly reported and now defunct of these organizations was created within the DHS and was called the Disinformation Governance Board or Disinformation Board.[8] In February 2022 the Disinformation Board charter was approved by Secretary of the Department of Homeland Security Alejandro Mayorkas.

The existence of the group was announced in late April 2022 and the backlash was swift and brutal. Many immediately recognized the parallels between this new government disinformation operation and the "Ministry of Truth," the government propaganda machine in the book *1984* by George Orwell.

What catastrophic events prompted the government to start trying to protect us from disinformation? Everyone involved in promoting this new censorship operation was very vocal about the so-called facts that the Hunter Biden laptop scandal was Russian disinformation, the Steele dossier was proof of Trump's allegiance to Russia, Russians interfered with the 2020 presidential election attempting to hand it over to Trump, and that the Russians did collude with Trump to steal the 2016 presidential election from Hilary Clinton.[9]

Many in positions of authority had been working closely with Big Tech to promote these "truths" and suppress "disinformation" on these topics and others. They all promoted these lies right up to the very last minute, when they were disproven. And in April 2022 they were rewarded by the Biden administration with the ultimate power as arbiters of truth, the power to control information sources through a system of carrots and sticks, through generous support and vicious punishment. They were deputized as the Disinformation Governance Board! The party streamers flew wildly about the room, but only briefly.

The Biden administration and DHS were apparently a bit overconfident in their ability to control the narrative. The immediate and broad-based outcry forced the new censorship operation to be dissolved within a few weeks.[10] That is stunning! Democrats live in such isolation and are so out of touch with reality on the ground, they had no idea that such an outrageous overreach would be so loudly and universally condemned! We should all internalize that insight and allow it to be a principal factor when assessing the actions and motivations of politicians.

Apparently, they had not even considered the possibility that there might be resistance! They demonstrated an incredible level of confidence in their power to control the narrative and perceptions!

Republican members of Congress were among the most vocal opponents of this new censorship board. In May 2022, the secretary of DHS, Alejandro Mayorkas, was called to testify before the Senate Appropriations Committee on the purpose and scope of this new board. It was later learned that Mayorkas committed perjury during questioning. Mayorkas stated, "We at the Department of Homeland Security don't monitor American citizens," and claimed that the board had not yet begun its work. Both statements were false and Mayorkas knew it.[11] If you or I lied to Congress, under oath or not, or lied to a government agent during a casual conversation, we would go to jail. I guess high-profile government insiders fall under different laws?

In a hilarious twist, since everybody seems to love a victim, Nina Jankowicz, who led the Disinformation Governance Board all three weeks it operated, has started a crowdfunding campaign to finance a lawsuit. She is filing a suit against media organizations that exposed the truth about the censorship operation and her long history of disinformation hypocrisy. That is so 2023 of her. Hilarious!

Where government power meets legal resistance, the groupies step in and commit to victory by any means necessary.

In the fallout of this fiasco, the Select Subcommittee on the Weaponization of the Federal Government was established by the House of Representatives.[12] The subcommittee was created by House resolution HR12 in February 2023 to "investigate matters related to the collection, analysis, dissemination, and use of information on U.S. citizens by executive branch agencies, including whether such efforts are illegal, unconstitutional, or otherwise unethical." The group is doing good work in trying to uncover the details of collusion between Big Tech and various government agencies.

On February 9, 2023, House Judiciary Chairman Jim Jordan made the opening statement at the first meeting of the subcommittee. That statement can be found on most video hosting services with the title *Chairman Jordan's Opening Statement at the Weaponization of the Federal Government Hearing*[13]. It's well worth a watch. In the statement he summarizes several reports from whistleblowers inside the FBI and says there are many other reports from whistleblowers from the various enforcement agencies within the DOJ. Remember that the DOJ reports to the president and includes many enforcement agencies such as the DHS, FBI, DEA, ATF, US Marshal Service, and others.

The investigations and hearings are ongoing, but the Congressional subcommittee has already released many very disturbing reports, including the following:[14]

- Reining in Big Tech's Censorship of Conservatives 10.6.20
- Republicans Release 1,000 Page Report on FBI & DOJ Politicization 11.4.22
- The FTC: An Agency's Overreach to Harass Elon Musk's Twitter 3.7.23
- Weaponization Select Subcommittee and House Judiciary Committee Interim Report on AG Garland's Anti-Parent Memo 3.21.23
- Weaponization Select Subcommittee, House Judiciary Committee, and House Intelligence Committee Interim Report on How Senior Intelligence Officials and the Biden Campaign Worked to Mislead American Voters 5.10.23
- Report on FBI Whistleblower Testimony Highlights Government Abuse, Misallocation of Resources, and Retaliation 5.18.23
- The Murder of Kayla Hamilton: A Case for Immigration Enforcement and Border Security 5.23.23
- The Weaponization of CISA: How a "Cybersecurity" Agency Colluded with Big Tech and "Disinformation" Partners to Censor Americans 6.26.23
- The FBI's Collaboration with a Compromised Ukrainian Intelligence Agency to Censor American Speech 7.10.23
- Weaponization Select Subcommittee's Amicus Brief on *Missouri v. Biden* 8.8.23

It is so tempting to be comforted by the backlash and rest easy believing that this censorship issue has been dealt with and is behind us. However, that is far from the truth.

It is a complicated web of agencies and actors. The purpose of the Disinformation Governance Board was to consolidate existing operations to establish centralized messaging control. Those previously existing, dispersed censorship operations are still in full force. Unfortunately, they have had to face the bitter realization that they do not yet have the power to practice their craft in the light of day with impunity. They may take a lower profile briefly, but they are still working passionately behind the scenes to promote compliant messaging and eliminate dissent.

There is another category of companies that attempt to enforce "appropriate messaging" by pressuring companies to buy advertising space only from media outlets that promote compliant messaging. A small number of very powerful advertising and media associations are the gatekeepers of over 90% of the advertising spend in the United States. If you run a media company that sells advertising space, you have little choice but to comply. If those gatekeepers don't think you are loyal to the cause, your media company will be starved out of existence.

NewsGuard, for example,[15] "provides transparent tools to counter misinformation for readers, brands, and democracies." So they are not just protecting people from consuming misinformation, and companies from supporting misinformation with their advertising dollars, but they are also somehow protecting democracies?

Are democracies protected by making sure citizens can easily access "the approved truth" without having to concern themselves with the integrity of the source or what their allegiances and motivations might be? Is that really how democracy is strengthened? Not by rigorous and open debate but by ensuring that everyone agrees with those in charge?

NewsGuard has a well-documented history of downgrading media outlets for "disinformation" that is later determined to be factual.[16] In March of 2023, Florida state CFO Jimmy Patronis issued a letter of warning to NewsGuard titled "Florida Is Prepared to Protect Florida Businesses from NewsGuard."[17] The Media Research Center released a study in January 2023 that reveals NewsGuard rates liberal outlets very highly regardless of how inaccurate their reporting is and rates conservative outlets 25 points lower on the aggregate.[18]

NewsGuard information filtering is now being used broadly throughout public schools and is offered to parents free of charge![19] That should promote critical thinking skills development in public schools. Maybe not!

Global Alliance for Responsible Media (GARM), created by World Federation of Advertisers (WFA), represents itself as "the voice of marketers worldwide, representing 90% of global marketing communications spend." GARM was launched in 2019 "to address the challenge of harmful content on digital media platforms and its monetization via advertising." Their website also states, "GARM's ambition is to get the digital media ecosystem working together on the shared priorities that will lead to the removal of harmful content from advertiser-supported social media." Again, sounds great on the surface but is their mission to defund media companies that are out of compliance with messaging approved by GARM and their government clients?[20]

In March 2023 House Judiciary Committee Chair Jim Jordan (R-OH) subpoenaed officials from GARM and the WFA, saying that the two appeared to be facilitating "collusion among their members in a manner that may violate U.S. antitrust law."[21]

> Their control of advertising budgets empowers them to force news outlets and media companies to stick with approved messaging.

In December 2020 the British Broadcasting Corporation (BBC) created the Trusted News Initiative (TNI) agreement to bring legacy media and Big Tech together "to tackle harmful disinformation in real time." According to the BBC, the objective is to enlist members who commit to "alert each other to high risk disinformation so that content can be reviewed promptly by platforms, whilst publishers ensure they don't unwittingly share dangerous falsehoods."[22]

Through technology collaboration they have developed software that detects what they consider to be misinformation and triggers suppression alerts and algorithms. They have essentially gathered up all sources and primary distributors of news and information seen by most of the public in the United States and other countries. They control what information you can easily access. More importantly, they control who has a voice by fast-tracking those who agree with them and suppressing all others.

People who make a living only if they are heard understand that they must appease these gatekeepers if they are to continue providing for their families. Do you think that forces people out of the business entirely and forces those remaining to speak very carefully? Again, it almost seems like all the smart people in the room are saying all the same things, doesn't it? Members have priority, obviously, and the following companies are listed as members:

ABC (Australia), AFP, AP, BBC, CBC/Radio-Canada, Dawn (Pakistan), European Broadcasting Union (EBU), Financial Times, Information Futures Lab, Google/YouTube, the Hindu, Indian Express, Kompas (Indonesia), Meta, Microsoft, the Nation Media Group, NDTV (India), NHK (Japan), Reuters Institute for the Study of Journalism, SBS (Australia), Thomson Reuters, Twitter, the Washington Post

Trusted News Initiative has quickly gained tremendous influence over what discussions and information is allowed even in scientific and medical peer review systems. Peer review systems allow scientists to upload research results so other scientists with expertise in that area can provide initial review and comments on their methods and results. It is science and expert peers in the scientific community can applaud a study, thrash it harshly, or come down somewhere in the middle. However, if a study presents results that don't support the narrative, the Trusted News Initiative can pressure the publishing company to remove the paper without providing a science-based reason.[23]

So, how good are these organizations at preventing wrong-think? Are their detection and suppression algorithms effective? Try it out! Search the internet for information on Trusted News Initiative, Project Origin, C2PA, or any of the organizations mentioned in this chapter. You will find that they all seem to be universally loved by all. Nobody seems to have any concerns about the power they wield. They are either some of the nicest and most honorable people in the world or something else entirely.

The European Union (EU) has institutionalized censorship with a new law, the Digital Services Act (DSA), that applies to the 27 member countries. Enforcement from the ivory towers of Brussels, Belgium, began August 28, 2023. Thierry Brenton, EU commissioner of markets, and 230 staffers will determine the rules of acceptable content and the punishment for violating those rules. Let's make sure this type of government overlord insanity does not find a foothold in this country!

One of the best ways to keep an eye on these "protectors of truth" is to get your news and information from the sources listed in the final chapter of this book.

17

THE WEALTH MAGNET OF PUBLIC OFFICE

> *Liberty will not long survive the total extinction of morals.*
>
> SAMUEL ADAMS

Politics: The Art and Science of Self-Promotion

How do elected officials become so wealthy? Many are in significant debt when they arrive at their first state or federal position. Is it possible for them to leverage their influence to quickly move from being buried in debt to being very wealthy? It is not only possible, but the process is repeated regularly.

Everyone wants to be friends with the rich and powerful, the people who control the money. A wealthy fan base can bring a plethora of insider-only investment opportunities, book deals, speaker fees, silent partnerships, contributions to closely tied charitable foundations, and so on.

The Clinton Foundation took in donations of about $249 million in 2009, Hilary Clinton's first year as secretary of state. The Clinton Foundation also had exceptionally strong revenue while she was presumed to be the next president of the United States in 2014 and 2015 ($177 million, $116 million). As her campaign began to flounder, donations declined to $70.8 million in 2016. In the year following her election loss, 2017, donations dropped to $38.4 million. That is a 93% drop from 2009 donations.[1] Did the worthy and altruistic mission of the foundation suddenly become less worthy? Or did she simply no longer have the ability to sell government favor to the highest bidder?

Are you still skeptical? A 2016 report from the Associated Press highlighted that at least 85 of 154 individuals representing private interests who met with Hillary Clinton as secretary of state also donated to the Clinton Foundation and its global programs. In total, those 85 donors contributed as much as $156 million to the foundation.[2]

When it comes to cashing in on position and influence, there are many creative conduits for that money to flow. Even former Vice President Dan Quayle brings in up to $200,000 per speaking engagement! Imagine what popular politicians can bring in!

There are many paths to riches for those in power but none are as effortless and effective as good old-fashioned influence peddling. The Clintons have proven that over and over. Bill and Hillary Clinton set the standard by which all other self-serving politicians measure their own success. To get anywhere close to the success of the Clintons in this area, politicians must be very active and creative in making and supporting wealthy friends.

They make those relationships worthwhile by guiding government policy, regulation, and spending to benefit their most generous wealthy friends.

> The corrupt politician's final thought before drifting off to sleep: "Can I top the Clintons' haul?"

The Biden family provides a very informative study into the classic multigenerational wealth-building opportunities of those in power and their extended family. For decades Joe Biden and his extended family have enriched themselves by influencing government action to benefit those who have the millions of dollars needed to buy that kind of power.

Every close relative of Joe Biden has amassed far more wealth than their education and experience could possibly earn them. Much of that wealth has come from executive positions and board level positions at companies with multibillion-dollar government contracts or companies that are positioning themselves for government contracts or regulatory approvals needed to move projects forward.

The mechanisms used to solicit and deliver corrupt funds can be very complicated and difficult to trace. Many books have been written that step through the details. Peter Schweizer is the president of the Government Accountability Institute and has written books on the moneymaking machines created around the oval office. His book *Profiles in Corruption: Abuse of Power by America's Progressive Elite* provides details of the extensive influence-peddling systems of the Biden family and other high-profile elected officials. His book *Clinton Cash* covers the details of how the Clintons became incredibly wealthy through their close relationships with governments and businesses of foreign countries.

Sometimes the mechanisms used to buy influence with corrupt politicians are not all that complicated. Did you know that Hunter Biden is an amazing artist? According to reports in *Business Insider*, Hunter has made well over $1 million from sales of his works of art! A single undisclosed buyer paid nearly $900,000 for 11 of his works. I'm sure the purchases were made and prices were set based entirely on the value of Hunter's masterpieces. My editor tells me that sarcasm can be tricky in written form. How am I doing?

If we focus on current events, the news of the day, we see that Hunter Biden is in the headlines again for his business dealing with the governments of Ukraine and China, and businesses in those countries. On August 11, 2023, US Attorney General Merrick Garland elevated US Attorney David Weiss to the role of special counsel in the investigation into Hunter Biden's involvement in influence peddling. As a US Attorney, Weiss had been leading that investigation for over two years by the time he was appointed special counsel.

In June 2023 Hunter was charged with failure to pay income tax on nearly 5 million dollars of income. He was also charged with illegal possession of a firearm. The income was from Chinese and Ukrainian businesses.

Hunter was offered a sweet deal, allowing him to avoid prison time by pleading guilty to the tax-related charges. This deal would enable the Bidens and legacy media to aggressively drive the narrative that all of Hunter's legal matters had been resolved. They could then waive off any questions on Hunter's legal issues with "those issues were resolved" or similar dismissals. However, the charges were only a small part of the investigation into Hunter's business dealings. It is unlikely that many Republicans would go along with that narrative because well-informed conservative voters certainly would not.

The sweet plea deal was rejected by US District Judge Maryellen Noreika on June 26, 2023. This is very bad news for the Bidens. It looks like Hunter is going to trial, which is the last thing the Biden family wanted. They will certainly be embarrassed through the process. More frightening to them is the possibility that years of lies to investigators and their ongoing corrupt enterprises will be brought out in court filings and sworn testimony.

More bad news for the Bidens: a whistleblower, Devon Archer, has come forward with intimate details of the Biden machine and how Joe Biden, the "brand," was leveraged to convince foreign governments and businesses to pay Hunter millions through sham business deals and company titles. All of this has long been alleged but now there is proof. Hunter Biden received several million dollars over many years from China and Ukraine even though he had no competency in the businesses or technologies involved.

Recent reports state that the Biden family received well over $20 million dollars in recent years through their influence-peddling machine. Six different banks have filed 170 suspicious activity reports (SAR) on dozens of accounts tied to shell companies owned by Biden family members. These SAR filings with the Financial Crimes Enforcement Network were triggered by payments from enemy nations and other suspicious transactions possibly related to money laundering.

To make matters worse for Joe Biden, he has lied repeatedly for years to investigators and the press about Hunter's business dealings and his own involvement. This new information clearly indicates that Joe Biden also made multiple false sworn statements in court.

In related news, *The Epoch Times* reported in August 2023 that the Biden super PAC Future Forward did not report receiving nearly $12 million and has no explanation for not reporting it or where the money has gone.[3] Again, you or I would go to jail.

Should we give poor old Joe a pass because his corrupt earnings are minimal compared to those of the Clintons?

For those of us not closely watching the tendency for power to corrupt, it is hard to imagine that an elected official would sell out their country and significantly diminish opportunities available to future generations, for 10 or 20 million dollars. The cost to the people over decades is far too great in comparison. Yet it happens every day. *We the people* have no choice but to take the time to inform ourselves and do the work to hold those in government accountable.

Passionately embracing our role as citizens can involve risks. We know that those at the highest levels of government have the power of multiple government enforcement agencies. Those resources are at their disposal to encourage people to participate in and provide public support for their self-serving initiatives.

If high-profile influential people are not motivated by greed, they can be motivated by fear. Why do major corporations go along? Because they are run by influential people, individuals who have a lot to gain or a lot to lose, depending on which tool must be used to ensure their compliance. What government enforcement agencies? The IRS, FBI, CIA, EPA, FTC, FDA, NIH, Homeland Security, Immigration Services, ATF, DEA, and others.

Political corruption and payouts do not always involve international intrigue. Elected officials also build their wealth based on the insider knowledge they have of future legislation that will benefit specific companies or industries through taxpayer funding, preferential legislation, or budding catastrophes.

Insider knowledge of upcoming funding for specific infrastructure projects enables them to execute personal investment transactions in anticipation of future land value increases. Infrastructure projects often enhance land value due to government purchases of large tracts of land needed for the project and increased demand for adjacent land. They don't have to own the land needed by the government. They just need to own nearby land that will increase in value due to the new development.

Members of Congress also own stock in the companies they regulate, companies whose stock prices can be dramatically affected by legislation the members promote or by a few words they speak in public. Did you catch that? The regulators own stock in the companies they regulate! How do you think that affects fair and accurate application of the law? Are these companies held accountable by the regulators? Not if it could hurt the personal investments of the people who control those government entities.

Many elected politicians trade stocks and significantly outperform the S&P 500 year after year. Many experts agree it is impossible to achieve those results consistently on a relatively small number of stocks without insider information. Buying or selling stocks based on nonpublic information provided by insiders is known as insider trading and is a federal crime.

There are few effective limits on the ability of elected officials to take advantage of their insider knowledge. Martha Stewart went to prison for insider trading, but for some reason it appears to be incredibly difficult to apply the same standard to our elected officials. In 2012, the Stop Trading on Congressional Knowledge Act was passed in an attempt to curtail some of their insider trading and their conflicts of interest. The new law had little impact.

One of the more significant provisions of the law requires that members of Congress must publicly disclose their stock trades in a timely manner. This also applies to trades made by their spouses and dependent children. Compliance with the law has been spotty. Those who violate always have valid reasons for their noncompliance. Their accountant dropped the ball, there was a typo that prevented reporting, or they were just not able to understand the law. Really? Were they not just telling us that we should vote for them because they are so incredibly intelligent? Don't most of them have advanced degrees? Even law degrees in many cases?

If it is determined that a member has violated the Stop Trading on Congressional Knowledge Act, they could be forced to pay a fine as high as $200, if the penalty is not waived. So basically, the law is nothing but a circus act designed to convince voters that their elected officials are completely honest and are holding themselves accountable. This clever act of theater seems to be working for them, as usual.

Martha Stewart went to prison but members of Congress commit insider trading daily with no consequences.

Business Insider's investigative reporting project, *Conflicted Congress*, investigates and reports on financial disclosures made by members of Congress.[4] In December 2021, *Business Insider* published multiple reports on illegal or unethical investment transactions. Some of the findings released include:

- 57 members of Congress and 182 senior-level congressional staffers who have violated a federal conflicts-of-interest law
- Nearly 75 federal lawmakers who held stocks in COVID-19 vaccine makers Moderna, Johnson & Johnson, or Pfizer in 2020, with many of them buying or selling these stocks in the early weeks of the pandemic
- Senators, House members, and top Capitol Hill staffers who will help decide whether the government regulates cryptocurrency—and are themselves invested in Bitcoin and other altcoins
- Ratings of every member of Congress on their financial conflicts and commitment to financial transparency. 13 senators and House members have received a red "danger" rating on their three-tier stoplight scale, while 113 get a yellow "borderline" rating.

So, are they wealthy? The Open Secrets organization compiles and analyzes financial data for elected representatives. Their most recent data includes "Richest Members of Congress in 2018," "Poorest Members of Congress in 2018," and "Biggest Wealth Increase in Congress from 2008–2018."[5]

The wealth increase numbers are the most relevant because many arrive in Congress already extremely wealthy. Their net worth is far less interesting than the growth of that net worth since being elected. The percentage increase in some cases is staggering. Over 11,000% in one case!

Name	Wealth 2008	Wealth 2018	Percent Growth
Grace Napolitano (D-CA)	$8,000	$913,004	11,313%
Judy Chu (D-CA)	$92,007	$7,090,031	7,606%
Pete Olson (R-TX)	$85,514	$5,665,019	6,525%
Collin C. Peterson (D-MN)	$123,502	$4,241,504	3,334%
Chellie Pingree (D-ME)	$442,002	$9,938,006	2,148%
Steven Brett Guthrie (R-KY)	$421,506	$7,663,010	1,718%
Rob Wittman (R-VA)	$133,004	$1,645,563	1,137%
Rob Bishop (R-UT)	$3,501	$40,501	1,057%
Martin Heinrich (D-NM)	$27,317	$309,017	1031%
Eddie Bernice Johnson (D-TX)	$57,503	$615,501	970%

Figure 17.1 Biggest Wealth Increase in Congress from 2008–2018

Between influence peddling, sweetheart insider development deals, and insider stock trading, those holding office have a plethora of wealth building opportunities that are not available to the rest us. They win while we lose.

> *Lights flash madly, digit counters spin wildly, marking the capture of each new level of unimaginable wealth. There is only the game. No tomorrow. No consequence.*

18

NEVER LET A CRISIS GO TO WASTE!

> *Crisis is the rally cry of the tyrant.*
>
> JAMES MADISON

Government grows because the people in control of government agencies have a deep desire for more wealth and more power.

In the US federal government there is one president, one vice president, 100 senators, and 435 members of the House of Representatives. That comes to 537 elected officials who determine the size of the federal budget and how that money will be spent. Through legislation, they also indirectly determine which industries and businesses will thrive and which will be punished or even eliminated.

In the Constitution, the founding fathers created three separate and equal branches of the federal government, each with specific areas of responsibility. They are the legislative, executive, and judicial branches. This shared power and responsibility created vital checks and balances, accountability, that would prevent any branch from seizing too much power and becoming a threat to a government of, by, and for the people. Three branches, separate but equal, each enabled to hold the other two accountable.

The founders hoped that those blessed enough to be elected would fight to preserve the integrity and authority of each office they hold and thus uphold and protect the separation of powers created by the Constitution. They were concerned that the dynamics between the branches of government and office holders could devolve into a fraternal back-scratching circle where they work together toward self-serving objectives.

The founders did what they could to try to prevent that with separation of powers, accountability between branches, accountability to the people, and the intended role of the media. Despite their best efforts, the phrase "it's just politics" today roughly translates as "you help me get mine and I'll help you get yours." What we call "politics" is really just the art and science of self-promotion and is the slimy underbelly of our system of government.

> "Politics" is not "government." Politics is the art and science of self-promotion and is the slimy underbelly of our system of government.

So, in spite of the protections defined within our Constitution, here we are in a country where politicians are privately cooperating with each other for their mutual benefit instead of the benefit of the people who elected them. This is not true for all elected public servants, but it seems to be true for a large percentage.

If you studied the current 537 federal elected office holders, you would be hard-pressed to find more than a couple dozen who had not shown their true self-serving colors in one way or another. Most have done so by the legislation they support that is obviously not in the best interests of the country. Others by their ridiculous public statements designed to show the world how much love they have for the planet or for the latest self-proclaimed victim elevated to martyr status by the grievance industry.

Watch closely. Genuine concern for people or an issue looks very different than self-serving dialogues peppered and punctuated with obvious virtue-signaling. Watch closely! It'll come to you!

What does it mean to never let a crisis go to waste? Don't these problems need to be solved through legislation and spending taxpayer dollars? Sometimes yes, sometimes no. The question is not always whether the government should act. Sometimes the government should act. The question is, what action should government take? How can we ensure that the funded action is the best approach to solving the immediate problem? Is the proposed solution even designed to solve the problem?

In most cases "the solution" is just a convenient opportunity to package up a long list of existing agenda items not related to the current crisis. The bow on top is a very compelling official name that sounds entirely noble, intended to mislead the people into believing the legislation and required spending is actually the solution to the current crisis. If you or I did that, it would be called fraud and we could go to jail.

What recent legislation was passed even though it is not designed to address the crisis whose name it carries? The Inflation Reduction Act of 2022 is the most egregious recent example.[1] The current runaway inflation crisis has been caused by a massive increase in the money supply that was required to fund government spending. The cost to taxpayers for the federal response to COVID-19 was over $5.6 trillion.[2] The funds needed were not collected from taxpayers but were simply created out of thin air, driving the supply of money and the rate of inflation through the roof. How does spending another $739 billion, on top of that $5.6 trillion, help reduce inflation?

For perspective, during the financial meltdown of 2008 and 2009, a global economic disaster that threatened the stability of financial systems across the world, the solution cost US taxpayers about $800 billion. That solution was the American Recovery and Reinvestment Act (ARRA) of 2009.[3] It would be impossible to make a case that current inflation is a massive global crisis that requires a response on a scale similar to ARRA.

Government spending caused inflation in the first place! Even the Congressional Budget Office (CBO) admits that the law will have a negligible effect on inflation, which I think is about the most generous spin they could possibly put on it. Additional taxes. Increased costs to businesses. Increased taxes on energy. All cause the price paid by the consumer to go up. That's inflation directly caused by the Inflation Reduction Act of 2022.

ABC News referred to the Inflation Reduction Act of 2022 in an August 2022 web article titled "Senate Democrats Pass Climate, Tax and Health Care Bill after Marathon Voting Session" as "sprawling climate, tax and health care legislation" and stated that "Included in the bill, supporters are quick to highlight, are measures to foster job creation, raise taxes on large corporations and the wealthy, allow Medicare to negotiate down some prescription drug costs, expand the Affordable Care Act health care program and invest in combating climate change by implementing tax credits for clean energy initiatives, among other things."[4]

How does any of that reduce inflation? It doesn't. Contrary to the words they spoke, if they really are the smartest people in the room as they would like us to believe, not one person in Congress could have thought it would reduce inflation. In his remarks on August 16, 2023, at an event celebrating the Inflation Reduction Act of 2022, President Biden stepped through the goals of the act but made no mention of reducing inflation.[5]

Not a single Republican voted for it. This bill also added 87,000 new IRS agents. How will these new IRS employees paid with taxpayer dollars reduce inflation? The law also includes $369 billion in incentives for renewable energy, allowing the "most aggressive action ever" to meet Biden's climate goals. Inflation reduction? Biden appointed John Podesta, a scandal-plagued Clinton and Obama political operative, to manage the $369 billion in renewable energy incentives. That is an enormous amount of power to wield for a partisan operative known as "the Scandal Master."[6]

If our system of government was so brilliantly defined and signed into existence on September 17, 1787, over 230 years ago, how have we allowed those in office to get so out of control?

It is clear to many that the other two branches of government, the ultimate purveyors of accountability, have failed to perform their duty. Those branches are the press and the people. They are not really specified as branches of government in our Constitution, but they are arguably the most essential aspects of our system of government.

If those two groups do not conscientiously execute their duties, instead of a Constitution that defines and guides our system of government and protects the people from the government, the Constitution will become just an old piece of paper that is occasionally thought of fondly on July Fourth. Are we watching that unfold right now? Have we been watching it for decades with little concern? Perhaps we did not recognize the snail's pace of demise then, but we have no excuse now. That pace has accelerated exponentially and can only be ignored by the most determined of the willfully ignorant.

The press holds a special elevated place in this country. In the first constitutional amendment, freedom of the press is guaranteed. This freedom covers all forms of the press, such as print, radio, TV, internet sites, and others. This protects the press from censorship and the attempts of those in power to control press messaging. Many countries do not have free and independent media. In those countries, the press is just a mouthpiece for the criminals in control of the country's wealth and power. We in the United States are blessed to have these protections.

The press is a vital part of our system of government. The people cannot hold accountable the individuals in control of the government unless the press accurately informs the people of the activities of those individuals and the government entities they control. In previous chapters we covered how most of the press in the United States, platformed and promoted by Big Tech, operates in lockstep with those in control of the government. Now that we recognize that, we can take action to ensure that we are accurately informed. It takes effort but, if we are to accept our role as citizens in governing the country, we have no choice.

We can blame the press. We can blame elected office holders and unelected bureaucrats for acting with impunity while serving their own interests. However, the responsibility, the blame, rests on the shoulders of *we the people*! It is our fault that our government is controlled by self-serving individuals who have banded together to enable each other to achieve their objectives of more wealth and more power.

We the people have allowed ourselves to be pacified by reassuring and pleasant-sounding words from the government and their supporters.

We the people have allowed ourselves to be completely distracted from our responsibility by our own self-indulgences, our toys, our TVs, our streaming services, our sports, our porn, our intoxicants, our victimhood!

We the people have succumbed to our fear of being ridiculed or abandoned for questioning "common knowledge."

> *We the people* have failed! This country is controlled by people who seem to laugh at the oath of office they swore to uphold because *We the people* have made no perceivable attempt to hold them accountable!

In the United States, 93% of the population has access to the internet and 83% have smartphones. We have access to the actual facts, though they are sometimes as easy to find as health food at a 7-Eleven convenience store in 1985. The facts are there. Until we start holding our government accountable, they will repeat the well-known process of defining a crisis and then promoting themselves as our savior. All we have to do is give them another trillion or so dollars, just this once!

In the first 23 years of this century, the federal government has spent $84 trillion total.[7] However, it has only actually taken in $63 trillion from taxpayers. Where did the additional $21 trillion, or 25%, come from? It was spent, so it must have been real dollars from somewhere, right? The situation is far worse than that. At this time, in early 2024, our federal government is $34 trillion in debt. In the next chapter we explain how that is possible and the inevitable outcome of massive debt.

So, how have our elected public servants allowed, no, caused, this massive accumulation of debt? Let's look at just a 23-year period, 2000 through 2022.

When we discuss government spending, we should keep in mind that fraud, waste, and abuse are factored in by the government as expected. However, when massive emergency supplemental spending bills are rushed through the approval process and then rushed through the funding disbursement process, the opportunity for that fraud, waste, and abuse is far greater. I didn't say it is more likely to happen because it is always 100% likely to happen. There is always fraud, waste, and abuse. But the percentages lost are much greater with massive emergency supplemental spending bills.

Let's take a look at how the government legislates the use of taxpayer funding. The federal government has two primary spending categories that are funded through legislation: nondiscretionary and discretionary spending. Then there are supplemental spending bills that will be discussed in detail later.

> If we, the voters, understood how the mechanisms of government budgeting are manipulated to confuse and mislead us, we would be outraged.

A summary of those budgeting mechanisms is provided below. Also provided are pointers to some very good sources you can access to learn more. But I must warn you, as you begin to recognize the games politicians play, you will likely end up at the intersection of furious and curious. If thrust into that rabbit hole, remember it has no bottom. Tie a rope around your waist so someone can eventually pull you back out!

Discretionary:

The discretionary part of the budget includes funding for established and ongoing operations of the government like national defense, food safety, education, and federal employee salaries.

Discretionary spending is money formally approved by Congress and the president during the appropriations process each year. Generally, Congress allocates discretionary budget toward national defense, transportation, education, housing, and social service programs, as well as science and environmental organizations.

Nondiscretionary:

Nondiscretionary spending is referred to as mandatory spending. These programs are funded automatically based on formulas. This includes mandatory spending for programs like Medicare, Medicaid, Social Security, unemployment compensation, the Supplemental Nutrition Assistance Program, family support, child nutrition and foster care, retirement programs, veteran programs, and other programs.

When politicians and the media talk about the appropriations process or bills, they are referring to the annual legislative process for allocating funds to *discretionary* programs. When the negotiations stall, the phrase "government shutdown" gets thrown about with much consternation. In reality, the only government operations that could be shutdown are those deemed *nonessential in the discretionary spending budget*. Nondiscretionary spending continues as if on autopilot.

Discretionary spending is less than 24% of the actual government and only the nonessential areas of that discretionary budget are affected by a shutdown. All essential discretionary and all nondiscretionary functions continue to operate as usual. As scary as a government shutdown sounds, few would ever notice if it actually happened.

Emergency spending is additional spending funded through supplemental appropriations legislation and is over and above the annual budget. Since 1999, over 60 of these supplemental appropriations,[8] over $8.5 trillion, have been voted on and passed by our elected representatives.[9] The American Recovery and Reinvestment Act of 2009 alone was $787 billion. The Inflation Reduction Act of 2022 was $891 billion. Another $5.6 billion was spent between six COVID-related supplemental appropriations.

> We must heed James Madison's warning: "Crisis is the rally cry of the tyrant."

The supplemental appropriations bill process is often abused by politicians to fund nonemergency projects by circumventing the spending cap previously agreed to by Congress and celebrated in the press. They frequently gain a public relations win by limiting spending but still spend all they can get their hands on.

In the last 15 years, supplemental appropriations have added an average of over 25% to discretionary spending every year. In 2021 alone supplemental spending was over 171% of the discretionary budget approved for the year. That is an enormous level of "emergency" spending, considering the rushed distribution of that taxpayer money and the inability to apply reasonable oversight.

The table below provides a summary of each of the last 15 years in total supplemental appropriations in billions and in the percentage increase over budgeted discretionary spending per year. Figures are presented in real dollars spent, not the magical scoring calculations of the Congressional Budget Office.

Year	Supplemental Appropriation Total (Billions)	Supplemental Appropriation as Percentage of Discretionary
2022	$1,605.00	93.21%
2021	$2,813.05	171.90%
2020	$2,071.93	127.28%
2019	$25.39	1.90%
2018	$122.43	9.70%
2017	$25.55	2.13%
2016	$57.00	4.81%
2015	$0.00	0.00%
2014	$0.23	0.02%
2013	$60.51	5.03%
2012	$8.60	0.67%
2011	$0.00	0.00%
2010	$56.62	4.20%
2009	$894.90	72.32%
2008	$249.30	21.97%

Figure 18.1 Supplemental Appropriations in Billions by Year

The politicians' mantra of "never let a crisis go to waste" accurately characterizes the emergency spending bill scenario. Politicians can hardly contain their joy when discussing the latest threat to our existence and how the emergency funding they are rushing through is vital to the country's survival. They can always tell you exactly how many billions of dollars are needed to solve the problem but are vague on the details of how that money will be used to actually solve the problem. They can tell you that taxpayer money will be allocated to this department and that department, but they can't concern themselves with the details of, viability of, or value of the solution while they are in the throes of convincing citizens that it must be funded to avoid catastrophe.

Watch closely. It'll come to you.

Federal Government Debt in Trillions of Dollars
Raw, Inflation Adjusted

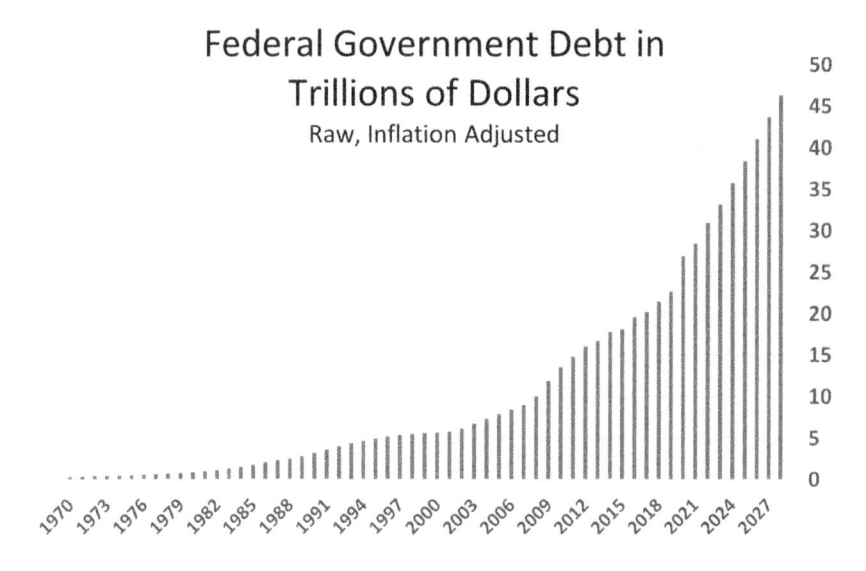

Figure 18.2 Federal Government Debt in Trillions of Dollars Raw, Inflation Adjusted

19

THE FED: ENABLING OUTRAGEOUS SPENDING AND UNSUSTAINABLE DEBT

> *Never has so much been owed by so many to so few.*
>
> WINSTON CHURCHILL

There seems to be an infinite number of "great ideas" for government programs, a euphemism for spending taxpayer money. Considering the current state of our government and accelerating government debt, the only reasonable position for the informed citizens to take is:

"Sounds great but unfortunately that money has already been spent."

The typical response from those who love massive, out of control government: "Oh, but there is plenty of money! The government just has to sell more bonds to investors to fund these new "investments"! It's a win-win. The government gets the cash needed and investors make money." Unfortunately, it is not a win-win-win because *we the people* eventually have to pay that investor back.

In the meantime, the government spends 16% of the annual budget on interest alone, nearly twice as much as two years prior. The holders of government debt see their risks increasing and are demanding more return on their investment in the form of interest. Interest payments on federal debt equate to about 1% of the US economy's GDP today. The Congressional Budget Office projects interest payments on federal debt will be 6.7% of GDP by 2053 and will be the government's single largest expense. Interest on debt!

In August 2023 Fitch Ratings downgraded the Long-Term Foreign-Currency Issuer Default Rating (IDR) of US national debt, citing "a steady deterioration in standards of governance over the last 20 years."[1]

Many economists believe the US debt will become unsustainable and trigger default in 20 years unless dramatic corrections are made very soon. The default will result in an economic crisis more devastating and widespread than any in US history. We will no longer have the wiggle room to print money to get out of the crisis because it will be the inevitable consequence of doing just that for decades.

Deficit spending is funded and debt is accumulated by selling bonds to whom? Let's look very briefly at who holds federal government debt and why we should be very concerned about some of these characters—especially foreign governments and the Fed!

It is important for us to understand who holds that debt, who we, the taxpayers, will pay trillions of dollars to, and the implications of that. To fund deficit spending, actual real money has to be secured by the government above and beyond the money collected from taxpayers.[2]

The federal government borrows those real dollars by selling marketable securities such as Treasury bonds, bills, notes, floating rate notes, and Treasury inflation-protected securities (TIPS). This debt can be broken down by whether it is nonmarketable or marketable and whether it is debt held by the public or debt held by the government itself, known as intragovernmental debt. The government owes itself money? Why? How does that work?

The federal government uses the phrase "debt held by the public" to refer to the following holders:

> *Any person or entity that is not a US federal government agency. This includes individuals, corporations, state or local governments, Federal Reserve Banks, foreign investors, foreign governments, and other entities outside the United States Government. Debt held by the public does not include intragovernmental debt.*[3]

Intragovernmental debt? It almost sounds like the federal government can sell securities to itself. How does that make sense? It'll come to you!

But note that "debt held by the public" excludes US federal government agencies but *includes* Federal Reserve banks. So, Federal Reserve banks are not government entities? Correct!

That construct known as the Federal Reserve, or the Fed, was created to provide a smoke screen that obscures the actual magnitude of the problem. More on that in a minute.

So, what is *intragovernmental* debt? The federal government uses that phrase to refer to the following holders:

> *Debt that one part of the US Federal Government owes to another part. This represents cases where Social Security, Medicare, and other federal programs collect more revenue than they need in a year and then purchase Treasury debt for their trust funds.*

If the federal government can loan itself money and, in the process take on debt, why does it need to borrow that money? From itself?

The table below breaks federal debt into broad categories of debt holders. A quick look reveals that the federal government is not being completely honest on the nature of this debt. If they were being honest, they would move the debt held by the Federal Reserve to the Intragovernmental Holdings category where it really belongs. However, they would never do that because, if they did, the amount of debt held by the federal government increases 100%! The federal government holds nearly half of its own debt! How could that possibly make sense? Only in the government!

The tables below are based on data from the federal government as of September 30, 2021.

Accumulated national debt at that time: $28.42 trillion.

DETHRONING THE RULING CLASS

Debt Holder	Debt Held by the Public	Intragov Debt	% of Category	% of Total
Domestic Individuals, Corporations, State or Local Governments, Other[4]	$8.64 trillion		38.7%	30.40%
Federal Reserve Banks[5]	**$6.14 trillion**		**27.6%**	**21.60%**
Foreign Investors mostly governments[6,7]	$7.5 trillion		33.7%	26.39%
Public Holdings Total	$22.28 trillion			78.39%
Social Security Trust[8]		$2.82 trillion	46%	9.92%
Military Retirement and Health Care Funds		$1.35 trillion	22%	4.75%
Civil Service Retirement and Disability Fund		$0.92 trillion	15%	3.24%
Medicare Trust Funds		$0.31 trillion	5%	1.09%
Other Federal Government Programs and Trust Funds		$0.74 trillion	12%	2.60%
Intragovernmental Holdings Total		$6.14 trillion		21.60%

Figure 19.1 Federal Debt by Holder Category as Reported

Debt Holder	Debt Held by the Public	Intragov Debt	% of Category	% of Total
Domestic Individuals, Corporations, State or Local Governments, other[4]	$8.64 trillion		53.5%	30.40%
Foreign Investors mostly governments[6][7]	$7.5 trillion		46.5%	26.39%
Public Holdings Total	$16.14 trillion			56.79%
Federal Reserve Banks[5]		$6.14 trillion	50%	21.60%
Social Security Trust[8]		$2.82 trillion	22.96%	9.92%
Military Retirement and Health Care Funds		$1.35 trillion	10.99%	4.75%
Civil Service Retirement and Disability Fund		$0.92 trillion	7.49%	3.24%
Medicare Trust Funds		$0.31 trillion	2.53%	1.09%
Other Federal Government Programs and Trust Funds		$0.74 trillion	6.03%	2.60%
Intragovernmental Holdings Total		$12.28 trillion		43.2%

Figure 19.2 Federal Debt by Holder Category More Accurately Portrayed

Endnotes: [4] [5] [6] [7] [8]

Again, the federal government holds nearly half of its own debt! Yes, the Fed is not technically part of the government but it clearly is operating as a governing body and an extremely impactful one at that!

The question we should all be asking is this: If the federal government has the cash on hand to buy its own debt, why does it have debt? It has the cash already, right?

The government and its extremely vocal, and sometimes vicious supporters, want you to believe that it just isn't that simple. The bad news is that they are right. The smoke screen created by the Federal Reserve, or the Fed, is intentionally so complicated that only wealthy insiders, their hopeful future billionaire supporters, and those willing to pretend they understand it, will claim they understand it.

The Fed uses a tool known as quantitative easing, or QE, to purchase large amounts of so-called assets that include Treasury bonds, mortgage-backed securities, and other types of debt. These assets, a deceptive term for government debt, appear on their balance sheet.

In 2007 the Fed's balance sheet had "assets" of about $900 billion. By 2015 it had exploded to $4.5 trillion, a 500% increase! From January 2015 to September 2019 the balance sheet was reduced to $3.7 trillion through "quantitative tightening."[9] What a relief! No, not really much relief at all.

In March of 2020, responding to the COVID-19 pandemic, the Fed began aggressively buying more assets (government debt). By 2022, the Fed's balance sheet had bloated to nearly $9 trillion in assets (government debt), a 1000% increase in 13 years!

If the Fed can buy $9 trillion in federal bonds and commercial debt, how can the federal government be over $30 trillion in debt?

First of all, the Fed is not technically part of the government. The Fed's role is to control interest rates, employment rates, inflation rates, money supply, and other crucial aspects of the US economy. The Fed essentially has absolute control of our economy. The Fed is also a private entity, which is not part of our elected representative government and is not accountable to voters. That's interesting, isn't it? Again, a very elaborate smokescreen that is intentionally very difficult to understand and prevents citizens from holding anyone accountable for exploding unsustainable debt and the resulting economic malaise.

The Fed is technically not part of the government but clearly it is a central part of the government!

So, where did the Fed get $9 trillion to buy this government debt? That's a lot of money! Where did it come from?

The Fed does not buy bonds directly from the federal government. It buys bonds already held by financial institutions through a very American-sounding program known as Open Market Operations. Open market? Who could find fault with that? The Fed's eagerness to buy bonds from financial institutions creates a zero-risk, all-upside opportunity for those institutions. They will put as much money as possible into government debt because they know the Fed will buy it from them. I think that is known as a back-scratching circle at the frat house.

You've probably heard people say things like, "The Fed is just printing money!" Those who benefit from big government, and the accompanying big spending, respond to that with, "You're an idiot! That is obviously not true!"

Well, technically the Fed does not actually print money. They are way too smart to take on that logistics nightmare. They just ask the US Treasury to do it for them. But that is old-school physical money. The real action is in digital transfers. The Fed doesn't need actual cash to buy government debt. When the Fed buys government bonds or debt from a financial institution, the Fed simply credits the financial institution's account the agreed dollar amount.

The Fed creates money almost at will to buy these assets from financial institutions. They essentially type a number in a field on their computer screen and click the Create Money button, magically creating billions of new dollars with a mouse click.[10]

The Fed has clicked the Create button to buy an additional $5.4 trillion in assets since September 2019, nearly tripling the Fed's balance sheet, government debt, in just a few short years.

Those newly created dollars enter the US money supply the moment the seller's account is credited.

Where did that additional $5.4 trillion go? Indirectly to the federal government and ultimately into the daily money flow of the US economy. According to the Center for Financial Stability (CFS), the growth of money in the US economy has averaged 5.6% per year since 1967. In March of 2021 the money growth rate hit 23.8%. The supply of money circulating in the United States economy grew by over 23%!

> Flooding the economy with cash impacted everyone in the country by triggering a catastrophic rate of inflation.

As we discussed earlier, comparing debt to GDP is useful because it enables us to evaluate debt as a percentage of the economic production. In terms of accumulated debt to GDP ratio, a study by the World Bank found that countries whose debt-to-GDP ratios exceed 77% for prolonged periods experience significant slowdowns in economic growth. The US ratio was 118% for 2022, or 153% of the warning level according to the World Bank.[11]

Warning! Warning!

The federal debt has far exceeded the World Bank warning threshold! Who allowed that to happen? *We the people* did! But now we are paying attention! Remember, "Sounds great but unfortunately that money has already been spent."

For reference, 2008 debt was $12.6 trillion. At 68% of GDP, well below but rapidly approaching the warning level according to the World Bank.

It is also helpful to analyze money supply using GDP as kind of a reference point from year to year. Over the past 50 years, the yearly increase in GDP and the yearly increase of the money supply have tracked each other fairly closely, with GDP growth being a bit higher than money supply growth. In 2008 the relationship flipped and money supply began growing significantly faster than GDP. From 1990 to 2008 both grew about 145%. From 2008 to 2022, money supply grew at three times the rate of GDP. Get that! From 2008 to 2022, money supply grew at three times the normal rate, a rate that was guaranteed to bring devastating consequences. Who allowed, or encouraged, that to happen? We can thank the Fed for continually clicking the Create Money button!

> From 2008 to 2022, money supply grew at three times the normal rate. The wealthy ruling class got richer. The rest of us suffered massive price increases.

An incredibly strong GDP can cover a lot of sins, for a while. Unfortunately, those sins, if not corrected, will eventually choke the golden goose of GDP, creating a death spiral that is impossible to pull out of! Not really impossible. No situation is beyond recovery for the US taxpayer, or so the world hopes. We saved the world from tyranny in World War II. Sadly, in the next "war" we'll be trying to save us from ourselves.

Some would argue that the government had to create and spend that money to save our economy or to save us from the pandemic. Again, the question is not if the government should act. The question is, what is the appropriate action that solves the actual problem without creating larger problems for future generations? We are quickly becoming that future generation.

We can try to "print" our way out of a cash shortage for only so long. But we can never print our way out of debt, only deeper into debt. People don't seem to understand that printing money actually makes the problem worse. As of mid-2023 the Fed pays over $750 million in interest every day. The previous year the Fed's daily interest payments were only $18 million per day.[12]

As a nation we are deliberately choosing to evade the current unpleasant reality at the inescapable cost of long-term devastation. For our children and grandchildren, their natural longing for self-actualization will be trampled under that burden.

When those oxygen masks drop from the ceiling during the economy's inevitable death spiral, we will all be strapping our money masks onto that debt monster who has fallen onto the flight controls. We will sacrifice at levels not seen in generations, desperately hoping that debt monster will recover before the economy hits the ground!

Again, this recovery will require that the government take obscene amounts of real dollars from taxpayers in the form of new and increased taxes to battle the inevitable repercussions of our incredibly short-sighted and indulgent past. Taxpayers will already be struggling to survive day-to-day on a substantially devalued US dollar due to out-of-control inflation. Without exaggeration, we can expect the struggle of our day-to-day lives, in terms of trying to survive financially, to approach the financial misery experienced on the US home front during World War II.

Instead of the trauma of war, death, permanent injury, and loss of those we love, we will be dealing with the trauma of knowing we did this to ourselves.

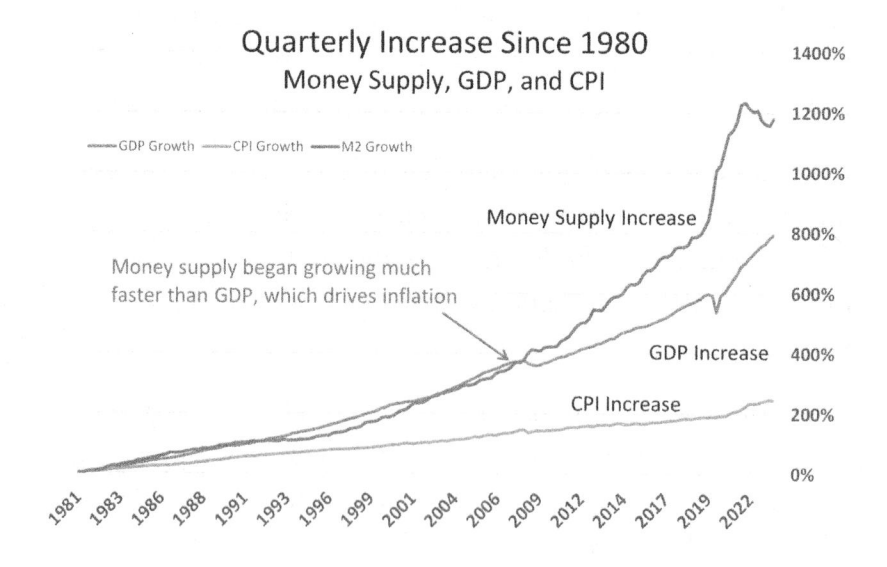

Figure 19.3 Quarterly Increase Since 1980 Money Supply, GDP, and CPI

Since 2019 the Fed has been flooding the economy with cash by buying federal government debt, causing money supply to outpace GDP at an unsustainable rate.[16] Any questions about what drove the US economy to a debilitating rate of inflation?

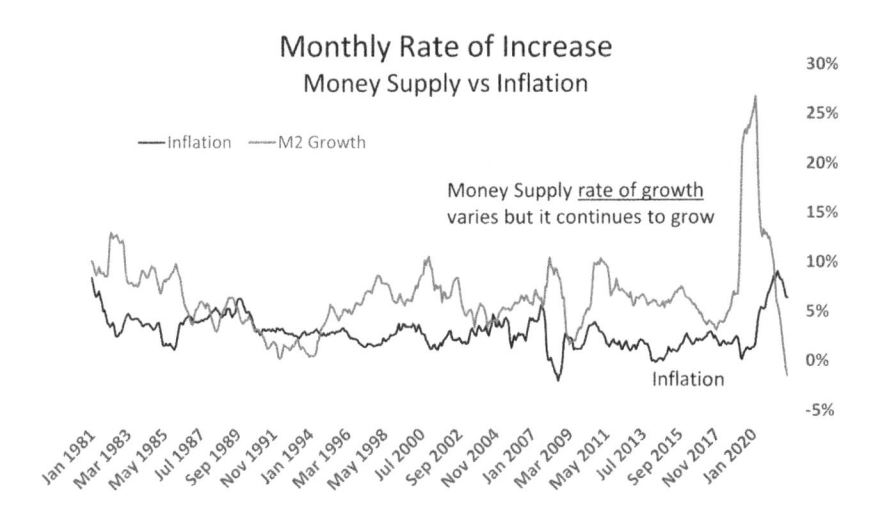

Figure 19.4 Monthly Rate of Increase Money Supply vs Inflation

17 18

PART 3

INCITING CITIZEN ENGAGEMENT

20

YOU ARE AN INFLUENCER!

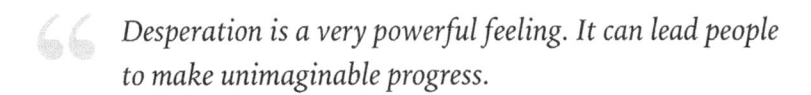

> *Desperation is a very powerful feeling. It can lead people to make unimaginable progress.*

You may not realize it, but you are an influencer. You have worked hard to reach a station in life where you have a wide range of internal and external resources available to you. Those resources may include day-to-day life skills, job skills, job title, income, knowledge, perspective, reputation, a powerful life story, or many other types of resources. You are gifted.

You are empowered to use those gifts to the benefit of everyone around you. Take a minute to think about the many ways you can share those gifts with your family, friends, coworkers, community, and those you meet on social media.

Many of us have reached positions in our careers and in our communities that enable us to be very powerful influencers based on the credibility that we have garnered through our professional careers and our reputations. You may be a very good manager, salesperson, executive, auto mechanic, electrician, plumber, HVAC tech, computer specialist, dog trainer, beauty specialist, parent, volunteer, or one of thousands of other highly visible or somewhat invisible roles. In any case, the success you have created through your dedication to your craft has helped elevate you to the role of influencer.

Some career choices bring with them a higher profile and sometimes a very comfortable income. If you are an attorney, a medical professional, an educator, involved in nonprofit organizations, or are a company executive, you have an amazing opportunity to be a positive force in the world around you. While these careers are often thought of as being very influential, the rest of us have just as much opportunity to be role models.

Many of us have life stories that may be difficult to tell. We may have been born into a difficult situation that we had to claw our way out of. Or we may have been born into a good situation but then later made choices that lead to a life of despair and dysfunction that we have worked hard to overcome. Today, your story is not about where you started or the choices you made. Your story is about how you fought your way to a better life and a better you.

In the process of building a better you, you were forced to create and maintain within yourself life-saving levels of self-awareness, discipline, and focus. Levels that few people can truly comprehend. The story of how you got through those challenges is a survival guide for people who desperately need to know that the battle they are facing is one that they can win. From where they sit, it doesn't look likely. They need to see it from your new perspective, from the other side of their challenges. You can't get more influential than that!

Do your mistakes disqualify you from the conversation of that topic? I believe that your mistakes, our mistakes, give us unique perspective and the ability to lead that conversation with deep understanding.

We can't all be Eric Stratton, rush chairman, thankfully! But the world probably has more than enough of those influencers already.

> It is our time to accept the role and do the work of influencing! If not us, who?

Today, at this moment in our history, we need just normal everyday people like you and me. People who are willing to stand up, courageously and politely, to boldly represent the principles and the massive size of the conservative movement. The world needs influencers like you to use your resources and your story to guide others out of their despair and into the hope offered by the conservative movement.

Did I say politely? How does that work in this social media cesspit of vicious trolls? It works amazingly well actually!

As an influencer, the purpose of an interaction should be to get people to think more deeply about the topic without triggering an excessively strong reaction from them. If your words are carefully chosen and civil, you improve your chances of triggering thought instead of mindless frantic typing. In some cases, if you have effectively presented the core question of an idea or principle, you may get no response at all, other than a few likes. People in disagreement are less likely to respond to a comment that is well thought-out, fact-based, and civil. Commenters who find joy in starting a feeding frenzy may mumble the words "thread-killer" at you. We accept that as a badge of honor!

Heated threads are often filled with superficial back-and-forth volleys of talking points and accusations that participants are ignorant, uneducated, uninformed, science deniers, stuck in an outdated mindset, hate the poor, hate the planet, or are afraid of change. Some start throwing around labels like capitalist, socialist, fascist, communist, or even Nazi. The Urban Dictionary humorously defines these terms as "A person who has a different opinion than you." OK, that is funny, but it is sadly accurate in this context.

Vitriolic threads can be entertaining. They attract a lot of onlookers. But nobody is being informed or influenced by them. You have an opportunity to change that. If you can thoughtfully and accurately craft a respectful comment that brings the focus back to the underlying principle, your message will be difficult to scroll past because it will be entirely unique within that thread.

Take your time. Do your research. Maximize the value of the opportunity to influence. What is the difficult to deny, underlying question that motivated you to take a position with so much conviction that you want to help others see it? What fundamental aspect of the issue have others lost sight of in the contentious and frenzied debate? They need you, the most influential person sitting at your keyboard, to bring them back to that!

> I'm only responsible for what I say, not for what others hear...unless I'm trying to lead others to truth and hope.

Believe me, you can live your best influencer life through mature, calm, and well-thought-out discussions of the issues we currently face. A key part of that best life is knowing the types of people and topics to avoid. Identifying and avoiding useless rabbit holes is a skill that is developed over time and will greatly improve your peace and effectiveness.

Useless rabbit holes we will discuss later. Let's discuss toxic commenters. What would motivate someone on social media to resort to personal attacks and name-calling? Logically wouldn't it make more sense for them to communicate their beliefs on a hot topic in language that is welcoming, clear, concise, and compelling? Why don't they just do that instead of immediately going mad dog on someone who presented a different view?

On the other hand, you will also see threads dominated by well-informed commenters who speak very intelligently on complex issues. They seem to be extremely knowledgeable of government processes, specific legislation or government action, the long-term impact of that action, and reasons people have for supporting or opposing that action. You may think the commenter does not appear to be your average person with a life outside of politics and social media. Their knowledge is just too deep. And you are right about that. Some are just interested in the topic. Others are employed by interest groups to influence public opinion using social media platforms and issue-oriented websites they create and maintain.

Interest groups are organizations whose purpose is to influence public opinion and government legislation for their clients.

Much of the information you encounter online is created and promoted by one type of interest group or another. These groups also participate in discussion threads on the most popular platforms.

If a commenter seems to have invested tremendous time and effort researching and gathering facts, maybe they are a policy nerd and maybe they did. Those people are rare. More often these people are paid masters of copy and paste. They could be intelligent and articulate, but normally they are just adjusting the text to fit the context of the thread and pasting it in. It is challenging but not impossible to be an influencer on these threads. Hang in there. It'll come to you!

In my experience, it appears that the motivation for active participation in these threads can be boiled down to five or six primary categories of commenters. The benefit to understanding these broad categories is that it enables us to develop some sense of why a person would react in a particular way to views that conflict with their own.

It is possible that you are such a skilled influencer that you are able to post compelling and thought-provoking comments without triggering vicious responses. For all of us that should be our goal. However, it takes time to develop that level of skill and there are plenty of people trolling around social media just looking for a fight. Then there are others who just get emotional, cannot restrain themselves, and just start flaming people. We will never be free of them.

If you can identify the group that a person likely falls into, you may be able to adjust the way you engage with that person to increase your level of influence on them or on those witnessing your interaction with them. In many cases you may have zero opportunity to influence the person you are interacting with, but you probably can provoke thought in those who are exposed to your calm, polite, well-reasoned statements.

Here are the six categories of those who attack opposing views instead of calmly discussing the issues:

1. Emotionally and intellectually challenged: According to the National Alliance on Mental Illness, one in 20 adults in the United States experience serious mental illness each year.
2. Love a good drama: There is a small number of people who just love drama. If there is a lack of drama in their presence, they will create some quickly with great enthusiasm.
3. Uninformed or misinformed yet very vocal: This is probably the thick part of the bell curve. We discussed earlier that 95% of people believe that they are self-aware but only about 15% actually are. A similar distribution probably applies to the informed versus those believing they are informed.
4. Deeply invested emotionally: Many have been steeped in bias through public education, celebrities, news outlets, and social media. It is all they have ever known. To call it into question is to call into question their personal belief system, personal identity, and everything they have stood for most of their lives.
5. Financially invested: Many who vocally defend a philosophy, agenda, policy, or organization, do so out of financial motivation. They either receive or hope to receive money or other resources. The individual, their

employer, their business, their nonprofit, or their industry may benefit from their advocacy.
6. Paid advocates: Influencers are paid to actively support the objectives of their clients on social media. Their mission is to present topics as positively as possible, refute dissent, and create the appearance that the agenda has broad support among the general population.

Remember, it is not a message you are delivering, but a conversation you are participating in that may lead to a relationship.

People will engage in a conversation but will quickly tune out a sermon blasted at them.

> *When we avoid difficult conversations, we trade short-term discomfort for long-term dysfunction.*
>
> PETER BROMBERG

21

DEBATING THE...CHALLENGED

> *Never argue with stupid people. They will drag you down to their level and beat you with experience.*
>
> AUTHOR DISPUTED BUT LIKELY MARK TWAIN OR JEAN COCTEAU

The first three categories of toxic commenters listed in the previous chapter have many traits in common. The key common trait is that of honest belief in their positions. They honestly believe that they are informed on the issues and that their position on those issues is the most reasonable.

Why is it important to understand that?

It is important because, while some are compelled to destroy all dissent no matter how politely that dissent is presented, this group is normally not so quick to mount an attack. If you present your facts and opinions in a welcoming, clear, concise, and compelling manner, with honesty and humility, you may still be verbally attacked but it will likely be a very brief attack, a sentence or two. Your response to that attack is where you will find your greatest opportunity to influence the bystanders, if not the attacker.

Let's cover the differences between these three groups briefly.

Emotionally and intellectually challenged:

There are often indicators when a person posting on social media is dealing with challenges that limit their ability to calmly reason things out with you. The words, phrases, and spelling used are often clues. How they organize the details of their posts can be another clue. Spelling and grammar may or may not be clues because different cultures and generations use words differently and have different standards for social media interactions. The possible use of shorthand and phrases specific to another culture, even in the same country, should be taken into consideration.

When interacting with people you suspect may be in this category, I think the principle to keep in mind is that of kindness, regardless of what they post to or about you. There is no benefit to drawing attention to mistakes in their comments. If their statements are incoherent or entirely void of logic, you cannot help them or anyone else by pointing that out.

On the other hand, you have an opportunity to influence here because bystanders may see the person's comments and be on the edge of their seats waiting for brutal retorts and hoping to see the situation escalate into an all-out brawl. Your kind response may disappoint them on a superficial level, but it will likely leave a memorable impression as well.

Be careful not to let your assumptions about the person lead you to respond in a way that may be perceived as condescending or dismissive. Be the kind and supportive slightly older sibling that you always wanted.

Love a good drama:

People in this category can just never get enough drama. There is never a shortage of drama in their presence. They make sure of that. Every response from you will be met with personal attacks. Those attacks may be sprinkled into an incredibly frustrating and useless "hit-and-run" style of argument resembling a "but what about" debate. They seize control of the debate and run from topic to topic by responding to your point with an inflammatory statement completely unrelated to the topic you thought you were discussing.

This type of debate provides no value to the participants or those watching. In the end you will feel like you have been strapped to the end of a whip being relentlessly cracked.

This is one of the few scenarios where a little snark might be due. You may want to gracefully bow out of the discussion with something to this effect:

Well friend, you don't seem to be interested in healthy productive discussion so I'm out. Best of luck to you.

Brutal, right? No, not really. But that's about as nasty as we ever need to be. It's a little snarky because the two of you are not friends and you probably don't care one way or the other how their luck goes! Or maybe you do. Who am I to judge?

Do not argue. There is no benefit. Don't get down in the gutter with them. They live for the gutter fight, where they can impress the world with their witty punches and devastating counterpunches. There is no point in giving them that opportunity. As stated previously, your kind response may disappoint bystanders on a superficial level but it will likely leave a memorable impression as well.

Uninformed or misinformed yet very vocal:

Again, this is probably the thick part of the bell curve. Most of the people you encounter will fall into this category.

These people can normally be identified by their repetitive use of superficial talking points. They often repost shallow memes and comments from sources you will over time begin to view as "the usual suspects." In many cases they haven't really thought through the facts or logic behind the statements. They simply copy and paste something that "sounds about right" to them, often without any concern for the validity of the information or the source.

This group represents your biggest opportunity to influence. They have put very little thought into the beliefs that they hold. They have basically bought into the ideas presented in the virtue-signaling narrative that dominates public schools, traditional media, and social media. They think that most people seem to be saying about the same thing and it sure sounds loving and kind, so it must be right. That is the end of their analysis.

Rule one for this group: most of their posts and comments should just be ignored. Not every silly post is an opportunity to influence. Most are just nonsense that should be scrolled past to avoid a pointless "I'm rubber and you're glue" playground tiff.

Most should be ignored but sometimes these people provide opportunities. Some of these people, and certainly many of the bystanders, can be gently stunned into taking a deeper look into the authenticity of the ideas they have been going along with. By carefully crafting a message that is free of vitriol, free of any offense, and is welcoming, clear, concise, and compelling, you can help encourage some to research the topics for themselves.

How can you "stun" them without vitriol or offense? That's where the hard work begins to lead to the most rewarding results. There is a formula that you can use to create a response. The approach involves the following steps:

1. Read their post four or five times.
2. Try to imagine their life experience and how they were informed on the issue.
3. Try to put yourself in their frame of mind.
4. Specific to the issue and their comments, what deeper relatable truth are they missing?
5. What key words and phrases can you use to get them to start thinking about that deeper truth?
6. Look for something in their statement that you can use to create common ground to build on.

Create a response that attempts to establish some level of agreement and builds on that to present a more effective path forward. You don't necessarily need to point out the flaws in their understanding or disagree with them directly. Offer up better ideas and explain how the end result is more beneficial than other alternatives.

22

DEBATING THE EMOTIONALLY INVESTED

> *Many on the left are so entranced by the beauty of their vision that they cannot see the ugly reality they are creating in the real world.*
>
> THOMAS SOWELL

This group is completely dedicated to promoting liberal causes. They are more likely to consider themselves to be informed or well-informed on the liberal perspective. They are committed to all things liberal and are passionate about sticking to and supporting the narrative. They feel a responsibility to be aware of the current messaging coming from the people they believe to be brilliant humanitarians who love the oppressed and the planet more than anything else. They immerse themselves in every talking point, headline, and meme posted by their luminaries.

Unfortunately, you can soak up every talking point, headline, and meme that ever existed and still be entirely uninformed. In that case you wouldn't really be misinformed because you are not informed at all. But you could be misinformed about the fact that you are uninformed. That would be the worst-case scenario, being completely unaware of the fact that you possess nearly no actual knowledge on the issues that you so passionately defend.

What they lack in knowledge they make up for with passion and exuberance.

Members of this group have been steeped in bias through public education, celebrities, news outlets, and social media. It is all they have ever known. To call liberal doctrine into question is to call into question their personal belief system, personal identity, and everything they have stood for most of their lives. Few have the ability to explore other views objectively without perceiving those views as a threat to their own. For most people, challenges to their beliefs can be a major anxiety trigger, especially those who are deeply invested emotionally.

Group members have a massive arsenal of copy-paste ammo, and they will fire every single round if needed to convince a dissenter of their foolish ways, or at least send them off to bandage their wounds.

With this group it is normally very difficult to gain a concession or even a willingness to consider another view. Trading talking points in a breathless rapid-fire succession will accomplish nothing but boost their ego as they, in their minds, shut you down and demonstrate their brilliance point by point. Again, in their minds.

To get their attention, and that of onlookers, you will need to break the typical patterns of back-and-forth ping-pong of clichés and derogatory statements about each other's intellectual shortcomings. You will need to make a statement that takes them somewhat by surprise. Show them behavior that they have seen rarely, if ever, from those evil heartless conservatives who hate the planet and think the old, sick, and poor should just die. Remember, that's what they have been told about conservatives for years or even decades and that's what they believe.

What behavior would that be? It depends on the situation. You may have the opportunity to agree with them on some aspect of their assertions. There may actually be some common ground or at least the appearance of common ground. In some cases, it may be a bit of a stretch to get there but it may be worth the effort, as long as it doesn't stretch your credibility.

Keep in mind that many people do not have in-depth knowledge of the positions they take in the debate. Their knowledge may have been casually gleaned almost entirely from talking points, headlines, and memes that are consistent with their beliefs. Confirmation bias algorithms used by social media platforms show them again and again information that reinforces their beliefs and leads them to think that their perspective is perfectly in line with that of all thinking people, anyone who is not a complete moron. Their political views have been instilled in an ecosystem completely void of intellectual challenges. It's an "of course everyone knows that" environment.

Since their logic and beliefs are not often challenged, they may not have ever been forced to dig into the issues to develop a more thorough understanding of underlying principles and the connections between them. What scenarios force us to improve our skills or even develop new skills? Difficult situations where there is risk of loss and where we must find within ourselves the determination and focus required to avert disaster.

What risk? What possible loss? Credibility, reputation, community standing, and the cascading losses that can be the result. For those who have no concern for such things, the risk of losing doesn't register in their minds at all and therefore does not motivate them to do the work to avoid it. For others, that potential loss, or maybe just the opportunity to engage in iron-sharpens-iron community, motivates them to build knowledge and refine their ability to intelligently discuss the issues.

It is very likely that people in this group will unknowingly mix concepts in their comments and present conflicting principles without being aware of the contradictions that are obvious to you and others. We need to be careful to avoid pouncing on their poor understanding of principles they claim to espouse. It is an opportunity to capture their attention and draw them closer to us.

In cases like this we can build rapport by demonstrating that we are reasonable and honest debaters. Agree with them on the point they mistakenly made. Then in the same response, in case they suddenly realize their folly, give them a way out by graciously agreeing that the issues are complicated and full of contradictions that make it difficult for anyone to completely commit to either side of the topic.

You are friends now! Or at least possibly no longer mortal enemies.

Now that you have proven yourself flexible and generous, follow that with actual evidence that validates your position. To fully capitalize on the opportunity, make sure that the information is unoffensive, well-reasoned, and indicates that you possess a solid understanding of the issue and underlying factors.

If their comments don't contain wording that you can leverage to create common ground, you can often use a similar technique to accomplish the same end result. You may have to reach a little further or stretch the immediate context slightly, but you can normally gain ground by kindly pointing out, in a "yeah I get it" manner, that the issue is complicated and it is difficult to fully embrace either side.

23

DEBATING THE FINANCIALLY INVESTED

> *Try not to become a man of success, but rather try to become a man of value.*
>
> — ALBERT EINSTEIN

Who has a financial motivation to viciously and vocally defend a philosophy, agenda, policy, or organization? Let's start at the top.

Insiders:

This group includes those close to the political elites. It includes their sponsors, handlers, staff, family, and friends. It also includes a loose collection of those who stand to profit from membership in the friends and family network: business owners, their employees, public relations firms, nonprofits and others.

Many who cross the line in defending a philosophy, agenda, policy, or organization do so out of financial motivation. They either receive or hope to receive money or other rewards in return for their loyalty. They themselves, their employer, their business, their nonprofit, or their industry may benefit from their advocacy.

How much of the information you see on social media and in the news today is generated by these financially invested parties and blasted to all corners of consciousness by their powerful supporters in Big Tech? How much of it seems to be broadly accepted based on the fact that there appears to be little or no visible disagreement? Is there any opposition or are these ideas so universally accepted that no knowledgeable and sane person could possibly disagree?

As we discussed in a previous chapter, "the narrative" promotes compliance among the general population and is the key to amassing more power now and even more power in the future. Politicians, or rather their incredibly brilliant sponsors, handlers, and staff ultimately determine the narrative and the most effective methods for winning public opinion over to their side.

Powerful and well-rehearsed organizations work together to present a consistent message with the goal of convincing the general population to accept their messaging as conventional wisdom. How else would dozens of news anchors and commentators use the exact same phrases and focus on the same topics every day?

Politicians, their sponsors, handlers, staff, family, and friends are often very active in the debate. However, they are focused on defining the debate through powerful outlets of news, information, and political analysis. We are not likely to ever be in the same virtual room with any of them. We will probably never have the opportunity to debate them or exchange comments with them directly, but their posts do present opportunities for us to engage in the public debate and influence others.

Business owners, their employees, and public relations machines are often very vocal and visible influencers of public opinion. Since they are accepted as the smartest people in the virtual room, they have an elevated and amplified platform that often enables them to immediately affect public opinion with just a few words. They often use their influence to perpetuate the narrative through the same powerful outlets of news and political analysis. Media outlets, bloggers, and podcasters seize on their statements and repeat them relentlessly for days. The story and related memes are posted, reposted, and shared on social media millions of times. We are not likely to ever be in the same virtual room with anyone in this group either, but their posts do offer opportunities to influence.

Remember that the most vocal supporters of the narrative are high-profile influential people who have enormous followings and either receive or hope to receive money or other rewards in return for their efforts. The less vocal, or more passive "supporters," in this category are painfully aware that the US government, and the people who control its resources and enforcement agencies, can be a very dangerous adversary. The people who control the offices of the US government also control the IRS, FBI, CIA, EPA, FTC, FDA, NIH, Homeland Security, Immigration Services, ATF, DEA, and others. These agencies in the hands of the self-serving can be incredibly destructive to individuals and businesses. This helps explain how the narrative is perpetuated enthusiastically with little visible opposition from high-profile individuals.

Paid Advocates:

Lobbyists and other organizations are paid to promote ideas to the public and to politicians. We generally think of lobbyists as people who are paid to convince politicians to support or oppose legislation. The lobbyist is paid by a company or an industry to represent their interests and work with politicians to encourage policies that benefit their clients in some way.

Lobbyists primarily directly interact with politicians and their staff to sell them on the benefits of their agenda to the public. Lobbyists also use advertising and other tools to move public opinion in their favor and use that public opinion as a lever to convince politicians to move in that same direction.

In the age of social media, the lobbying game has changed dramatically. Lobbyists now have the ability to affect public opinion dramatically and quickly. If they can quickly and cost-effectively win public opinion to their side, the case they present to politicians becomes much stronger.

Prior to the ubiquitous use of social media, their messaging was delivered through advertisements placed with legacy TV, newspapers, and magazine outlets. With those mediums there are relatively long lead times involved between conceiving of a message and actually delivering it to the public. It could take months to produce a TV commercial or to create a print ad campaign along with the supporting articles written by industry experts that appear in the same outlets.

Social media has compressed the lead time to a few days, or even a few hours in some cases. Lobbyists can now create and execute a campaign in a matter of days instead of months and reach far more people at much lower cost. Social media also offers a level of agility that traditional media just cannot match. If a social media campaign is not as effective as anticipated, the message, target audience, and delivery platform can be adjusted very rapidly. Campaign effectiveness can be determined almost in real time by tracking key metrics such as impressions (ad views), click-through rate, cost per click, mentions, and sentiment. If the metrics indicate weak results, the message and ad buys can be redirected quickly to try to improve the effectiveness of the campaign.

Lobbyists have become masters of using social media to shape public opinion and then using social media metrics to convince politicians that the objectives of the lobbyist's client fall in the sweet spot of what the public wants from government. Since the primary goal of the politician is to be reelected, that can be a powerful lever for moving them in the preferred direction.

According to Opensecrets.org, companies, labor unions, trade associations, and other influential organizations spend billions of dollars each year to lobby Congress and federal agencies. For 2022 about $4 billion was spent by companies on lobbying.

How much of the information you see on social media and in the news today is generated by these financially motivated parties?

Investigate the people and companies behind public relations initiatives that concern you. Research the opinions of trusted conservative sources.

Use your influence to help others recognize the disingenuous actors attempting to create the appearance of broad-based public opinion.

24

THE KINGS OF ASTROTURFING: FAKE GRASSROOTS MOVEMENTS

> *The past was erased, the erasure was forgotten, the lie became the truth.*
>
> GEORGE ORWELL, *1984*

Much of the information you encounter online is created and promoted by one type of interest group or another. Some of those groups have truly noble ambitions to improve the lives of those less fortunate or to promote economic development in underserved areas. Others deviously use the cover of philanthropic advocacy to promote their own self-interests or the interests of their industry. Of course, their personal interest is often simply to be well paid to promote ideas supporting a political agenda. The validity or integrity of the ideas and agenda promoted are of no concern to them as long as the checks clear.

To help avoid confusion, be aware that the following terms are often used interchangeably:

- Interest group
- Advocacy group
- Pressure group

These terms refer to organizations whose purpose is to influence government legislation and public opinion. To succeed in their mission, they must gain recognition among the general public, in political circles, or at least in their community of interest.

If they fail to elevate their profile and their platform, they fail in their mission.

These groups also participate in discussion threads on the most popular platforms. The members of these groups are well-funded and vigilant in online discussions. They have created extremely effective processes for promoting their interests online and encouraging their detractors to remain silent. Their marketing teams have assembled an arsenal of highly refined posts, comments, and responses that staffers can rapid-fire copy and paste to dominate the conversation and drive home the message.

Lobbyists fall under a broad category generally known as interest groups. However, we are differentiating between organizations regulated by lobbying laws, other types of interest groups regulated based on their tax-exempt status, and other unregulated groups.

In the US there are laws that govern the extent that certain groups can engage in political activism and lobbying of politicians. As a result, tax-exempt interest groups normally focus more on creating compelling messaging and swaying public opinion on an issue. Traditionally many tactics have been used, including meetings, rallies, protests, petitions, and press releases. However, interest groups now focus most of their resources on building a following on popular social media platforms and using that influence to flood the zone, creating the appearance of commonly held beliefs.

Think about how easy it would be for a small number of people to seed social media platforms with thousands of posts, memes, and discussion threads, all singing from the same book and page. It is incredibly easy and is happening daily on a scale you probably cannot even imagine. This is known as flooding the zone to create the perception that everyone is in agreement. Anyone disagreeing in the face of near universal support would have to be a complete moron.

Some of these groups are completely aboveboard and legitimate, with backing from leaders and other organizations with shared interests. However, there are many so-called advocacy groups on social media platforms that do not appear to be connected to any company, organization, or person. The sites list no founders, leaders, partner companies, or other identifying information. That is very strange to me. When I encounter messaging on social media that I find interesting, my first two questions are, who is behind this and what is their agenda? If I can't quickly and easily answer those questions, I begin to have doubts about the legitimacy of the group and the message it promotes.

Why would the people behind an advocacy group be entirely anonymous? Aren't they proud of their accomplishments? Their pages are often very professional and compelling. Someone has skills! Don't they want to be recognized as a leader on that issue? Don't they want to promote the issue through interviews and public appearances? If they are legitimate and honestly leading on the issue, they would do everything within their power to promote it publicly based on their good name and reputation. Wouldn't they?

Why is it important to understand who is providing you with information and the true nature of their agenda? You need to know if they are a credible objective source or if they are entirely driven by their own self-interests. What self-interests?

Let's look at a scenario that may or may not be fictitious. The history of high-speed rail in the United States has been less than spectacular, to say the least. Massive taxpayer funded projects have failed entirely, fallen far short of their advertised capabilities, and cost taxpayers far more to complete and operate than was promised in the sales pitch. That is true in nearly every single case in history.

California's disastrous $33 billion 520-mile high-speed rail project was approved in 2008 with a target completion date of 2020.[1] Fifteen years on, costs have exploded to $128 billion and not one mile of track has been installed. The project has been scaled back to 171 miles of eventual rail.[2]

Such spectacular failures burden the industry with an enormous amount of baggage to overcome. But overcome they must because they stand to rake in billions or trillions more in taxpayer dollars if they can get the government to fund future high-speed rail projects.

So, how do wealthy insiders overcome this massive weight of past failures to secure future high-speed rail development projects? Well, they need a very impressive sales pitch on the new technology that promises rapid completion of new rail developments that are far less expensive to build and far less expensive to operate. Then they need to employ their lobbyists to convince politicians that this is what the public wants because it will clearly save the planet. To convince those politicians, they very aggressively promote the same messaging in the public square of social media to gain a large following of the gullible that politicians cannot ignore.

Keep in mind that there are hundreds of billions of taxpayer dollars up for grabs. They can afford to invest several million to win a very luxurious future funded by never-ending paydays from taxpayers in the billions.

However, their legitimate "public education" campaigns and government lobbying will not be enough. Those efforts are closely monitored and the promises made in the sales pitch must be within the realm of facts and reason. They must define and control the narrative on social media if they are to succeed. The legitimate companies have already stretched the facts as far as they possibly can. Their reputations are at stake. Their "facts" must be close enough to reality to provide them with a defensible position under the cover of "according to expert consultants we hired," "based on industry accepted research and forecasting," and other assertions of plausible deniability.

What do they do if those facts, stretched to their limits, are not compelling enough to win the battle for public opinion? Don't worry. The solution is just a few shadowy steps away, on the other side of a string of sketchy contracts and payouts for "unspecified services." Those services are provided by nameless and faceless people who have nothing to lose. They provide multiple layers of separation and plausible deniability to their clients, who do have everything to lose.

The services provided by these anonymous organizations could be described as, and often appear to be, advocacy for an issue. However, what they really provide is false hope to a gullible public looking for solutions to the world's most difficult challenges.

They manage very professional-looking websites and social media pages. Their sites have page after page of extremely compelling articles, posts, and memes overflowing with glowing analysis from "industry experts" on why their industry is uniquely positioned above all to save the planet. And it appears that all followers and commenters agree that they are the hope of the world.

They appear to be completely legitimate on the surface. When you start asking questions, like who is behind this and what is their agenda, the answers are difficult or impossible to find. The organization is investing significant resources to provide volumes of compelling and informative memes, posts, and articles. Wouldn't the individuals and organizations behind these highly polished sites and in-depth analyses be proud to be associated with their work? Apparently not.

The separation they provide to their clients is key to their success. The false information they broadcast to every corner of the internet must not be traced back through the obfuscation cloud of multiple companies to their actual client. If you cannot easily identify those responsible for running the misinformation sites, it will be difficult for you to trace them back to their client. It is a major win for the client, the wealthy insiders attempting to overcome a massive burden of past failures to secure future high-speed rail development projects.

Through this arrangement, the distant contractor aggressively seeds false information and false hope throughout social media and helps create an echo chamber that grows louder and louder as more misguided voices join in. Legacy media, bloggers, influencers, newspapers, and magazines use the site as an authoritative source for their stories, further promoting the agenda of the wealthy insiders.[3]

Over time the misinformation is reposted, shared, mentioned, and cited so much that it eventually dominates the results returned by search engines, in one form or another. Many will accept the information as credible after searching the topic, using various search terms and always receiving results with glowing reviews of the organization. A new cubic zirconia of "conventional wisdom" has been forged, not by heat, but by false prophets and the feel-good virtue-signaling of the uninformed.

Isn't this new conventional wisdom challenged by experts and skeptics? If it were challenged, how would you ever know? Do you think they would allow disagreement or off-message comments on their pages? Not a chance. Those comments are scrubbed immediately before they are seen. This creates a situation where there is little opportunity to challenge the narrative and encourage people to do their own research. Any dissent that is able to see the light of day seems to be unanimously dismissed as "out of context" or "not credible." No credible challengers? No convincing skeptics? Must be good data, right? Wrong!

This type of manipulation of public opinion has become known as "astroturfing," where companies create fake grassroots movements to promote their agendas. As Sharyl Attkisson, investigative journalist and bestselling author, puts it:

> *Astroturfers often disguise themselves and publish blogs, write letters to the editor, produce ads, start non-profits, establish Facebook and Twitter accounts, edit Wikipedia pages or simply post comments online to try to fool you into thinking an independent or grassroots movement is speaking.*

Sharyl Attkisson has a very interesting TED Talk titled "Astroturf and Manipulation of Media Messages." You can find the video and more of her investigative reporting at SharylAttkisson.com.

To put the power of astroturfing into perspective, she states that "surreptitious astroturf methods are now more important to these interests than traditional lobbying of Congress. There's an entire PR industry built around it in Washington." According to Sharyl Attkisson, using social media to win public opinion with false data and fake grassroots movements is now more important than traditional lobbying of Congress!

Is it effective? Let's complete the discussion of our scenario that may or may not be fictitious. Amtrak was created in 1970 by the federal government to take over 20 passenger rail companies that were on the verge of collapsing. Amtrak is owned by the federal government but is controlled by a private corporation. Amtrak generates revenue from passengers but also receives funding from state governments and the federal government.

According to the Epoch Times, from inception until the middle of 2021 Amtrak had received $45 billion in funding from the federal government. In a single legislative act in fall of 2021 in Washington, Amtrak received $66 billion in funding from the federal government as part of the $1.2 trillion Infrastructure Investment and Jobs Act. From $45 billion in funding over 50 years, to an additional $66 billion in funding in one act of Congress! Is astroturfing effective? You have your answer!

On December 8, 2023, the Biden Whitehouse announced that an additional $8.2 billion in taxpayer money would be spent on 10 major passenger rail projects across the country. Is astroturfing effective? Apparently!

Again, how much of the information you see on social media and in the news today is generated by wealthy insiders who control the narrative?[4]

Investigate the people and companies behind public relations initiatives that concern you. Research the opinions of trusted conservative sources.

Use your influence to help others recognize the disingenuous actors attempting to create the appearance of broad-based public opinion.

PART 4
COURAGE TO SEE THE TRUTH

25

COVID RESPONSE – EPIC POWER CONSOLIDATION

> *Those who expect to reap the blessings of freedom must, like men, undergo the fatigue of supporting it.*
>
> — THOMAS PAINE

This chapter and the three following it present four different case studies based on recent events that have dominated our lives. Here we review the events and how information was represented in the media and other sources. In all four cases, our perceptions and beliefs were manipulated using tactics covered in earlier chapters. Here you will recognize those tactics, how they were used to encourage compliance, and how they were used to punish dissent.

In these chapters you will also see opportunities to do your own research and find the truth.

The COVID pandemic and the US response to it are complex topics. Many complete books have been written and will be written on how brilliantly or incompetently the crisis was handled. I cannot possibly provide comprehensive coverage here, but I can provide some context and perspective from my point of view.

No medical advice or debate is presented here. Work with your healthcare professionals to address your healthcare concerns.

The response to COVID has changed this world forever. I did not say that COVID changed this world forever. It was the response that was devastating. Many believe that the response was carefully calculated to achieve a specific objective.

The "people," the mindless and soulless worker bees in the streets, us, now fully understand that we cannot possibly survive without the protections and sustenance provided day-to-day by our all-powerful and generous ruling class. We are doomed to a miserable death if not for the elites brilliantly managing the small details of our everyday lives.

At least they hope that is the lesson we have all learned. They spent trillions of taxpayer dollars trying to teach us that. I sincerely hope we are a huge disappointment to them in this case!

A couple of quotes from influential leaders of the radical left seem to shed some light on the evolution of this crisis:

> *You never let a serious crisis go to waste. And what I mean by that it's an opportunity to do things you think you could not do before.*
>
> RAHM EMANUEL, WHITE HOUSE CHIEF OF STAFF FOR BARACK OBAMA, 2009 TO 2010

> *In the arena of action, a threat or a crisis becomes almost a precondition to communication.*
>
> SAUL D. ALINSKY, RULES FOR RADICALS

COVID is a very serious and devastating virus. There is no question about that. However, there are many questions about the efficacy of how it was handled and the accuracy of the data and "accepted science" that were pushed by officials and were allowed on social media platforms. "Allowed" on social media? Allowed by who? It'll come to you!

According to the Centers for Disease Control and Prevention (CDC), over 1 million people have died from COVID in the United States since the first case was reported in Wuhan, China, on November 17, 2019:[1]

- 2023: 70,224
- 2022: 255,621
- 2021: 469,966
- 2020: 367,209

Unfortunately, the numbers are unreliable because only in 6% of those cases was COVID the only cause. The CDC has clarified that the other 94% had other "conditions and contributing causes" in addition to COVID.[2] Those contributing causes include heart decease or failure, respiratory decease or failure, diabetes, renal failure, influenza, pneumonia, Alzheimer's disease, obesity, sepsis, cancer, and many others.

Perhaps the most startling "contributing" causes counted as death by COVID are those related to "intentional and unintentional injury, poisoning, and other adverse events." In other words, *even physical injury resulting in death is counted as death by COVID!*

How could the numbers be so badly skewed? Aren't these people scientists? We now know that doctors were told to mark cause of death as COVID if there was any suspicion that the patient had been exposed to COVID. Many doctors resisted the directive and were strongly encouraged to comply or suffer consequences.

So, what is the real death toll from COVID? Is it 20% of the reported count? Possibly 10%? We will never know the accurate COVID death count. However, it is evident to nearly everyone in hindsight what many saw from the beginning.

The response was detrimental to the entire nation on many levels. The response enabled a small number of people to seize control of our lives and our futures to a degree unimaginable to most of us before January 2020. I say "most of us" because some did raise concerns from the very beginning and were systematically and publicly dismissed as Neanderthal science deniers.

The facts are out there but, by design, are about as easy to find as a vegan organic snack in a California biker bar in 1982.

During the pandemic, vaccine mandates were implemented by the federal government and some state governments. In September of 2021 President Biden issued two executive orders mandating vaccines for approximately 100 million employees of health care providers, large employers, and the federal government and associated contractors.[3]

Thousands of people who resisted getting vaccinated were fired from their jobs. *Military Times* magazine reports that about 1% of marines were discharged for refusing to take the vaccine. Many fired workers have recently won lawsuits against their employers, who were forced, in some cases, to reinstate the employee in their job and pay back wages. Many such lawsuits are not yet resolved.

More data to consider: in August 2022, 58% of COVID deaths were people who had been vaccinated.[4]

> In hindsight, were warnings of overreaction ignored?
> Who was impacted by the overreaction?
> Who benefited from the overreaction?

We now know, based on science, that the most devastating measures forced upon us were also the most ineffective. Scientists are now admitting that they were wrong to support public health officials who overstated results and misused science to mislead the public. The scientific community seemingly spoke with one voice on the matter beginning in early 2020. Some of those same scientists are now admitting that broad indiscriminate vaccinations, long-term lockdowns, school closures, and mask mandates were ineffective and had serious long-term effects on real people.

We now know from a November 2022 study by the American College of Cardiology that an alarming number of young people who were vaccinated, a very low-risk group, are suffering from heart diseases like myocarditis at extremely high rates.[5] The study reported those rates at 35.6 cases per million for Moderna and 12.6 per million for Pfizer. For comparison, in 2018 the rate of myocarditis in the general population was 2.01 per million people under age 40, according to the study. People under 40 who were given the Moderna vaccination are 17 times more likely to develop myocarditis than the 2018 unvaccinated general population. *17 times!* Not 17% more likely. Seventeen times more likely!

Remember that for over two years those who raised questions about the potential danger of an untested vaccine were viciously berated as ignorant science deniers.

So, now we suddenly remember that any time the scientific community seems to speak with one voice, we should be very concerned. In the voice of Edward Norton from the movie *Fight Club*: "The first rule of science, you always question the science!" If scientists are not allowed to question it, it is not science and truth is not the agenda.

At this point it is very difficult to find actual debate on the pandemic. A quick search of the internet indicates that we all seem to be in full agreement on every aspect, right? Any question or disagreement is buried under mountains of articles and posts consistent with the approved narrative, which is parroted continuously and verbosely by Big Tech and legacy media. Few of us have the time or the patience needed to wade through the bilge to eventually find well-reasoned debate on the validity of that data.

The approved narrative and the laughable far edges of the opposing side seem to be amplified above the doctors and scientists, those who have the expertise and data to present a credible opposing view. The outrageous kooks and crackpots are allowed to be heard and mocked for entertainment value. These ridiculous outliers are effectively elevated to the role of opposition leaders by the media. All who raise questions about the response to COVID are immediately associated with this lunatic fringe and dismissed. Those in power discredit as hicks and hayseeds all who are not convinced of the safety of the vaccine. But credible debate and dissent are forbidden. Violators, if they are credible and have something to lose, will be punished and will suffer tremendous personal loss.

Remember when "racist," "xenophobic," "backward," and "ignorant" people believed that COVID originated in a lab in Wuhan, China? Turns out most experts now admit a lab in Wuhan was the likely source. Former head of the CDC, Robert Redfield, has stated that evidence suggests that is the case. The Wuhan Institute of Virology, funded partially by US taxpayer dollars at the request of Dr. Anthony Fauci, was performing gain of function experiments with the virus, attempting to mutate it to jump from animals to humans. There is evidence that that they were successful and that the mutated virus was not effectively contained.

> Why would they bother to suppress the Wuhan lab origins? Because our government funded that lab.

Dr. Fauci served as the director of the National Institute of Allergy and Infectious Diseases from 1984 to 2022. He was reported to be the highest paid employee of the federal government, at $480,000 in 2021.[6] Now that he is retired, he is paid over $355,000 per year, the highest pension from the federal government in history.

While many still believe Dr. Fauci is the most well-respected physician in the country, reports of his fabrications of "truth," suppression of debate, and mishandling of the COVID response have left many wondering what his motives have been through his tenure as the nation's top doctor. In 2019 he reported a net worth of $7.5 million. As the pandemic subsided in 2022, his net worth had grown to over $12.6 million, a 68% increase in three years.

When questions about this taxpayer-funded research in China began to surface, Dr. Fauci realized that his legacy and career would evaporate if the public learned he encouraged and funded this research. To prevent that, he went on a mission to obscure the facts under a mountain of newly fabricated data.

> Step one, have scientists under his control hurriedly write and publish a paper in the March 17, 2020 issue of *Nature Medicine* designed to disprove the lab leak origins theory.[7]

> Step two, respond to questions by casually stating that "there was some study recently" that reports the virus

likely evolved over time and mutated, enabling it to jump to humans.

Just some study he heard about somewhere and he had no part in creating. Or so the story goes. And thus, all those ignorant science deniers and their "crackpot theories" could be easily dismissed by Fauci and his groupies in the media and Big Tech. Foolish dissenters with a platform could be and were suppressed with great force!

In June 2023 the US House of Representatives Select Subcommittee on the Coronavirus Pandemic issued a subpoena demanding information on communications related to the *Nature Medicine* report from the primary author, Dr. Kristian Andersen.[8] Former CDC director Robert Redfield has come forward with details of cover-up steps taken to suppress the lab leak theory, Dr. Fauci's connections to the Wuhan lab, and the fraudulent report intended to stop discussion of the lab leak theory. Many scientists are now demanding that *Nature Medicine* remove the report.

It is a very tangled web that honest reporters have begun to unravel. Please do your own research through trusted independent sources.

Just one example of the dangers of deviating from the approved narrative is the debate on the use of Ivermectin. Doctors were viciously ridiculed for prescribing "animal medication" and lost their licenses to practice when they promoted Ivermectin as a treatment for certain COVID patients. Those same doctors reported more than a 99.9% success rate for their thousands of patients. Many celebrities have admitted taking Ivermectin to treat COVID and have been mercilessly attacked on social media for it.

These transgressions triggered many alarming headlines such as:

- ABC News August 23, 2021: "Ivermectin, a Deworming Drug, Should Not Be Used to Treat COVID, Health Officials Say"
- AARP September 1, 2021: "Warnings Mount against Taking Livestock Dewormer to Prevent, Treat COVID-19"
- BBC October 6, 2021: "Ivermectin: How False Science Created a COVID 'Miracle' Drug"
- *The Guardian* September 24, 2021: "Fraudulent Ivermectin Studies Open Up New Battleground between Science and Misinformation"
- The FDA December 2021: "Why You Should Not Use Ivermectin to Treat or Prevent COVID-19"

When you dig into the FDA article listed above you'll see that it is almost amusing. They provide a link to a database of related medical studies intended to support the headline. Unfortunately for the FDA, the study results do not support the headline but contradict the headline.[9]

Of the 89 related studies in the database, 32 had been completed and provided results. Of those 32 studies, 16 reported results that supported the use of Ivermectin, six reported mixed results indicating it could be beneficial, 10 reported that no evidence was found to indicate that Ivermectin was effective in treating COVID. So, the studies used as evidence by the FDA to claim Ivermectin should not be used are 69% supportive of using Ivermectin to treat COVID! Mildly amusing but strongly infuriating.

Let me say here, with great emphasis, I am not a doctor and I am not advocating for Ivermectin. I'm advocating for the free and open exchange of ideas and actual facts. The use of Ivermectin is just one case of many where that debate was not allowed to happen.

Again, I am not a doctor and I am not giving medical advice. Always follow the advice of your doctor.

The FDA, Health and Human Services, the pharmaceutical companies are on a mission to save lives, right?

The backlash against Ivermectin is even more curious, considering it was approved for human use in 1987 and many billions of doses have been administered since then. Despite that, the FDA issued strong warnings on the dangers and risks of using Ivermectin to treat COVID. The FDA even tweeted the following on August 21, 2021:[10]

> *You are not a horse. You are not a cow. Seriously, y'all. Stop it.*
>
> *Why You Should Not Use Ivermectin to Treat or Prevent COVID-19*
>
> *Using the Drug ivermectin to treat COVID can be dangerous and even lethal. The FDA has not approved the drug for that purpose.*

Why would the leaders of our health care industry aggressively discourage the use of a readily available and inexpensive drug to save lives? The FDA, Health and Human Services, the pharmaceutical companies? Is their mission not entirely focused on saving lives and improving the quality of life? No, that is not their mission at all, regardless of what their websites and public relations firms tell us. The mission of those at the top of government organizations is to acquire more funding and to cozy up to the most successful businesses in the industry they regulate. The mission of pharmaceutical companies is profit. You see how those missions come together to support each other nicely?

Studies have since validated the benefits of using Ivermectin to treat COVID. The FDA has dramatically softened its position on its use as well. Those who publicly ridiculed doctors and their patients now just shrug their shoulders as if to say that those decisions were above their pay grade and they were only following orders. Orders from whom?

David R. Henderson and Charles L. Hooper published a very enlightening article on this topic entitled "The FDA's War against the Truth on Ivermectin." It can be found on the American Institute for Economic Research website.[11]

Families in the United States and around the world were financially devastated by lockdowns, loss of income, and extreme levels of inflation. Those in control of government and certain industries fared far better:

- 573 new billionaires were created in two years during the COVID crisis.
- 2,668 billionaires owned $12.7 trillion in wealth.

This information was covered in an earlier chapter. It is repeated here because it is directly related to this case study and brilliantly validates the most fundamental beliefs held by conservatives. Oxfam International (Oxfam.org) reported those figures in a May 23, 2022 report. They also reported that the wealth of those billionaires rose more in the first 24 months of the crisis than in the previous 23 years combined. In 24 months! Think about how that is even possible!

At the time of this report, 2,668 billionaires owned $12.7 trillion in wealth. That is a very small number of people in control of a staggering level of wealth that exceeds that of more than 100 countries combined. Only the top 10 wealthiest countries in the world have more wealth than these 2,668 individuals.

The holders of $12.7 trillion in wealth are able to make a long list of very influential people incredibly wealthy and still have $12.7 trillion. Think about the impact of legislation, regulations, news coverage, and information flow all angled to support their agendas. That is true power!

Again, COVID is a very serious and devastating virus. It must be dealt with in a scientific, logic-based manner. It is very real. Most of us know multiple people who have died from COVID. I personally know of a family of six siblings in their fifties that was reduced to a single survivor by the virus. They were reasonably healthy, hardworking people and five of them were taken by it. COVID should not be dismissed as just another sensational headline.

However, we should also take very seriously the massive government and corporate overreaches justified and excused in response to the pandemic. We should take very seriously the more than $245 billion stolen by criminals when the government rolled the presses to quickly spread free money generously across the country after businesses were shut down.

The seemly endless supply of free money also drove inflation and interest rates to debilitating levels not seen in decades. I guess $245 billion stolen out of $5.6 trillion in taxpayer dollars spent on the COVID response is considered to be a minor rounding error by the ruling class.

Was there fraud? Of course! But that was just pennies tossed into the frenzied mosh pit by the wealthy ruling class to give us something other than them to focus on.

The Small Business Administration (SBA) alone disbursed approximately $1.2 trillion of COVID-19 Economic Injury Disaster Loan (EIDL) and Paycheck Protection Program (PPP) funds. Of that, the SBA estimates that at least $200 billion was handed over to people who submitted fraudulent applications.[12] The US Department of Labor estimated that more than $45 billion in taxpayer dollars were lost to unemployment fraud.[13] Many of those fraudulent unemployment claims were filed by government employees who were still on the job.[14]

You may find it difficult to believe that federal spending nearly doubled during the pandemic. Just in case you are skeptical, the spending bills that enabled that outrageous level of government spending are listed below.

$ Billions	Public Law	Law Name
$8.30	116-123 (2020)	Coronavirus Preparedness and Response Supplemental Appropriations Act, 2020[15]
$104	116-127 (2020)	Families First Coronavirus Response Act[16]
$2,200	116-136 (2020)	Coronavirus Aid, Relief, and Economic Security Act[17]
$484	116-139 (2020)	Paycheck Protection Program and Health Care Enhancement[18]
$900	116-260 (2021)	Consolidated Appropriations Act, 2021 [including coronavirus stimulus and relief ($900 billion COVID-related)[19]
$1,900	117-2 (2021)	American Rescue Plan Act of 2021[20]

Figure 25.1 COVID Related Federal Spending Legislation

Endnotes: [15] [16] [17] [18] [19] [20]

When over $5.6 trillion was created by clicking a button repeatedly, how did that impact our families? The long-term impact is the enormous government debt that our children and grandchildren must carry on their backs. The more immediate impact is out-of-control inflation at rates not seen in over 40 years. Since January 2020, the value of that dollar in your pocket dropped below 80 cents in just four years. That has a very real and tangible impact on you, your family, and organizations you support.

The economic fallout of the government's COVID response will be felt by families for many years as they attempt to recapture their American Dream. Over 20 million jobs were lost due to the COVID response. Unemployment skyrocketed from 3.5% to 15% in just two months and eventually reached 17%.[21]

Most of those job losses were in the leisure and hospitality industries, which experienced a 49% decline in employees. The poor, the young, and those who had only recently set out on their own were the hardest hit. Among those, women suffered the highest number of job losses because they held a higher percentage of jobs in the industries hit the hardest, according to the US Bureau of Labor Statistics.

> Every person in the United States who has a job, buys groceries, or supports dependents, was seriously impacted.

For those of us who support buy-local initiatives, we have suffered setbacks that will take years to recover from, if it is even possible. While big business growth surged, small business suffered irrecoverable losses. Early in the pandemic the number of operating small businesses dropped by over 34%.[22]

It is difficult to keep a small business running when employees cannot come to work, customers can't come to your business, and your business can't go to the customer. Business expenses raged on while revenue plummeted. Rent, utilities, loans payments, insurance, licenses, equipment, and other costs continue day in and day out. Business owners also must continue to be paid a subsistence salary, if possible, so they can meet their personal financial obligations.

Further complicating business operations and recovery, supply chain issues quickly developed early in the pandemic. As the pandemic dragged on, the impact of the disruption grew into the worst supply shortage of the past 50 years. This exacerbated the pandemic fallout for businesses, small and large, that rely on suppliers for the materials, components, and inventory needed to deliver products and services to their customers.

Why did this happen? Supply chains are very labor-intensive. It takes a lot of people and human interaction to source, refine, manufacture, and transport the products and materials most companies need to operate. Many of those suppliers were US-based and were forced to shut down. However, for many industries, suppliers are concentrated in China. According to a Deloitte report on managing supply chain risk, 200 of the Fortune 500 companies have a presence in Wuhan, China.

Remember that Wuhan is where the virus first spread after it was escorted out of a local lab, knowingly or not. Wuhan is a manufacturing hub for high-tech industries and the automotive industry. It is home to hundreds of facilities that manufacture semiconductors, electronic components, and car parts. While China as a whole was on lockdown, Wuhan was the first to be locked down and isolated as much as possible from the rest of the country and the world. The inability to source supplies from Wuhan and other areas of China had a devastating effect on economies across the globe.

As restrictions began to be lifted, businesses were forced to struggle through the hangover effects of very limited supplies, a smaller workforce willing to resume public interactions, rapidly accelerating inflation, and significantly higher business loan costs due to inflation and interest rate increases. Consumers were also saving more of their income. The highest savings rate recorded in history was 32% in April

2020.[23] As of January 2024, the savings rate has settled at 3.8%. A dollar saved is a dollar not spent on a smoothie at a local business.

The impact on students of being out of the classroom for months or even years has been detrimental to their education, their community connectedness, and their mental health. Researchers at the Center for Education Policy Research at Harvard University (CEPR) and Stanford University's Educational Opportunity Project, estimate that students lost as much as 1.5 years of progress in math education during the pandemic.[24] If that gap is to be closed, those students would need to learn 50% more math than typical every year for three years. It is not likely that such an ambitious learning plan is being implemented in public schools.

In the September 2022 report from the National Assessment of Educational Progress (NAEP), reading scores for nine-year-old students dropped 5%, the largest decline since 1990.[25] The report also stated that math scores for those students dropped 7%, the first decline the NAEP had ever recorded. The study estimates that the students impacted by school lockdowns will lose an average of 5.6% of lifetime earnings.

In terms of mental well-being, the CDC reported that, in 2021, 37% of high school students reported experiencing poor mental health during the COVID pandemic, and 44% reported they persistently felt sad or hopeless during the past year. The report also indicated that a significant percentage of students suffered some form of emotional or physical abuse in the home during that time.[26]

The devastating effects of lockdowns on students were predictable, as some tried to warn early in the crisis.

According to a survey released in June 2022 by the National Center for Education Statistics, leaders in 87% of public schools agreed or strongly agreed that the pandemic has negatively impacted student socio-emotional development. The survey also noted that 84% agreed or strongly agreed that students' behavioral development has been negatively impacted.[27]

The taxpayer-funded American Rescue Plan response to COVID allocated an additional $122 billion to K-12 education. Unfortunately, public schools spend more time managing chaos of their own creation than actually teaching kids the skills they will need to become functioning adults. All of this probably helps explain why 6% of K¬–12 students in the United States were homeschooled during the 2021–2022 school year.[28]

College students have suffered setbacks as well. For them, the pandemic disrupted their eagerly anticipated transition into adulthood. The number of undergrad students in US colleges declined 6.5% over the first two years of the pandemic, the largest two-year decline in 50 years, according to the National Student Clearinghouse Research Center.[29] Studies show that people who delay the start of their college education significantly reduce their future earning potential.

According to one study of 4,714 college students, stress levels have been high in many areas. Of the students in the survey, 49% reported either losing their employment or having their hours reduced. About 37% reported being "very much or extremely" impacted financially, and 29% reported they were at least somewhat concerned about being able to afford food.

Some of that can be attributed to the normal college experience, but they reported other areas of anxiety that can be tied directly to the national COVID response. Over 73% reported connecting less with family and friends. Over 67% reported more frequent feelings of loneliness. The study is titled "The Psychological, Academic, and Economic Impact of COVID on College Students in the Epicenter of the Pandemic" and can be found on SagePub.com.[30]

According to the CDC, drug overdose deaths increased by 30% in 2020 and nearly 15% in 2021.[31] That is a 45% increase in just two years! Experts believe that increase may be attributed to a combination of increased hopelessness caused by lockdowns and the fact that recovering addicts could not access services and group meetings that are vital to their sobriety. An environment dominated by fear and hopelessness could make it easier to surrender to the persistent beckoning of easy escape offered by intoxication.

The three-part documentary, *Life of Crime: 1984–2020* by director Jon Alpert, follows a group of young petty criminals for nearly 40 years as they struggle through prison, addiction, and recovery. The final episode is difficult to sit through, as it reveals in very raw terms how the loss of hope, brought on by persistent fear and lockdowns, devastated the vulnerable. It is a very somber conclusion to an extremely emotional journey of hopelessness occasionally interrupted by cautious optimism.

> Drug overdoses up 45%! The intersection of boredom, hopelessness, and an endless supply of cheap fentanyl is devastating.

Dozens of research reports have been released in recent months comparing lockdown levels across US states and how people in those states were impacted by COVID and the response to COVID. States that did not implement long-term lockdowns did not suffer significantly more COVID cases or deaths. However, the lives of the people in those states, especially the young and most vulnerable, were not saddled with permanent setbacks.

One of the experts that raised concerns about lockdowns in the first months of the pandemic was Dr. Jay Bhattacharya, a well-respected epidemiologist and Stanford Medical School professor. Dr. Bhattacharya was coauthor of the April 2020 Santa Clara Study titled "COVID-19 Antibody Seroprevalence in Santa Clara County, California," one of the first comprehensive studies of how the disease spread and the impact on populations.[32]

The study concluded that cases of COVID were already far more widespread in early 2020 than was thought and the mortality rate was much lower than reported. At the time, there was widespread criticism of Dr. Bhattacharya and the report. However, hundreds of later studies confirmed the findings. Dr. Bhattacharya was also coauthor of the "Great Barrington Declaration," one of the first public declarations by scientists and doctors to raise questions and concerns on lockdowns being implemented across the world at the time.[33]

If you are wondering why you have never heard of Dr. Bhattacharya, he was one of many experts who were shadow-banned by Twitter and other platforms to prevent "misinformation" spread. They were not openly locked out or kicked off the platforms, but algorithms were used to make sure few people, if any, would be able to access their posts.

Why would the platforms suppress the free exchange of ideas? It is no surprise to you by now that platforms ban or shadow-ban users when pressured to do so, or when they anticipate they may be pressured to do so by government agencies. See the interview of Dr. Jay Bhattacharya conducted by Peter Robinson of the Hoover Institution for more information on how honest scientists and doctors view the devastation inflicted on real people and communities by the response to COVID.[34]

You should know the primary experts who perpetrated this tragedy in the United States. They are:

- Dr. Anthony Fauci, director of the National Institute of Allergy and Infectious Diseases from 1984 to 2022
- Dr. Francis Collins, director of the National Institutes of Health from 2009 to 2021
- Dr. Tedros Adhanom Ghebreyesus, general director of the World Health Organization from 2017 to the present

For reference and context:

- During the 2017–2018 flu season, 52,000 people in the United States died from the flu and 710,000 were hospitalized.
- According to the CDC, more than 480,000 people die annually from smoking and secondhand smoke in the United States each year.
- According to the CDC, more than 140,000 people die from excessive alcohol use in the United States each year. A 2022 study published in *JAMA Network Open* indicates that an estimated one in five deaths of adults

ages 20 to 49 was due to excessive use of alcohol. In addition, the number was one in eight for people between the ages of 20 and 64.
- According to the CDC, more than 100,000 people die from drug overdose in the United States each year. Overdose deaths from fentanyl, a cheap and extremely powerful synthetic opioid, increased nearly 300% from 2016 to 2021.

The response to COVID has changed this world forever. Did we learn the lesson they intended for us? Are we now living in constant fear that we are doomed to a miserable death if we don't allow the elites to manage the small details of our everyday lives and protect us from our own ignorance?

Are we going to continue to be the mindless and soulless worker bees in the streets that cannot possibly survive without the protections and sustenance provided day-to-day by our all-powerful and generous ruling class?

Or are we going to stand strong, take back our lives, and put the people in control of our government back in their place, serving the people instead of being generously served by the people?

> *The world will not be destroyed by those who do evil, but by those who watch them and do nothing.*
>
> ALBERT EINSTEIN

26

DONALD TRUMP DISRUPTOR-IN-CHIEF

> *The obedient always think of themselves as virtuous rather than cowardly.*
>
> GEORGE CARLIN

In this case study, we are not rehashing how information was represented in the media and other sources. Since we were all immersed in it for years, it is intuitively obvious by now. Instead, we go over facts that were suppressed, who participated in the cover-up, and how government officials committed serious crimes to protect insiders and the loyal, knowing they would in turn be protected by the ruling class.

Sentiment on Donald Trump runs the gamut in the conservative community. Some think he was the greatest president of the last 50 years. They can rightfully point to the tremendous economic growth and the lowest unemployment in many decades that were the result of significant reduction of regulation and taxes. Unemployment for women was at the lowest point in nearly 70 years. The United States was much less reliant on other countries for energy and became a net energy exporter. The United States withdrew from laughable international agreements, including the Trans-Pacific Partnership and the Iran nuclear agreement. Trump returned the United States to a position on the international stage of powerful and trusted partner, or serious opponent not to be trifled with.[1]

Others consider Trump a complete disaster as president. Most would likely agree that he often behaved in a manner that was less than presidential. Sometimes he responded to critics in ways not acceptable for a president of the United States. Sometimes he spoke off the cuff instead of taking time to think things through and confer with his advisors. At times he picked petty fights on social media instead of creating a mic-drop moment with a few well-articulated words from the president of the United States. As usual, the truth is probably found somewhere between those two extremes of opinion.

But let's not forget that Trump was hired by *we the people* to protect our interests. He was a political outsider, willing to ruthlessly use any legal means necessary to stop the ultra-wealthy ruling class and return power to the people. He made it clear in his inauguration speech that his mission was to transfer "power from Washington DC and give it back to you, the people." In that speech he called out establishment politicians as entirely self-serving in multiple statements including this one: "Washington flourished, but the people did not share in its wealth. Politicians prospered, but the jobs left and the factories closed."

The establishment politicians, the ultra-wealthy ruling class, were put on notice! At that moment, they realized that Donald Trump was not going to play nice or go along to get along. During the campaign they had suspected that he might actually mean what he said, and now they were sure of it. At this point those who lived in luxury from their status in the ruling class made a joint decision: Donald Trump must be destroyed and all those who profit from the swamp (both conservative and liberal) must work together along with the media and Big Tech to keep the status quo in place.

They have only themselves to blame for his election in what I consider to be the most hilarious demonstration of unintended consequences in recent history, triggered by an enormous miscalculation on the part of the Democratic Party. They were convinced he could not win the final ballot and did everything they could to make sure he was on that ballot opposite Hillary Clinton.

As they had calculated, at the end of the primary election he had won that ballot spot opposing Hillary. At that point they turned on a dime and began to do everything they could to make sure he did not win the general election. Their friends in legacy media and Big Tech went to great lengths to enthusiastically prove their loyalty throughout the election cycle. They dragged up and amplified every old story and allegation they could find to convince voters that he lacked the moral character to hold the office. They believed that Hillary would stand out head and shoulders above as a policy expert, articulate communicator, survivor of a cheating husband, and a beloved beacon of virtue. Hilary was all that? Really? The Democratic Party seemed to think so!

The singular unifying mission at the time: Trump must be destroyed before the election. Those who contribute to the success of the mission in a significant way will be generously rewarded!

The most energized and well-known attack on Trump was known as the Steele dossier, or Russiagate. The week of the presidential election, an article by David Corn in *Mother Jones News* was titled "A Veteran Spy Has Given the FBI Information Alleging a Russian Operation to Cultivate Donald Trump."[2] Trump was a Russian plant in US politics! A week hence a Russian spy could be elected president of the United States! Or so the story went.

The so-called facts of the report were essentially "someone told the FBI something and there might be something going on here," also known as unverifiable allegations. The legacy media and Big Tech didn't care that the story was entirely unsubstantiated. They didn't care that the piece did not rise to the level of the journalistic ethics of a checkout stand gossip rag. They went wild with it, wall to wall, just a few days before the election.

How did Trump win the election in the face of such damning allegations? I guess the citizens have higher journalistic standards than the actual journalists do! Voters saw through this latest charade, which had been spread out like a camouflage throw blanket over Hillary's email server related crimes, and many others.

We now know that the FBI was aware of these allegations at least three months before they became public. Their investigation into it, code-named Crossfire Hurricane, began in July 2016. It was later proven that FBI director James Comey and CIA director John Brennan knew the Russia-collusion narrative was false, a hoax played on voters, even before the Crossfire Hurricane investigation was initiated by the FBI.[3] In fact, Brennan had already received information that Hillary Clinton had personally approved the execution of a campaign effort to tie Trump directly to Putin and the hacking of Democratic National Committee emails by the Russians. The plan was initiated in April 2016 when it became clear that Trump would be on the final ballot for president against Hillary Clinton.[4]

Again, FBI director James Comey and CIA director John Brennan knew it was a lie before they started investigating in July. But still the media ran wild with the story. The directors of the FBI and CIA, knowing it was false, stepped back and let the story consume an enormous amount of page space and airtime.

The FBI and CIA knew the allegations were false but let voters continue to believe an investigation was needed.

After Trump was elected the FBI offered Christopher Steele, the dossier's namesake, $1 million if he could prove the allegations in the 35-page document were true. He could not and did not receive the money. However, those who opposed Trump continued to speak of the Steele dossier as if it were settled science that definitively proved that Trump was evil.

From there it is a very tangled web so convoluted that most voters have given up trying to decipher it. A few milestones and names of note may help alleviate some of the confusion:

May 2017, during Trump's presidency, former FBI director Robert Mueller is appointed special counsel to investigate alleged ties between Trump and Russia.

April 2018, *New York Times* and the *Washington Post* win a Pulitzer Prize for their investigative report on Trump's relationship with the Russians and their joint election interference initiatives. Pulitzer Prize! For absolutely fictitious "investigative" reporting! *New York Times* is considered the paper of record in the United States and many parts of the world. No matter how outrageously dishonest their reporting is, they always get a standing ovation from the ruling class, the media, and their glassy-eyed misinformed readers. Most other news and information organizations rely on them for guidance on what stories to cover and how to cover them. That fact provides some insight into why legacy media should be avoided when searching for the truth.

March 2019, the Mueller report is released and states there is no evidence that Trump had ties to the Russians but that the Russians, among other countries, have been and continue to be involved in election interference activities. As usual, the report received little honest press coverage.

May 2019, John Durham is selected by Attorney General William Barr to investigate the origins of the Trump-Russia collusion allegations, and the actions taken by government officials based on those allegations. Get that! Mueller investigated the allegations. When they were proven false, Durham investigated the people involved in creating and perpetuating those false allegations. Someone lied to the FBI and should go to jail. Probably many people. It seems that even the FBI itself lied to the FBI! You would go to jail for doing that.

December 2020, John Durham's appointment is upgraded to special counsel to allow the use of additional investigative capabilities.

May 2023, the Durham report is released and includes many alarming details of criminal actions taken by employees of the FBI related to the Crossfire Hurricane investigation.[5]

Special Counsel John Durham's report in May of 2023 contained many details that all of us should be concerned about. I'm not that concerned that the primary source for the dossier, Russian intelligence operative Oleg Deripaska, admits to making it up. He's a Russian spy with no self-imposed boundaries. What would you expect?

Very concerning, however, is the fact that the Durham report confirmed that the creation of the dossier was funded by operatives associated with the Hillary Clinton campaign and other Trump opponents.

All citizens should be very concerned that the FBI knew that many details in the dossier were entirely fictitious but continued to present it as factual evidence to the Foreign Intelligence Surveillance Act (FISA) court to secure secret warrants for fishing expeditions against Trump associates. The goal was to entrap his associates as a means of getting to Trump himself.

So, let that sink in for a while. The FBI used information that it knew to be false to secure warrants to spy on members of a presidential campaign! For what reason, or for whose benefit, would the FBI spy on a presidential campaign when there were no credible suspicions of criminal behavior? Did the sitting president, Obama, and his preferred candidate, Hillary Clinton, benefit from the information collected illegally on a political opponent? Of course they did!

Former FBI lawyers admitted to Durham investigators to lying to the FISA courts on many occasions! Who went to jail for that? Nobody!

The Durham report contains many other concerning details, including the fact that the FBI made payments to the primary source for the dossier, Oleg Deripaska, for three and a half years, from March 2017 to October 2020. At the time FBI officials knew that Deripaska was still an intelligence operative for the Kremlin. The FBI knew Deripaska very well as it had investigated him for nearly 10 years related to his attempts to acquire classified information from government employees.

The Durham report provides details of many false statements made by the FBI on forms, reports, and in interviews. Those false statements were related to the FBI relationship with Deripaska, his relationship with the Kremlin, and a long list of other questionable details of the Crossfire Hurricane investigation targeting Trump.

Former FBI lawyers admitted to Durham investigators to lying to the FISA courts on many occasions about the details and sources of the Steele dossier while seeking secret warrants against Trump associates. If you or I lie to a federal agent or court, we go to prison. The law is obviously not applied blindly or without preference.

On January 19, 2021, his final day in office, President Trump declassified hundreds of pages of documents related to Crossfire Hurricane. These documents could contain more revelations on corrupt behavior of government employees involved in the investigation. Over three years later, those documents have not yet been released. President Trump issued a direct and lawful order that these documents be released to the public. Biden's attorney general continues to refuse to follow the order issued by a sitting president and many Freedom of Information Act (FOIA) requests submitted by citizens.[6]

If the public had access to those documents, the outrage and legal fallout would be devastating to the CIA, FBI, and the ruling class. Those who would be punished for their crimes live in fear, knowing that Trump likely has copies of the documents and plans to use them to take legal action. The FBI raided Trump's Mar-a-Lago estate on August 8, 2022, searching for classified documents. This was about four months after Trump filed a lawsuit for damages against Hillary Clinton and many others. The suit was dismissed but the 108-page filing contained details that may have been pulled from the declassified documents that are still buried somewhere in the DOJ. Interesting timing of the raid. Were they looking for the documents or just trying to make a point?

At this time, it is not known if the Durham report will result in anyone in government being punished for their crimes. There have been repeated calls for indictments against FBI agents and other government employees for lying to the FBI, being a liar in the FBI, colluding with foreign agents to interfere with a US presidential election, lying to Congress, lying repeatedly to the FISA courts, surveilling a presidential candidate and their staff, leaking confidential documents to the press to embarrass a political opponent, or any of the other untold numbers of crimes committed by people in our government.

We can only hope that someone, many people, will finally be arrested and charged. Several months after the release of the Durham report there have been no charges filed and no arrests. None of the powerful heads or staff of the CIA and FBI have been held accountable for their obvious violations of the law and their oath of office. This is one example of why more and more people believe that those in control can use the resources of the government to openly punish their opposition. As for those who believe in the existence of the deep state, their numbers are growing at an accelerating rate.

For more information, see the report titled "FBI Whistleblower Testimony Highlights Government Abuse, Misallocation of Resources, and Retaliation" published by the Select Subcommittee on the Weaponization of the Federal Government. In the words of one whistleblower within the FBI, the current state of the FBI is "cancerous," as the Bureau has "let itself become enveloped in this politicization and weaponization."[7]

Sadly, the depth and breadth of the crimes and corruption are not widely known by the public. Those in power agree that it was not in their interests for the public to be aware that corrupt self-serving individuals operate with impunity within the FBI and other agencies. The information is out there. However, you will not find it in the legacy media or using a popular search engine. If you want to find the truth, you will have to dig well past the normal default information sources.

Have you had enough of the weaponization of federal agencies? Unfortunately, it didn't end there.

The attacks did not stop after Trump won the election. At that point they transitioned their efforts from discrediting a candidate for president to attempting to destroy a sitting president. These attempts included continuing the false allegations of colluding with Russia to win the 2016 election, manufactured outrage over the firing of FBI director James Comey in May 2017, and more manufactured outrage over the resignation of Lieutenant General Michael Flynn.

In General Flynn's case, he made a mistake that tarnished his reputation and ended his career. In February of 2017 it came to light that General Flynn lied to the White House about his meetings with a Russian ambassador to the United States. No political intrigue. He was just conducting business as usual for politics, not realizing everyone associated with Trump would be scrutinized mercilessly for inconsequential actions while insiders committed serious self-serving crimes with impunity.

Trump was also impeached by the House and acquitted by the Senate in December 2019 on allegations that he pressured Ukraine to provide evidence of Biden's corruption. The House charged that Trump was effectively trying to influence the 2020 presidential election by digging up dirt on his opponent. The fact that there is recorded evidence of Biden admitting to corrupt dealings in Ukraine seems less important than Trump's so-called crime of trying to hold Biden accountable for his corruption.[8]

Trump was under attack 24/7 from all sides. He, and everyone else in the world, could not open their eyes in the morning without witnessing another attack from disingenuous, hypocritical, and dishonorable people. Is he a flawed man who has made many mistakes throughout his life and often responds to critics in a petulant manner? Absolutely! Was he the worst president in the history of our nation? Obviously not. Most would admit that anyone could have been worn down by the constant flimsy attacks from people of far less moral character and personal substance, who were none the less promoted as the epitome of virtue by legacy media and Big Tech.

The extensive criminal collusion between the Hillary Clinton campaign, people within government agencies, and foreign actors could fill many books. Attorney and author Hans Mahncke recently released the book *Swiftboating America*, which covers many of these activities through the eyes of private citizens turned internet sleuths who helped peel back the layers of crimes and cover-ups. Hans Mahncke can be found on Twitter, where he regularly offers insight and perspective into the wealthy ruling class and the government agencies they control.

What about the Stormy Daniels scandal? Doesn't that prove Trump is not a man of good moral character? Most of us believe that, in 2006, while married to his third wife, Trump did demonstrate poor judgment and bad character when he had consensual sex with Stormy Daniels, an adult film actor.

I suppose there might be a few among us who think that was an inconsequential decision and action. Most of us probably recognize it as behavior inconsistent with efforts to build a functional and productive marriage and life. But that's not what got him into trouble.

In October 2016, days before the election, Trump's attorney Michael Cohen wired $130,000 to Daniels's attorney after Daniels signed an agreement to keep her relationship with Trump private. No crime there. Happens every day. Allegations of falsifying business documents to cover up the hush-money payments were investigated. The question was whether or not the payment could be considered an unreported campaign contribution.

The DOJ and the Federal Election Commission (FEC) both investigated. In the end Michael Cohen pleaded guilty to a number of crimes but federal prosecutors did not charge Trump. He wasn't charged but he was relentlessly pilloried in the legacy media.

In March 2023, after Trump indicated he would run for president again in 2024, Manhattan District Attorney Alvin Bragg in a bizarre turn of events indicted Trump on unspecified sealed charges related to the hush money. In the words of legal scholar Alan Dershowitz, who taught at Harvard Law for 50 years, "In 60 years of practice, this is the worst case of prosecutorial abuse I have ever seen."

The indictment was sealed but legal experts agreed any charges remotely possible were misdemeanor and fall outside of the statute of limitations. Does that sound like a worthwhile use of enormous amounts of taxpayer funded time and resources? I guess so, if your objective is to punish people who pose a threat to your corrupt empire! Well-played lawfare!

After the indictment was unsealed, there was immediate disappointment within the wealthy ruling class as they realized that the case had no merit. Bragg likely initially sealed the indictment to allow time for buzz and anticipation to fuel narrative momentum before reality caused legal experts to shrug and walk away.[9]

Former US House speaker Nancy Pelosi responded to these new charges with "No one is above the law, and everyone has the right to a trial to prove innocence." So, he has to prove his innocence? She appears to be operating under a different set of laws than the rest of us. I guess we have all suspected that for a long time.

Congress has been doling out hush money to accusers anonymously for decades. Ironic?

In a related twist of hypocrisy, a deceptively named 1995 law called the Congressional Accountability Act allowed taxpayer funds to be used for paying settlements when members of Congress were accused of sexual misconduct. Since then, $17 million of taxpayer money has been paid out in 264 individual cases, according to GovTrack.us. In December 2018, the Congressional Accountability Act (CAA) Reform Act was signed into law, which states members of Congress must reimburse the treasury for settlements in some cases.

If we had access to enough facts to realize the extent of the hypocrisy overflowing from modern political theater, it would likely trigger more outrage than mere mortals could withstand.

Was Trump a good president? I believe that Donald Trump entered the race based on ego but through the campaign process saw more clearly the insidious depth of the evil we face from within as a nation. From there I believe he began to recognize that he had an opportunity to try to return power to the people, to stop the ambitions of the ultra-wealthy ruling class. I believe that became his mission and he did everything he could to execute that mission in the face of unimaginable opposition. People across all demographics believe they know his heart and are willing to be incredibly loyal to him regardless of his faults. They see his faults but believe his heart, passion, and mission far outweigh them.

The *Epoch Times* magazine summarized the impact of Trump, saying:[10]

> *The Trump MAGA legacy is now largely institutionalized. All Republican candidates will run on secure borders, energy independence, deregulation, Jacksonian foreign policy, a populist middle-class, nationalism, and deterrence against China—albeit with much-needed new emphasis on destructive deficit spending.*

Remember, the enemy of my enemy is my friend! He alone has the resources needed to expose the wealthy ruling class, if he will.

27

THE JANUARY 6 "INSURRECTION"

> *Who controls the past controls the future. Who controls the present controls the past.*
>
> GEORGE ORWELL, *1984*

We have all lived through the media presentation of the approved storyline of the January 6 "insurrection" for three years now. In this chapter and the next we go through a case study focusing on the facts on the ground before, during, and after the events of January 6. For people whose perceptions are based on the reporting by legacy media, they will likely find that reality is something very different.

Context and backstory are vital to understanding what led up to and what happened during the January 6, 2021, protest turned riot at the Capitol building in Washington DC. Liberals, Democrats, legacy media, and others refer to it as a violent insurrection intended to overthrow the government.

Was it really an insurrection? Did thousands of people converge on Washington DC to overthrow the US government? No, of course not. Did a very small number of people have plans to use violence to prevent Congress from certifying the Electoral College vote of Joe Biden as president of the United States. Yes, nine people to be exact!

However, the following lies have been repeated relentlessly by so many that few can find the facts beyond the lies:

President Joe Biden May 28, 2021: *"killed two police officers"*

President Joe Biden March 2, 2021: *"five cops killed"*

White House Press Secretary Karine Jean-Pierre: *"the worst attack on our democracy since the Civil War"*

Vice President Kamala Harris: *"Certain dates echo throughout history…December 7, 1941. September 11, 2001. And January 6, 2021."*

Senate Majority Leader Chuck Schumer: *"violent insurrection"*

Former FBI agent Peter Strzok: *"9/11 is nothing compared to January 6"*

January 6 Committee Chairman Bennie Thompson: *"seven people lost their lives"*

While those on the left refer to it as a violent revolutionary insurrection, they celebrated the leftist groups that stormed the Capitol building and many state capitol buildings before the January 6 incident and after.

In February 2011 about 12,000 protesters occupied the Wisconsin State Capitol building for multiple days, causing approximately $7 million in damage. They were attempting to disrupt passage of a Republican initiative to rein in government labor unions. Protesters were cheered on at the time by many national level politicians including Nancy Pelosi.

In July 2013, hundreds of pro-abortion protesters entered the Texas State Capitol and attempted to block the legislative process by screaming loudly to prevent discussion and voting.

In October 2014, climate activists forced their way into the Interior Department, vandalized the building, and sent police officers to the hospital.

In October 2018, thousands of liberal protesters, encouraged by incendiary rhetoric from Massachusetts Democratic senator Elizabeth Warren and a collection of well-known liberal celebrities, entered the US Capitol building to protest Brett Kavanaugh's nomination to the Supreme Court. Over 300 were arrested and charged with unlawfully demonstrating in Senate office buildings, but none were charged with insurrection or kept in solitary confinement for months while awaiting trial.

In June 2020 the Secret Service arrested protesters who had illegally entered the White House grounds. The president and his family were moved to a secure bunker during the breach.

In July 2020, Antifa attacked the Portland Federal Courthouse. Occupants were threatened, windows were broken, fires were set, and police were assaulted. Most of the charges were dropped. Those convicted received little or no jail time.

In October 2021, dozens of climate activists entered the Interior Department to try to prevent approval of projects that they opposed.

October 18, 2023 hundreds of pro-Palestinian protesters, egged on by Congresswoman Rashida Tlaib (D-MI), rampaged through and vandalized the congressional office building Cannon House and refused to leave. They were physically removed. Approximately 300 were arrested for unlawful demonstration. A small number were charged with assaulting police officers.

Bad behavior never justifies more bad behavior. The point is that, if the incursions listed above are not felonious, if they are not passionately reported by the media as vicious attacks on democracy, if they are actually celebrated by the media, celebrities, and liberal politicians, we should question their cries of insurrection regarding the events of January 6, 2021.

As we work through the details it will become clear that laws are being selectively applied based on political views. You will see clear patterns of lawfare perpetrated by the ruling class to punish the opposition and remind the rest of us that we have much to lose.

It is important to remember the events leading up to January 6. At the time, the results and integrity of the November 2020 presidential election were being hotly debated and contested as we moved toward the inauguration of president-elect Joe Biden. Hundreds of cases of election irregularities were reported the day of and in the days following the November 3 vote. President

Trump and many of his high-profile supporters were very vocal about the fact that they believed that Trump had won the election honestly but the scales were tipped toward Joe Biden through a variety of election fraud tactics.

The Stop the Steal movement and Ali Alexander, the lead organizer of the movement, are key to this story. After the November 3 election, Ali Alexander organized Stop the Steal rallies in every state to raise awareness of possible fraud in the election. On November 14, hundreds of thousands of people attended a Stop the Steal rally in Washington DC. The general public had no idea how strong the movement was, or that it even existed, because legacy media provided very little coverage of the events and the movement. Facebook, Twitter, and other Big Tech companies removed accounts and posts related to the movement. Sadly, that is not a surprise to anyone by now.

The Stop the Steal mission was to pressure elected officials and government agencies to investigate the integrity of the election. They believed that an investigation would reveal to the public that the election had been impacted by significant intentional irregularities and fraud. Their hope was that officials and the public would stand with those who believe election fraud enabled Joe Biden to win.

In the end, 127 Republicans in congress objected to certifying election results in Arizona and 145 Republicans objected to certifying election results in Pennsylvania. I think most would agree that the Stop the Steal movement and others like it at the time did sway some lawmakers to not simply go along to get along but to stand strong on the belief that our elections must be conducted in a manner that protects the integrity of the results and enables voters to be confident in the process and the outcomes.

What evidence is there of fraud in the election? Should their claims be taken seriously? Election integrity should always be taken seriously. There are documentaries, investigative reports, and entire websites dedicated to election fraud allegations in the 2020 US presidential election. Do your own research but be aware that the most popular search engines will only show you one side of the story.

Liberals reveal their lack of objectivity by responding to every story on election fraud with the standard clichés: "debunked," "discredited," "no proof," "minor errors," "voter suppression," "threat to democracy," "civil rights violation," "most secure election in history," and so on. There's your winning bingo card!

If you want the facts, you will have to abandon the legacy media and popular search engines. The truth is out there if you are willing to face it and know where to look. See the list of reliable sources at the end of this book. The *Epoch Times* article "Voter Fraud Convictions Challenge Narrative of Secure Elections" is a good place to start.[1]

> People want to believe that there is no significant level of election fraud because it is comforting.

The greatest opportunity for fraud exists in absentee voting submitted through contractors, collection boxes, and the mail. In-person voting greatly reduces the chance of fraud. If you want to ensure elections results accurately reflect the will of the people, eliminate absentee voting except for reasonable hardship cases. Voting by mail across all states now accounts for nearly 50% of all votes. Again, the greatest opportunity for fraud.

In Europe, most countries have banned mail-in voting. To reduce the opportunity for fraud, those that do allow voting by mail have strict controls in place including limiting it to very few clearly defined circumstances. All of those countries require that the voter present a photo ID to vote in person. Of those that allow vote by mail, most require the voter to pick up a ballot in person and present a photo ID. In fact, most countries in the world require a photo ID to vote.

Why have countries in Europe implemented voting regulations that liberals in the US claim are essentially voter suppression tactics? These countries were forced to implement more effective voting controls after seeing widespread election fraud in their countries and in others.[2]

In contrast to Europe's strict controls, in the United States, 10 liberal-leaning states mail ballots to every voter in the state. Every voter in the state! That's millions of ballots that can be filled out and returned by anyone. In 2020, the election commissions in many states relaxed their verification processes and deadlines for absentee ballots, in violation of state election law, seemingly to reduce the burden of processing millions of ballots.

Georgia, Pennsylvania, Michigan, and Wisconsin committed the most well-publicized violations of their own election laws. Laws that have been thoroughly debated and negotiated by legislative bodies are intended to represent the will of the people. Election commissions cannot just ignore those laws and make up rules that are more convenient to their agenda.

Does the dramatic difference in results between absentee voting and in-person voting indicate fraud?

How is this seemingly unfettered absentee voting system working out in the United States? The ABC News website FiveThirtyEight.com analyzes the massive increase in absentee voting in their post, "What Absentee Voting Looked Like In All 50 States."[3] One startling revelation from the 2020 election is that Biden won in the absentee vote count in 14 of 15 states by a very wide margin. In those same states Trump won in election day voting in 14 of 15 states by a much larger margin. The analysts had access to data from only 15 states. Based on those results, yes, we should all be very concerned about the greater risk of fraud with absentee ballots.

In 2020 there was an underlying driver for the massive increase in absentee voting and the fact that Biden campaigned almost entirely from the emotional comfort of his basement. That driver was COVID lockdowns. Will we see a repeat of lockdowns leading up to the presidential election of 2024? We are already seeing hints of it. Biden's rapid mental decline is obvious to even his most glassy-eyed supporters. He cannot possibly survive politically in an actual face-to-face debate. Another round of COVID lockdowns for 2024 could work out well for him!

Do voters believe the election was secure and accurate?

According to a March 2022 Rasmussen survey, 52% of voters believe that "cheating affected the outcome of the 2020 US presidential election."[4] By party affiliation the numbers are 75% of Republicans, 34% of Democrats, and 48% of independents.

That is a huge percentage of people, 52%, who believe fraud determined the outcome of the election! Even 34% of Democrats! In the United States of America! Will the 34% of Democrats who believe the election was stolen still vote for the election thieves? Anything could happen in 2024!

In June 2023, John McCormack published an article in the *National Review*, "Sorry, Trump Lost," which provides a well-reasoned response to Trump's claims of widespread election fraud. He also addresses Dinesh D'Souza's election fraud documentary *2000 Mules*.[5] John McCormack follows the data, does the math, and in the end, believes that it is unlikely that election fraud was responsible for swinging enough votes to Biden to give him the win.

Others do not agree with John McCormack's assessment and there is evidence supporting their position. It is deceptive to claim that vote recounts prove there was no significant fraud. The point is that the votes were submitted fraudulently. Once they are accepted and placed on the stack, you can count them a thousand times and get roughly the same result every time. Claims that Dinesh D'Souza's *2000 Mules* documentary has been disproven are greatly exaggerated.

In the 2020 election the margins were extremely close in some states. Based on reporting by Domenico Montanaro of National Public Radio (NPR), "just 44,000 votes in Georgia, Arizona and Wisconsin separated Biden and Trump from a tie in the Electoral College."[6] According to research released in May 2022 by John Lott Jr. of Real Clear Politics, Biden received between 255,000 and 368,000 fraudulent excess votes across six states: Arizona, Georgia, Michigan, Nevada, Pennsylvania, and Wisconsin, where Biden won by a margin of 313,253 votes.[7]

That's really not a lot of "excess votes" across six states but is enough to cover the spread between winning and losing.

Those claiming that there is no significant level of election fraud are completely ignoring the long list of recent arrests and convictions. If they were interested in having the information, they could go to one of many websites, such as the *Western Journal* or *Epoch Times*, and search for the "election fraud" tag. They would find hundreds of articles detailing those arrests and convictions. The list grows weekly.

Clearly election laws and processes must be updated after this fiasco to ensure that we can be confident each legitimate vote is counted, and the results are indisputable.

Even with the evidence noted above, if the election was stolen, it was effectively stolen long before the first vote was cast. When the resources of the government, Big Tech, and the media are enthusiastically focused on protecting one candidate and destroying the other, the results are locked in long before voting even begins. That's not a fight the losing candidate can win after the fact.

There is a reason the phrase "hindsight is 20/20" is used so frequently. Who doesn't wish for a do-over at some point in their lives? Without the benefit of hindsight, on January 6, 2021, the Stop the Steal movement culminated in a massive rally at a park in Washington DC known as the Ellipse. The organization had held hundreds of rallies across the nation since the election without incident and had every expectation that this one would be no different.

Another organization, March for Trump, planned a rally at the same location and date. Early projections by organizers indicated that up to 1.5 million people would attend. Trump announced just days before the rally that he would attend and be one of the speakers. Several speakers were planned, and the rally was to start at 9:00 a.m. At 1:00 p.m. attendees would walk to the Capitol building to protest the certification of the election.

As the event unfolded that day, there were delays that threw off the timing of speakers at the rally and they spoke well past the planned 1:00 p.m. walk to the Capitol building. At about 2:00 p.m. approximately 10,000 rally attendees began walking toward the Capitol building. Reports are that the other protesters had started gathering at the Capitol much earlier. In fact, protests at the Capitol are very common. There were 26 separate protests registered for that day: 17 were explicitly pro-Trump, three were anti-Trump, and the rest were either religious or interest-group gatherings appearing to lean conservative.

At about 11:00 a.m., well before the end of the rally, the Capitol was approached by two to three hundred people led by the Proud Boys organization, which is known for civil disobedience and sometimes violence.

A summary of the initial timeline of events as recounted by a senate report,[8] the *Wall Street Journal*,[9] and later released recordings of police radio communications [10] provide the following insights:

11:57 a.m. President Trump began his remarks.

12:19 p.m. The first fence breach was reported.

12:57 p.m. It was reported that protesters pushed through one of the bike rack barricades and rushed toward the building.

1:06 p.m. Deputy Chief Waldow ordered the use of force on the crowd.

1:07 p.m. Joshua Black, a protester standing peacefully near the police line, was shot in the face with a crowd-control projectile.

1:10 p.m. Protesters in the area where Joshua Black had been injured became agitated and began pushing against the police line.

1:11 p.m. President Trump concluded his remarks.

2:08 p.m. Protesters were reportedly on the east and west steps and started trying to enter the building.

2:14 p.m. The Capitol building was entered by the first protesters through broken windows.

The timeline indicates that the protests at the Capitol started well before President Trump started speaking at the park and were quickly escalating well before he concluded his remarks. The claim that Trump got on stage, whipped the crowd into a frenzy, and then unleashed them on the Capitol is just not credible. Search for and view the video recording of his comments to get more accurate insight into the nature of his remarks that day. He called for a peaceful protest.

Clearly protesters should not have physically engaged with law enforcement and should not have forced their way through locked doors and windows to enter the Capitol building. The moment they crossed those lines, they became a threat to lawmakers, their staff, and security personnel in the building and were subject to the potential consequences of being seen as a threat.

After entering the building, nearly all protesters wandered around somewhat aimlessly and were essentially sightseers. Some chanted or vocalized their frustrations. A very small number of them had plans to commit acts of vandalism on property. A much smaller number were unhinged to the point that they may have committed acts of violence against other people. Both of those groups were chastised by the more levelheaded protesters and were told to knock it off.

In the end, the Capitol building suffered about $1.5 million in damage and approximately 140 police officers were assaulted.

Four people died during or as a direct result of the riot, and they were all protesters. Ashli Babbitt was shot and killed by a police officer, two protesters died from heart attack or stroke, and one other protester was initially reported to have died of an overdose of her prescription ADD medication. However, it was later revealed that the reported drug overdose victim, Rosanne Boyland, died as a result of losing consciousness, being trampled, and then being struck by police with a baton multiple times. The initial trigger of her medical distress was a large amount of pepper spray she inhaled when it was released in the very close quarters of a tunnel entrance. Video of the events leading up to the death of Rosanne Boyland is available on many websites.

Capitol Police Officer Brian Sicknick died on January 7, 2021, the next day, after suffering two strokes. The *New York Times* incorrectly reported on January 8, 2021, that officer Sicknick had died from a head injury after being beaten over the head with a fire extinguisher by protesters during the January 6 riot. They later updated the story after it had been confirmed that officer Sicknick had returned to police headquarters without a head injury and was texting with family after the riot. By then, news outlets throughout the world had followed the lead of the *New York Times* and had made the murder of officer Sicknick by rioters their top headline.

Many people still believe and continue to repeat the lie that officer Sicknick was murdered by rioters at the Capitol on January 6. Do they really still believe the lie or are they simply using it to promote their narrative? The *New York Times* headline still incorrectly reads to this day "Capitol Police Officer Dies from Injuries in pro-Trump Rampage" even after the text of the article was corrected. Even President Biden recently incorrectly stated in a speech that two officers were killed by rioters.

How did this protest escalate into a riot?

Did a relatively small number of very aggressive agitators successfully trigger the chaos that ensued? Couple these agitators with the mistakes of a handful of officers on the scene and you have a full-blown riot on your hands. The term *full-blown* is probably exaggerating the reality quite a bit. In fact, the small number of agitators were gaining little traction in their attempts to create a frenzy. A few of the officers on the scene helped them out by terribly mishandling the situation and further inciting the crowd instead of calmly trying to de-escalate and disperse the crowd.

Video indicates that some of the officers were clearly not adequately supervised and not sufficiently trained for their jobs. A small number of officers are seen in the video quickly reacting to protesters in anger, further escalating the tensions. They used unnecessary physical force on people who were obviously not a threat and, in some cases, were already moving away from the officers. Prior to the unnecessary show of force by officers, individuals in the crowd were making progress in stopping the agitators and de-escalating the situation.

To be clear, most of the officers on the scene attempted to remain calm and de-escalate from the beginning. A few officers clearly had other ideas. Unfortunately, once the situation started getting out of control, it quickly became difficult to distinguish the agitators from those encouraging calm on both sides.

Recently released videos show a few officers throwing exploding munitions into tight crowds of people who were simply standing there or moving slowly around, posing no threat. Some of these exploding canisters disperse tear gas. Others spray people nearby with rubber pellets. Using these munitions in tight crowds is a violation of law enforcement policy. They are intended to be used on the edges of crowds to encourage the crowd to disperse. In this case, there was significant risk of panicked trampling by the crowd because they were blocked in and had nowhere to go.

It is extremely dangerous to throw exploding munitions into a dense crowd where the explosion, flash of fire, and pellets will undoubtedly be very close to individuals who could be badly injured. The videos show protesters with fire in their hair and clothing being helped by other protesters, who can be seen patting out and pouring water on the fire.

Did a few intentionally antagonize protesters?

It is clear in the videos, and accompanying audio, that some officers used these tactics to punish people, not to disperse or arrest them. Metropolitan Police Department officer Daniel Thau's body cam video shows him repeatedly punishing nonthreatening protesters by tasing at least four of them, throwing several exploding munitions into the crowd, and blasting people with pepper spray who were standing together and making no threatening statements or gestures.

All of this took place outside of and away from the Capitol entrance. His own body cam shows him gathering up exploding munitions from other officers after he exhausted his own supply. The video shows that each time another officer handed him one, he immediately pulled the pin and threw the exploding canister into the crowd. At one point, Thau was able to grab a projectile launcher, which he immediately used to launch a variety of canister types into the crowd. A few other officers engaged in the same punishment tactics and many protesters were seriously injured as a result. These attacks triggered a very angry response from the crowd.

Mark Griffin of Canadensis, Pennsylvania, was struck in the knee by a canister that split his femur. His crime? Standing at the police line talking to officers about why he and others had come to Washington DC to be heard. His multiple surgeries have cost him over $250,000 so far.

Other officers who were perched high above the protesters fired pepper balls and rubber bullets into the crowd. These tactics are intended to convince a threatening actor to flee the situation. The protesters shown on the video were not a threat and they were trapped there with nowhere to run. In the words of Stan Kephart, crowd control expert, "it was a shooting gallery."

One of the videos released recently shows protester Derrick Vargo fall more than 20 feet after being pushed off a wall by an officer, even though he was not a threat. He was seriously injured in the fall and had to be removed on a stretcher by paramedics. The law states that the officer's responsibility is to capture, arrest, and detain the protester, not push him off the wall to certain serious injury.[11]

Another protester, Victoria White, received at least 10 baton blows to the head and was struck in the face five times with a closed fist by an officer while she was trapped in a densely packed crowd and completely immobilized in the very tight space. She survived but was seriously injured.

Did the police attempt to deconflict the situation on the ground?

As if the situation was not volatile enough already that day, federal prosecutors recently admitted that three DC Metropolitan Police Department undercover officers actively incited the mob and engaged in provocateur behavior at the northwest steps of the Capitol building. This information came to light in March 2023, over two years after the riot, during the trail of William Pope of Topeka, Kansas. Part of the video evidence was posted on Rumble on March 24, 2023. Officers can be heard encouraging protesters to go join the mob on the steps. One of the undercover police officers can be heard multiple times chanting with the mob, "Our house! Our house! Our house!" "Drain the swamp!" "USA! USA! USA! USA!" "C'mon, go, go, go!" and "Keep going! Keep going! Keep going!"[12]

In April 2023, again over two years after the riot, during the trial of Proud Boys defendant Dominic Pezzola, it was revealed that over 50 undercover agents and informants were embedded in the crowd close to and monitoring Proud Boys group members.[13] I think *we the people* deserve to have far more detail on the actions of those 50 plus individuals as they participated in this so-called insurrection. Did they try to de-escalate? Did they encourage criminal activity?

About 80 unnamed and not arrested agitators, referred to as suspicious actors, are seen in video at the most contentious locations, encouraging people to commit various crimes. Many believe that these essential agitators were planted in the crowds to make sure they reached a frenzied state and crossed the line into criminal acts.

The most famous suspicious actor is Ray Epps, who is seen on video loudly encouraging people to enter the building. Some in the crowd chanted back at him, "No! No! No! Fed! Fed! Fed!" On September 18, 2023, Ray Epps was finally charged with a minor misdemeanor and was later sentenced to probation. The charge and sentence are wildly out of line with other defendants who did far less and were given much longer prison sentences. Now the media has started presenting him not as an insurrectionist or possibly a planted agitator, but as the victim of a campaign to smear an innocent man. Prosecutors believe that he has suffered great personal harm to his reputation by being labeled a government plant and has been punished enough. I wonder how that narrative started and how it came to dominate the story. It'll come to you!

> Fifty undercover agents and 80 unnamed agitators? Did they attempt to escalate the situation?

The investigation into these suspicious actors is a quickly evolving situation due to the recent release of 41,000 hours of previously unseen video. You can keep up with the latest information by following a few people who are actively engaged in the investigation of these suspicious actors. Defense attorney Brad Geyer spent months investigating more than 100 of these suspicious actors.

Attorney Michael Hamilton was at the Capitol that day and saw firsthand three large vans of agitators arriving on the scene with a police escort. They were dressed as Trump supporters but were clearly not who they pretended to be. They were angry and were very active in trying to whip the crowd into a frenzy. Hamilton left the area when he saw the energy shifting in a dangerous direction.

Hamilton states that it was later determined that the three vans the group arrived in belong to Antifa. Joseph Hanneman, investigative reporter, is also following this very closely. You will not likely find this information using popular search engines but, if you are resourceful, you should be able to locate testimony, reports, and posts from those mentioned.

Regardless of how you feel about the events of January 6, those involved should be able to expect the government to honor their civil rights and basic human rights. We should all expect the same for any person suspected of a crime. We should also expect law enforcement to use reasonable force and a proportional response based on the nature of the alleged crime and any threat. Those basic principles were completely discarded in the aftermath of January 6.

If you are seen as a vocal and passionate opponent to someone with unlimited power, someone not accountable to anyone, how do you think that is going to work out for you? If you weren't sure before January 6, it is probably pretty clear to you now. Would you like to get up close and personal with a SWAT team in takedown mode?

Future generations are begging us to hold accountable the people in control of our government!

28

JANUARY 6 SCORCHED EARTH AFTERMATH

> *They justify absolute authority as necessary to protect their compliant servants from the trauma of self-determination.*

The largest investigation in FBI history, larger than the 9/11 investigation, hundreds of SWAT-style takedown arrests, revelations that proactive requests for adequate security were rejected, video of security personnel attempting to incite a peaceful crowd, and many other appalling details have been brought to light in the aftermath of January 6.

How many were arrested and what were the charges? Seems like something we should know considering the massive scale of the FBI investigation and the intense media coverage of this so-called violent attempt to overthrow the government. How many traitorous violent revolutionaries were sent to prison for life for their evil murderous plot? Our prisons must be packed beyond capacity with tens of thousands of these domestic terrorists who attempted to violently seize control of our nation, right?

No, far from it.

About 16 were charged with seditious conspiracy. Nine of them were convicted or pleaded guilty. The rest were charged with much less serious offenses, such as entering or remaining in a restricted federal building or grounds.

So far, over 1,200 arrests have been made on over 900 felony charges and 2,000 misdemeanor charges.[1] About 850 people have pleaded guilty or been found guilty on about 505 misdemeanor charges and 345 on felony charges. Most were charged with interfering with police, obstruction of an official proceeding, or trespassing. About 185 individuals were charged with using a deadly or dangerous weapon or causing serious bodily injury to an officer. Approximately 10 individuals were arrested on charges that relate to assaulting a member of the media or damaging their equipment.

Again, of the over 1,200 charged, nine were convicted of anything related to insurrection. If the riot at the Capitol building were an insurrection, wouldn't hundreds or thousands of participants have been charged with sedition or seditious conspiracy?

Over 330 of the defendants have been charged under a white-collar crime law known as the Sarbanes-Oxley Act of 2002. Sarbanes-Oxley was enacted to prosecute publicly traded companies and their executives for fraud. Federal prosecutors have taken the position that protesters violated that act when they attempted to delay certification of the Electoral College vote. Many of those convictions are being appealed. The Supreme Court has agreed to hear the first case and that outcome will lead to either affirming those convictions or reversing them. Many are anticipating the cases will be reversed.

It is interesting that people charged with white-collar fraud crimes were arrested in early morning SWAT-style raids involving dozens of guns-out officers. The DOJ needs to decide if these people are highly armed and dangerous revolutionaries or just common fraudsters.

Again, of the estimated 250,000 people present that day, only nine were convicted of anything related to insurrection.

The videos, testimony, recordings of radio transmissions, and other details that have surfaced recently provide new evidence needed to appeal many of the convictions. Many of the appeals are based on claims that prosecutors and the DOJ withheld evidence that would have proven the defendant's innocence. A significant number of convictions are likely to be reversed. However, damage has already been done to their families, careers, and futures by arrests, convictions, press coverage, and incarceration both pretrial and post-trial.

In the end, most of those arrested on sedition-related charges were the usual fringe suspects who have earned their tarnished reputations through their own words and actions over many years. Most were associated with either the Proud Boys or the Oath Keepers organizations. About 100 of the protesters present that day were known to be associated with the Proud Boys. Key members can be seen in video of the event vocally encouraging the mob to push past officers and enter the building.

About 30 people associated with the Oath Keepers and about 25 associated with the Proud Boys have been charged with crimes for their participation in the riot. Most are charged with conspiracy to obstruct an official proceeding and assaulting, resisting, or impeding a law enforcement officer, but nothing related to sedition or insurrection.

Five Proud Boys leaders were charged and four were convicted or pleaded guilty to charges of seditious conspiracy. They received sentences ranging from 15 to 22 years in prison. The four were Enrique Tarrio, Ethan Nordean, Joe Biggs, and Zachary Rehl. The fifth, Dominic Pezzola, was acquitted of seditious conspiracy but was convicted of other crimes and received a 10-year sentence.

Eleven associated with the Oath Keepers were charged with seditious conspiracy. Five were convicted or pleaded guilty to seditious conspiracy. They are Elmer Stewart Rhodes III, Edward Vallejo, Joshua James, Brian Ulrich, and William Todd Wilson. The others were acquitted of seditious conspiracy but were convicted of other crimes. Some are still awaiting sentencing.

In some cases minimum sentencing requirements were prompted based on the judge's determination that their actions constituted an official act of terrorism. Note that January 6 defendants are being tried before Washington DC juries. Joe Biden won 93% of Washington DC votes in 2020. It seems unlikely that an objective jury can be assembled in that environment for these defendants.

Again, based on convictions, nine people associated with these two groups had planned and coordinated seditious acts. The rest were just overzealous fools engaging in protest, with no intent to overthrow the government and no knowledge of a plan to do so. This is the formula used routinely by those determined to start a riot: gather as many useful idiots as possible to demonstrate for a noble cause and then do everything possible to escalate the situation into a full-blown riot. Only this time there was no looting, no arson, and little vandalism.

On January 13, 2021, one week after the riot, the House voted to impeach Trump for incitement of insurrection related to the January 6 riots. The vote was 232 for and 197 against, mostly along party lines with 10 Republicans voting with Democrats to impeach. Essentially that means that the "prosecutor," the US House of Representatives, decided to bring charges. It would then be up to the US Senate to then conduct the trial. One month later, on February 13, the Senate voted to acquit Trump of the charges. This is a great example of political theatrics that serve no purpose other than to punish opponents and warn potential future opponents of the danger they may face. All designed to protect the ruling class.

> It is an extremely high-risk venture to take on those who control law enforcement, the trial system, and the jury pool. Everyone now realizes that and will behave accordingly.

Protesters should not have entered the Capitol and should not have injured or threatened anyone. That should have been clear to everyone with any sense of morality, ethics, or patriotism.

However, in the months following, the heavy-handed response made up of SWAT-style arrests, no-bond solitary confinement, and extremely long prison sentences, is well beyond excessive when compared to other protests and even recent violent riots.

During the riots of 2020, BLM protesters looted and burned hundreds of businesses, causing $2 billion in damages. Many protesters were arrested but well over 90% of them were released with charges dropped. The few that were convicted received very light sentences, even those with long criminal records. A few received as little as probation or as much as seven years for burning down businesses. Montez Terriel was sentenced to just 10 years for setting fire to pawnshop and, in so doing, causing the death of a 30 year-old man inside the building. That is just 10 years for arson and murder!

In contrast, the Proud Boys members were given sentences ranging from 10 to 22 years for little more than trespassing and damaging a fence.

Again, if the riot at the Capitol Building had been an insurrection, wouldn't hundreds or thousands of participants have been charged with sedition or seditious conspiracy and wouldn't most of them have been convicted?

Since the media seems to like to diminish people by associating them with fringe groups, let's take a closer look at the actual facts around the two most publicized groups in this event.

The Oath Keepers organization was founded by Stewart Rhodes in 2009 with a mission to encourage members of law enforcement and the military to honor the commitment they had made to defend the Constitution against enemies foreign and domestic. Members agreed to resist orders that Rhodes saw as a violation of constitutional rights, including warrantless searches, disarming citizens, and using the enemy combatant designation to hold citizens without bail.

In the words of Stewart Rhodes, "We know that if a day should come in this country when a full-blown dictatorship would come or tyranny, from the left or from the right, we know that it can only happen if those men, our brothers in arms, go along and comply with unconstitutional, unlawful orders." Their original mission was to make people aware that tyranny can only thrive in this country if law enforcement and the military support and enable their unconstitutional objectives and tactics.

From there the group has veered into more dangerous activities in recent years. They took to inserting themselves and their weapons into volatile situations where they could only serve to further destabilize and increase the risk of violent confrontation. They were present at the Bundy Ranch standoff with federal agents in 2014. That same year they converged on Ferguson, Missouri, armed and ready to protect businesses from rioters. Those riots were triggered when a grand jury did not charge a police officer in the fatal shooting of 18-year-old Michael Brown. In 2015 they took up positions to prevent the government from taking control of a disputed Oregon gold mine.

Oath Keepers claims about 38,000 members. However, most of those "members" are subscribers to their information site. The number of active participants is estimated to be less than 5,000.

The Oath Keepers claim that on January 6, 2021, they were at the Capitol building to assist in security in case President

Trump invoked the Insurrection Act and that triggered Antifa to riot. There is video evidence of three instances where they did assist law enforcement in de-escalating tensions and helped to protect officers from protesters. Those cases do appear to support their claims, but other video evidence clearly indicates that they were not just innocent bystanders to the chaos either.

The Proud Boys organization was founded by Gavin McInnes, who was a well-known Canadian political commentator. The Proud Boys describe themselves as promoters of "Western chauvinism," believing that Western European culture is superior to all others. This, coupled with their rhetoric promoting the use of violence against those who oppose them, has helped earn them a "terrorist organization" designation from the Canadian government. They claim to be racially diverse and to only use violence when necessary to defend themselves.

Criminal convictions for violence, prison sentences, and statements against Jews, women, and other groups have made it impossible for the group to be taken seriously in any debate. The group attempts to portray itself as a fraternity of drinking buddies with good-natured and silly rituals. The initiation ceremony reportedly requires that the prospect take punches from members while yelling out the names of at least five breakfast cereals.

Today they may prefer to portray themselves as just another community men's group but let's step back and think about the nature of this organization.

When a group of men gather for the purposes of drinking heavily, boisterously exchanging ideas on self-defense, showing off their weapons, bragging about their brave adventures, and openly denigrating women and others not like them, anything can happen and most of the possibilities are not good. Most of those men are just looking for a place to hang out with other guys. A small number are likely deeply committed to the lifestyle and the rhetoric. A very small handful are undoubtedly likely to do something stupid that will thrill the deeply committed members and embarrass the rest.

For those just looking for a place to hang out, they should remember: if you hang out with five intellectuals, you will be the sixth. If you hang out with five idiots, you will be the sixth. At one time the group counted about 22,000 members worldwide.

After January 6, excessive-force SWAT-style arrests, complete with flash grenades, were made at the homes of those suspected of participating in the protest. Families were terrified and even children were handcuffed. Some defendants were, and are over two years later, being held in solitary confinement without bail in Washington DC's Correctional Treatment Facility while they wait to go to trial. More details can be found by following Joseph Hanneman, investigative reporter, and Stan Kephart, well-known security expert with over 40 years of experience.

From the earliest days of January 6 defendants being held in the District of Columbia jail, allegations of abuse have been made against the jail and its employees. Attorney Joseph D. McBride has been very vocal about the deplorable conditions and treatment the detainees have suffered for many months, or even years, while held without bail. McBride initially represented Richard Barnett of Arkansas but later represented many others associated with January 6. The allegations are too numerous and detailed to cover here but details are provided in the following reports from attorney Joseph D. McBride[2] and Congresswoman Marjorie Taylor Greene:[3]

> Attorney Joseph D. McBride: "Emergency Request to Investigate Mistreatment of Pre-Trial Detainees from the January 6, 2021 US Capitol Protest"

> Congresswoman Marjorie Taylor Greene: "Unusually Cruel: An Eyewitness Report from Inside the DC Jail"

On the three-year anniversary of the event, U.S. Attorney Matthew Graves stated in a press briefing that thousands of people who merely entered the grounds outside the Capitol without authorization could still be charged. The DOJ does not yet seem to be satisfied that adequate punishment has been administered to those foolish enough to openly oppose the wealthy ruling class.

On March 1, 2024, journalist Steve Baker was arrested on four misdemeanor charges related to his reporting at the U.S. Capitol on January 6, 2021. Baker was arrested, his wrists were chained around his waist, and his ankles were bound by leg chains before he was placed in a cage with dangerous criminals. Cases like this are normally handled as a misdemeanor order to appear before the court where the defendant would walk into the courtroom at the designated time with their attorney, acknowledge the charges, and agree to return for trial at a later date. Then they would walk out.

It seems that the federal government has decided to make a point by charging Baker in the first place and then piling on extraordinary levels of humiliation. Of more than 60 journalists who entered the Capitol that day, only a few have been charged and they are all considered right of center journalists.

No doubt, after seeing political protesters brutalized through the arrest process and months of inhumane treatment awaiting trial, many who are concerned about the intentions of those in control have decided to quietly go about their day to avoid being noticed. That seems to have been the intended purpose anyway.

———

The size of the crowd was in line with previous estimates. How could they be completely unprepared?

How could Capitol security be so utterly unprepared to manage a crowd that was anticipated weeks earlier? The Government Accountability Office (GAO) released a 122-page report in February 2023 that revealed the FBI and Capitol Police had identified "credible threats" before January 6, 2021.[4] It goes on to say that the threat information was not fully processed and was not shared with other security agencies. The report states that the FBI and other agencies did not follow procedure for such threats. It further states that the Capitol Police *did not share threat products with its frontline officers.*

If that information had been handled properly, the Capitol building would have been secured and agents on the ground would have been instructed not to open the gates and wave the protesters into the protected area around the building.

Former federal prosecutor Tim Heaphy was the January 6 committee's chief investigative counsel and confirmed what many in law enforcement and many casual observers suspected from the beginning. He revealed in multiple interviews that steps could have and should have been taken by the FBI and other agencies to prevent the mob from entering the Capitol. Those agencies should have acted proactively based on the significant direct intelligence they had collected before January 6. Heaphy specifically told NBC News, "That said, what happened at the Capitol was also affected by law enforcement failures to operationalize the ample intelligence that was present before January 6 about the threats of violence."[5] [6] The written report from the committee included a dramatically stripped and sanitized overview of these security failures in an appendix.

Peace through strength is the tried-and-true principle that should have been applied here. Adequate security would have convinced all but the most hopelessly irretrievable fools that proper etiquette for peaceful protest must be held in the highest regard. Those very few morons who could not control themselves would have been swiftly dealt with, saving 10,000 other people from being marked as terrorists attempting to overthrow the US government.

House Speaker Pelosi rejected multiple requests for National Guard assistance before January 6.

More facts highlighting inexplicable security failures were brought to light in December 2022 when House Republicans released a 144-page report in which they blame House Speaker Nancy Pelosi for failing to protect the Capitol. Supporting these claims are the public statements made by former Capitol police chief Steven Sund, who has repeatedly stated that that House Speaker Pelosi turned down requests for preemptive deployment of the National Guard six times before January 6. Key details from that report:[7]

> There are several reasons the Capitol was left unprepared on January 6, 2021, including internal politics and unnecessary bureaucracy. Prior to that day, the US Capitol Police (USCP) had obtained sufficient information from an array of channels to anticipate and prepare for the violence that occurred. However, officers on the front lines and analysts in USCP's intelligence division were undermined by the misplaced priorities of their leadership. Those problems were exacerbated by the House Sergeant at Arms, who was distracted from giving full attention to the threat environment prior to January 6, 2021 by several other upcoming events.
>
> Specifically, the leader of the USCP Intelligence and Interagency Coordination Division (IICD) failed to warn USCP leadership and line officers about the threat of violence, despite the fact that IICD analysts gathered intelligence that clearly indicated a need for a hardened security posture.

The report went on to state:

> Similarly, then-House Sergeant at Arms Paul Irving—who served on the Capitol Police Board by virtue of his position—succumbed to political pressures from the Office of Speaker Pelosi and House Democrat leadership leading up to January 6, 2021. He coordinated closely with the Speaker and her staff and left Republicans out of important discussions related to security. As a

> critical member of the Capitol Police Board, the House Sergeant at Arms had an obligation to all Members, staff, and USCP officers to keep them safe by consulting stakeholders without partisan preference.
>
> But rather than coordinate in a meaningful way, Irving only provided information to Republicans after receiving instruction from the Speaker's office. In one case, Irving even asked a senior Democratic staffer to "act surprised" when he sent key information about plans for the Joint Session on January 6, 2021 to him and his Republican counterpart. The senior Democratic staffer replied: "I'm startled!"

For a firsthand account of security failures see the interview of former Capitol police chief Steven Sund on Tucker Carlson's Twitter episode 15.[8]

Again, protesters should not have physically engaged with law enforcement and should not have forced their way through locked doors and windows to enter the Capitol building. The moment they did that, they became a threat and were subject to the potential consequences of being seen as a threat. These were the acts of desperate people who believed that their country had been stolen from them by incredibly powerful elites who are accountable to no one.

How do we prevent this from happening again? We hold our government accountable and remove any possibility that an election could be compromised in the future.

Election integrity is one of the most important issues of our time. If our elections are a sham, if the wealthy and powerful can control the outcome of elections through fraud, do any of our other concerns really matter? If we cannot hold them accountable at the ballot box, we have no power and they are free to operate with impunity. For that reason, we must all be involved in the issue of election integrity.

Violence will not bring us to a solution. Knowledge and peaceful activism will!

29

TRUMP INDICTMENTS—PUNISHING THE RESISTANCE

This case study is very complicated because it involves technical details of specific laws, their intentions, and their historical application. In addition, this case study is live right now. It is a living, breathing, and growing thing. In the future, after these cases have been resolved, after the facts have been made known, those facts can be analyzed and conclusions can be made. For now, things change as new information is released almost every day. The base of understanding we establish here will be helpful as we follow unfolding events.

On August 1, 2023, Department of Justice special counsel Jack Smith indicted former President Donald Trump on four federal counts related to the November 2020 presidential election.[1] Even though the media refers to this as "Trump's January 6 insurrection indictments," there were no charges related to insurrection in any form and no charges related to the events at the Capitol building on January 6, 2021. The four-count indictment issued by a grand jury alleges that President Trump conspired to defraud the United States, obstruct an official proceeding, and deprive persons of their right to have their vote counted. These charges stem from Trump's claims that election fraud enabled Biden to win.

It is important to understand that achieving a conviction requires that they prove that President Trump knew his claims of a stolen election were false. If they can prove that, the next challenge is proving that he did more than exercise his right to free speech.

The Constitution protects even knowingly false statements. Special counsel Jack Smith must prove that Trump knew the election had been fairly decided and that he then took meaningful coordinated unlawful actions to prevent the implementation of the will of the people. That is a very high bar. Many legal scholars doubt the burden of proof can be met. Whether he is convicted or not, the message will be received loud and clear by those foolish enough to consider standing up to the ruling class.

Legacy media has repeated nonstop that the election had been the most secure and accurate election in the history of the nation. This is a classic gratuitous assertion, an unprovable claim that forms the pseudo-factual basis for a more far-reaching unsubstantiated assertion. This "well-known fact" provides the backdrop for the narrative that any statement to the contrary must be false and any action must therefore be criminal. Upon that foundation this indictment is built.[2]

> Many still believe what they heard on the news, that this was the most secure and accurate election in our history.

Remember that 127 Republicans in Congress objected to certifying election results in Arizona and 145 Republicans objected to certifying election results in Pennsylvania.

Obviously not everyone agreed that it had been the most secure and accurate election in our history. A myriad of election irregularities was reported during and after election day. In some states the election officials simply ignored the election laws of their state and conducted the election as they saw fit. Absentee and mail-in ballot submission and verification laws were blatantly disregarded and violated.

In multiple states election law prohibits the use of unmanned ballot collection boxes. That didn't prevent some election commissions from deploying hundreds of unmanned ballot collection boxes throughout their states. Georgia, Pennsylvania, Michigan, and Wisconsin committed the most well-publicized violations of their own election laws.

It has been reported that officials in four states, Arizona, Georgia, Pennsylvania, and Wisconsin, sent letters to Pence requesting that their electors be returned to the state until allegations of election law violations could be resolved. Those letters were received from state officials but were not necessarily a legal request to pause the vote certification process. However, that along with dozens of pending lawsuits alleging election law violations should have been sufficient to force federal election officials to investigate more thoroughly before the vote certification on January 6.

There is no question that election irregularities were plentiful in some states. We will never know if those issues were substantial enough to change the outcome. Many Trump supporters are quite open about their belief that fraud did determine the result. A few people seem to believe that there was no fraud at all. Others either believe that the level of fraud was not substantial or believe that it is to their benefit to go along to get along with those in power. That go-along group includes a handful of low-level Republicans who have released statements that there is "absolutely no evidence of widespread fraud" in the 2020 election. With that in their pockets, legacy media and Big Tech have boastfully declared to the average casual observer that they can now file the entire episode in the "settled science" drawer of their minds.

As mentioned in a previous chapter, research released in May 2022 by John Lott Jr. of Real Clear Politics, indicates that Biden received between 255,000 and 368,000 fraudulent excess votes. Based on reporting by Domenico Montanaro of National Public Radio, "just 44,000 votes in Georgia, Arizona and Wisconsin separated Biden and Trump from a tie in the Electoral College." How widespread would fraud, or even just irregularities, need to be to impact the result?

Did Trump violate a law by asking Pence to send results back to a few states for audit before certifying the vote?

Vice President Mike Pence is a central figure in the case and will likely testify if the case goes to trial, which will be very interesting since he and Trump were both campaigning to be the next president. Pence has since dropped out of the race.

The indictment alleges that President Trump unlawfully asked Vice President Pence to overturn the election. However, the lawyers advising President Trump at that time believed that the

Constitution gave the Vice President authority to pause the process of certifying the Electoral College vote and send the election back to some states for audit. Attempting to send it back to the states falls far short of attempting to overturn the election.

The conflict between Trump's attorneys and Pence arises from a disagreement on whether or not the Constitution allows the vice president to send the election back to states for audit. Trump is being charged in that count because his attorneys disagreed with Pence on what is allowed by law. Trump was advised by his attorneys on lawful recourse available to him. He is being charged in criminal court, not civil court, for following the advice of his legal experts.

It is frightening to realize that, when there is a debate on whether something is constitutional or not, one side is right and the other side is criminal. Trump was following the advice of his attorneys. It is not clear who advised Pence on the matter.

The indictment includes six co-conspirators. Four are lawyers who were advising Trump at the time on possible legal strategies. One other was a Department of Justice official who was also advising Trump.

Did those highly educated and incredibly intelligent legal experts really advise the president to conspire to defraud the people of the United States? Maybe they thought Trump could pull it off since he was universally loved and had gotten a free pass with barely a notice no matter what he had done in the past? Oh, but he was not universally loved and had been viciously persecuted using all available means for his entire presidency. Trump's advisors must have had very strong convictions to continue the fight knowing that the blowback would be devastating if they failed. Not "could be" but "would be" devastating.

Were Trump's actions reprehensible to some? Obviously, they were reprehensible to many but were his actions criminal? He did a bad thing so it must be illegal, right? Maybe not.

Many legal experts are of the opinion that the federal criminal laws being applied to bring these charges are being stretched beyond their intent and meaning. In an interview with Jan Jekielek on the "American Thought Leaders" program, Horace Cooper, a senior fellow at the National Center for Public Policy Research, commented on the irony that a law designed to protect the vulnerable from voter intimidation is being used to prosecute someone for trying to protect the votes of vulnerable voters. Mr. Cooper makes a very good point, and it will be interesting to see how prosecutors contort that law while trying to apply it to the facts of this case.

Who was criminally charged after the hotly contested election results of the Bush-Gore vote in 2000? Who was criminally charged when Democrats challenged election results in 2004? Who was criminally charged when JFK sent alternate electors to challenge Nixon's election results in 1960? Who was criminally charged when Hillary Clinton claimed the Russians had perpetrated election fraud when she lost the 2016 presidential race to Donald Trump? Nobody.

The indictment states that Trump conspired with fake Electoral College electors to have their votes counted instead of the legitimate electors. Supporting that charge, legacy media has reported that Trump conspired to organize "fake electors" with the intention of submitting fraudulent Electoral College votes for Trump.

Most of the people reporting this story probably don't understand the law well enough to know that they are not reporting the truth. It is a complicated legal matter. However, their media bosses, the people telling them to cover the story in that way, do know or should know they are perpetuating disinformation.

The electors from each state must submit their votes before a specified deadline. If that date passes and they have not submitted their vote, they have missed their opportunity to have their vote counted. If a challenge to the popular vote count has not been resolved by that date, both sets of electors should submit their votes. In the end, only one set of votes will be counted after the challenge has been settled. If one set of electors fails to submit their vote, the challenge becomes moot.

There were seven states where a challenge was not resolved by the deadline: Arizona, Georgia, Michigan, Nevada, New Mexico, Pennsylvania, and Wisconsin. To preserve the legitimacy of the challenge to the popular vote in those states, the Republican electors had to submit their votes before the deadline passed.

Michigan attorney general Dana Nessel (D) has filed criminal charges against 16 Republican electors for their participation in the 2020 presidential election.

In Georgia, district attorney Fani Willis has criminally charged Republican electors for their participation in the 2020 presidential election.

The Arizona attorney general recently stated that they are in fact-gathering mode and no charges have been filed yet.

In Wisconsin no criminal charges are planned but a group of Democrats has filed a civil suit against the state's 10 Republican electors.

At this time, it appears that New Mexico, Nevada, and Pennsylvania will not pursue charges against their Republican electors.

Regardless of the outcome of these cases, the defendants will likely be bankrupted as they attempt to defend themselves from politically motivated malicious prosecution.

To make sure Republican electors from these states suffer as much as possible for standing up to the wealthy ruling class, *Newsweek* published the names of each one involved in all seven states. Outrageous! In case you are thinking that just could not be true, see the *Newsweek* article, "Full List of Trump Fake Electors in Each State and the Charges against Them" and note that all are listed, whether or not they are charged with a crime.

Breaking News! "Communications Show Trump Team Was Involved in Georgia Voting-System Breach"

Really? Oh my! This is it for Trump! Or so you might think until you actually read the article.[3] In early January 2021 Coffee County elections official Misty Hampton invited Trump's team to audit Coffee County voting machines, where Trump had won by a 70% margin. On January 7, 2021, inspectors from Trump's team were given access to the machines by county election officials. Were laws broken? If so, by whom?

In Georgia, Fulton County district attorney Fani Willis filed charges on August 14, 2023, naming Trump and 18 others. They are facing a 41-count indictment, including solicitation of violation of oath of office, perjury, production of false statements and writings, forgery in the first degree, impersonating a public officer, influencing witnesses, conspiracy to commit election fraud, conspiracy to defraud the state, and others. The charges in this long list are bundled up and delivered with a RICO bow on top.

RICO stands for Racketeer Influenced and Corrupt Organizations. The federal RICO law was enacted in 1970 to overcome the difficulty in convicting organized crime bosses who lead criminal enterprises but are far removed from the actual crimes being committed. RICO makes it illegal to be part of a criminal enterprise in any capacity, regardless of whether or not you actually commit a crime or even conspire to commit a crime. With the ability to charge everyone, it is far more likely that someone will be willing to tell everything they know to stay out of jail. Accountants probably don't fare well in prison. Georgia and other states have enacted similar RICO laws.

The story is just breaking and we will see how it plays out.

In a less sensational case, Trump was indicted in June 2023 on charges related to mishandling classified documents. Of the 38 charges, 31 are charges that he unlawfully retained 31 separate documents.

The other seven charges are for process crimes related to how Trump responded to a 2022 grand jury subpoena related to those documents. Those charges involve conspiracy to obstruct justice, making false statements, concealing information covered by that subpoena, and lying to the FBI. That subpoena was for all documents with "classification markings" not for all classified documents. Based on that very careful wording, even documents that had been declassified at the president's prerogative had to be turned over if they still carried the classified marking.

It is too early to tell how defensible these charges are for Trump. This could become a serious legal matter for him. However, it should be noted that Hillary Clinton was never charged after it was determined that she stored thousands of pages of classified documents on an unsecured private and illegal email server and then destroyed the evidence after it came to light. Also, Joe Biden was never charged after leaving the vice president's office with boxes of classified documents. Selective prosecution? Of course! No one threatens the wealthy ruling class and survives!

At this time, organizations in at least 15 states are attempting to prevent Trump from appearing on the state's Republican primary ballot. In the end, the US Supreme Court will force states to allow him to be on the ballot. In the meantime, there will be endless hyper-enthusiastic legacy media reporting and political career making for each state that engages in this fool's errand.

Attempts to exclude Trump from state ballots are based on the Fourteenth Amendment to the Constitution, which was ratified in 1866, largely in response to the Civil War and the oppression of formerly enslaved people. Section 3 prevents a person from holding office if they had "engaged in insurrection or rebellion against the same, or given aid or comfort to the enemies thereof" after previously taking an oath of office. This was designed to prevent confederate leaders from holding office again.

Organizations in these states are attempting to apply a federal law to keep Trump off state ballots based on a federal crime that he has not been convicted of, or even charged with. High profile go-nowhere cases like this are as good an opportunity as any to get media attention, score major political points, and attempt to forge a political career!

On other charges, in a previous chapter we discussed Manhattan district attorney Alvin Bragg's March 2023 indictment of Trump related to the Stormy Daniels nondisclosure agreement hush money. Review that section for details.

Remember when Trump was also impeached by the House and acquitted by the Senate for trying to expose Biden's corrupt dealing in Ukraine? Attempting to expose crimes against the people seems to come with significant risk, depending on who the criminals are. In the words of the great Yogi Berra, it's like déjà vu all over again.

> *It is the first responsibility of every citizen to question authority.*
>
> BENJAMIN FRANKLIN

Again, this case study is alive and changing daily. Your challenge is to get past the narrative blanket spread out by the media and locate sources that you can trust to provide accurate information.

The list of organizations below is provided as a starting point. Research each and find one or two that align with your principles. Get involved by supporting the missions of these organizations and encouraging those around you to participate as well.

Republican National Committee Action Center https://www.gop.com/action-center

Pacific Legal Foundation https://pacificlegal.org

Foundation for Government Accountability https://thefga.org

Public Interest Legal Foundation https://publicinterestlegal.org

Judicial Watch https://www.judicialwatch.org

Conservative Partnership Institute https://www.cpi.org/category/election-integrity-network

Election Integrity Network https://whoscounting.us

Heritage Foundation https://www.heritage.org/electionscorecard

National Center for Public Policy Research https://nationalcenter.org

PART 5

TOGETHER WE ARE THE SOLUTION

30

OVERTHROWING ABSURDITY WITH REALITY

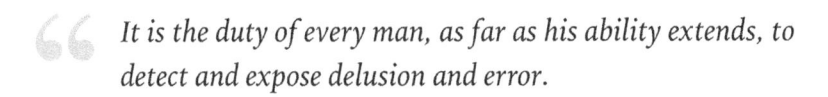

> *It is the duty of every man, as far as his ability extends, to detect and expose delusion and error.*
>
> THOMAS PAINE

> *It is your reaction to adversity, not the adversity itself, that determines how your life's story will develop.*
>
> DIETER F. UCHTDORF

Thank you for joining me on this journey! In this book I have attempted to share with you what I consider to be the essential truths that I have learned along the way. As I have said many times, we don't have to agree on everything. However, we must agree to be the resistance, the authentic resistance, not the fake resistance that supports and enables the wealthy ruling class.

We must accept our role in history as the resistance movement that successfully preserves a future providing the greatest opportunity for the greatest number of people.

Admittedly, you might be feeling a bit overwhelmed or disappointed that our country seems to have disintegrated so quickly. The same United States of America that celebrated its bicentennial in 1976 with over-the-top patriotism, with red, white, and blue and love of country splashed wall-to-wall, now often feels gray, angry, and dangerous. More and more Americans feel disenfranchised and shortchanged.

Feeling like a victim can rob you of hope. Being told that you are hated and aren't getting your fair share can make you despise those whom you are told are your enemies. The media circus makes it difficult to see beyond the approved narrative to access the truth about how we got here and who we can trust.

The truth must be told. We are blessed to live in an environment where we can thrive beyond our wildest dreams. We have the freedom that those in many other countries dream of. It is our responsibility not only to protect but to improve that environment, so future generations can experience even greater opportunities and achievements.

How do we preserve and enhance this environment to ensure that future generations have the same opportunity and more? We dedicate ourselves to accepting nothing less! We reach deep within ourselves to find the courage, commitment, and energy required to allow for nothing less!

It is time to arm ourselves with the truth as we politely and joyfully fight the good fight. Obviously not an actual physical fight or any type of violence, but the proverbial fight. How do we become effective resistance activists? By informing ourselves on the issues. By only consuming news, information, and opinion from trusted sources that support conservative values. By researching topics and events that can impact our families and our futures.

What steps can we take to promote conservative values and resist the accelerating decay of the principles that made this country the standard for freedom and opportunity for all? Step outside your front door and look around. Whatever you see, that is where you start. Be a role model of civility, peace, and joy. Tactfully and politely discuss current events with those around you. Share with them your beliefs on why conservative principles are the best hope for this country if it is to continue to provide freedom and economic opportunity to the greatest number of people. Focus on principles and not politicians or high-profile personalities.

As we learn and understand the truth and the importance of these essential conservative values, we must engage in discussion to sharpen our skills. This will enable us to gain the confidence and depth of understanding needed to effectively represent the conservative side of the dialogue. Nobody becomes the neighborhood chess champion by reading about chess strategies. They become the champion by engaging in matches hundreds of times and losing most of the early matches.

Speak out and be engaged with public schools, insisting that they focus on their original mission of functional education. We must demand an end to dividing our children into two groups—those who should be ashamed of who they are and those who are their victims. It is in the best interest of every member of society that our nation's children emerge from the classroom able to read, write, understand math and the sciences, and that they have a positive outlook on the future and their ability to succeed. This is vital to the future of our children and the country.

Take it slow. Your opportunity to influence is found with those who are already starting to question what they see in the media and on the political stage. They know things are moving very quickly in the wrong direction. Your biggest challenge may be in convincing them to reengage. They may have already checked out entirely and may have created filters around them that repel any information related to cultural or political conflict. Help them recognize that, yes, most of what they see can be very distressing, but there is hope and they can serve their community and future generations by bringing that hope to others who desperately need it.

Give others this book and your promise to study it together. Gift this book to as many people as you can! The light of truth and knowledge will begin to shine in their eyes as they read and understand it, and you can spend your time with them celebrating and acting on the truth instead of trying to convince them of the truth.

People are exhausted from the endless chaos. They are looking for logic, reason, and peace.

Reach out and help them find it!

We are in this together and we need to do everything we can to help the conservative movement continue to build momentum. We need to support organizations that promote conservative values and government accountability. We need to support them with our clicks, likes, comments, and money. They are the force that moves the needle of political affiliation in this country. They have the platforms, investigative teams, research analysts, and daily news and commentary on the events unfolding before our eyes. They don't have the big national sponsors that fund legacy media. These organizations need and deserve our support.

Do your research and decide which two or three you will support and rely on for news and information. Subscribe, follow on social media, and share their posts when they support your beliefs and engage our communities with civility, tact, peace, and joy.

I'm not asking you to give a thumbs-up to this mission. I'm asking you to fully engage in this mission as a resistance activist with your whole self. Your focus. Your energy. Your reputation. Your resources.

Let's apply all that we are and all that we can be to preserving opportunity and liberty for future generations. That's what is required to stop the ambitions of the ultra-wealthy ruling class that is slowly draining *we the people* of our shared heritage, identity, and principles.

> *Violence is not necessary to destroy a civilization. Each civilization dies from indifference toward the unique values which created it.*
>
> NICOLAS GOMEZ DAVILA

The following organizations are reliable sources of honest reporting and analysis:

Hillsdale College https://www.hillsdale.edu

Imprimus https://imprimis.hillsdale.edu

Daily Wire https://www.dailywire.com

PragerU https://www.prageru.com

The Epoch Times News https://www.theepochtimes.com

The Western Journal https://www.westernjournal.com/latest-news

The Federalist https://thefederalist.com

The Gateway Pundit https://www.thegatewaypundit.com

Town Hall https://townhall.com

Turning Point USA https://www.tpusa.com

The Atlas Society https://www.atlassociety.org

National Review https://www.nationalreview.com

John Stossel https://www.johnstossel.com

The Daily Signal https://www.dailysignal.com

Joe Pags https://joepags.com

Washington Times https://www.washingtontimes.com

Washington Examiner https://www.washingtonexaminer.com

The Russell Kirk Center https://kirkcenter.org

America First Legal https://aflegal.org

Heritage Foundation https://www.heritage.org/electionscorecard

Foundation for Government Accountability https://thefga.org

Pacific Legal Foundation https://pacificlegal.org

Public Interest Legal Foundation https://publicinterestlegal.org

Judicial Watch https://www.judicialwatch.org

Conservative Partnership Institute https://www.cpi.org/category/election-integrity-network

Election Integrity Network https://whoscounting.us

ABOUT THE AUTHOR

G.L. McGarvin is a software industry entrepreneur, compelling educator, and author of *Dethroning the Ruling Class: Rebuilding Community from the Rubble of Tyranny*.

Throughout his life G.L. has studied the world around him, especially culture and politics, to understand behaviors and motivations behind them. His relentless pursuit of clarity drives him to navigate complicated entanglements and discover the underlying truths.

As an entrepreneur, G.L. has established a reputation as a talented communicator on extremely complex topics. His role often includes establishing company brand by creating story-oriented content for marketing, sales, product launch, and customer enablement. "Clear, concise, and compelling" and "make the complex simple" are always his commitment.

G.L. has mastered his craft over the past three decades, bringing him success in both his personal and professional life. After living in and traveling to many places over the years, he and his wife now call Tulsa Oklahoma home.

NOTES

4. But I'm Not Racist, Sexist, or Homophobic?

1. Musa al-Gharbi, "How to Understand the Well-Being Gap between Liberals and Conservatives", American Affairs, March 21, 2023, https://glmcgarvin.com/4.1
2. Megan Brenan, "Media Confidence in U.S. Matches 2016 Record Low", Gallup, October 19, 2023, https://glmcgarvin.com/4.2

5. Complying with Reality

1. Russell Kirk, "Ten Conservative Principles", The Politics of Prudence (ISI Books, 1993), https://glmcgarvin.com/5.1

6. Opportunity for All

1. National Center for Education Statistics. (2023). Immediate College Enrollment Rate. Condition of Education. U.S. Department of Education, Institute of Education Sciences. Retrieved March 24, 2023, https://glmcgarvin.com/6.1
2. US Census Bureau, School Enrollment in the United States: October 2020 - Detailed Tables, Last Revised - May 23, 2022, https://glmcgarvin.com/6.2
3. Lorman Education Services, 39 Statistics that Prove the Value of Employee Training, September 1, 2021, https://glmcgarvin.com/6.3

7. Radically Generous

1. Thalia Beaty and Glenn Gamboa, "US charitable giving hit record in 2021 but inflation looms", AP News, June 21, 2022, https://glmcgarvin.com/7.1
2. AmeriCorps, Office of Research and Evaluation. (2021). Key Findings from the 2019 Current Population Survey: Civic Engagement and Volunteering Supplement. (by Laura Hanson Schlachter, Ph.D.). Washington, DC: Author, https://glmcgarvin.com/7.1
3. Ryan Messmore, "Does Advocating Limited Government Mean Abandoning the Poor?", The Heritage Foundation, May 4, 2011, https://glmcgarvin.com/7.3

NOTES

8. Engaged in Community

1. Constitution of the United States, September 17, 1787, https://glmcgarvin.com/8.1
2. Centers for Disease Control and Prevention, New CDC data illuminate youth mental health threats during the COVID-19 pandemic, Last Revised March 31, 2022, https://glmcgarvin.com/8.2
3. The Joint Economic Committee of the US Congress, An Overview of Social Capital in America, June 1, 2021, https://glmcgarvin.com/8.3
4. American Enterprise Institute, Sen. Mike Lee on localism and social capital | LIVE STREAM, July, 12, 2017, https://glmcgarvin.com/8.4
5. The U.S. Department of Health & Human Services, New Surgeon General Advisory Raises Alarm about the Devastating Impact of the Epidemic of Loneliness and Isolation in the United States, May 3, 2023, https://glmcgarvin.com/8.5
6. Mike Pence, "Renewing Our Commitment to Limited Government", The Heritage Foundation, June 7, 2004, https://glmcgarvin.com/8.6
7. William F. Buckley Jr., "Our Mission Statement", National Review, November 19, 1955, https://glmcgarvin.com/8.7

9. Partners in K–12 Education

1. Stanley Kurtz, "DeSantis's Triumph, Kemp's Test", National Review, December 20, 2022, https://glmcgarvin.com/9.1

10. Protecting Individual Rights

1. Ayn Rand, "Textbook of Americanism", 1946, https://glmcgarvin.com/10.1
2. National Archives, Declaration of Independence: A Transcription, July 4, 1776, https://glmcgarvin.com/10.2
3. National Archives, The Bill of Rights: A Transcription, Ratified December 15, 1791, https://glmcgarvin.com/10.3

11. Holding Government Accountable

1. Open the Books, Every Dime. Online. In Real Time. Join the Transparency Revolution!, https://glmcgarvin.com/11.1
2. Jim DeMint, "Tom Coburn, a Man of Integrity", National Review, March 31, 2020, https://glmcgarvin.com/11.2
3. Senator Rand Paul, "The Waste Report: Waste in the U.S. Government", December 2023, https://glmcgarvin.com/11.3

NOTES

4. Statista, Total number of government employees in the United States from 1982 to 2022, June 2023, https://glmcgarvin.com/11.4
5. Office of Management and Budget (OMB) and the Office of Personnel Management (OPM), Federal Workforce Statistics Sources: OPM and OMB, June 28, 2022, https://glmcgarvin.com/11.5
6. Congressional Research Service, Federal Employees' Retirement System: Summary of Recent Trends January 23, 2004 – December 12, 2023, Last Updated December 12, 2023, https://glmcgarvin.com/11.6
7. Statista, Forecast of the number of military retirees in the United States for fiscal years 2023 to 2033, May 2023, https://glmcgarvin.com/11.7
8. US Census Bureau, Annual Survey of Public Pensions: 2020, July 2012, https://glmcgarvin.com/11.8
9. U.S. Social Security Administration, Office of Retirement and Disability Policy, Office of Research, Evaluation, and Statistics, Annual Statistical Supplement, 2020, https://glmcgarvin.com/11.9
10. U.S. Social Security Administration, Office of Retirement and Disability Policy, Office of Research, Evaluation, and Statistics, Annual Statistical Supplement, 2020, https://glmcgarvin.com/11.10
11. G. Dautovic, "Straight Talk On Welfare Statistics", Fortunly, October 11,2023, https://glmcgarvin.com/11.11
12. US Census Bureau, Age and Sex Composition in the United States: 2019, April 2020, https://glmcgarvin.com/11.12

12. (In)Effective Use of Taxpayer Funds

1. Written by Anne Field; edited by Jasmine Suarez, "What caused the Great Recession? Understanding the key factors that led to one of the worst economic downturns in US history", Business Insider, Aug 8, 2022, https://glmcgarvin.com/12.1
2. Mark J. Perry, "The Lesson of Economic Damage From "Taxing the Rich" With the Punitive Luxury Tax in the 1990s", American Enterprise Institute, September 10, 2011, https://glmcgarvin.com/12.2
3. NBC New York, "Major Crimes Up 38% in NYC So Far This Year, NYPD Says", February 1, 2022, https://glmcgarvin.com/12.3
4. Alvin L. Bragg, Jr. District Attorney County of New York, "Achieving Fairness and Safety", January 3, 2022, https://glmcgarvin.com/12.4
5. Melissa Klein, "NYC convictions plummet, downgraded charges surge under Manhattan DA Bragg", New York Post, November 26, 2022, https://glmcgarvin.com/12.5
6. Charles Stimson and Zack Smith, "Progressive Prosecutors Sabotage the Rule of Law, Raise Crime Rates, and Ignore Victims", The Heritage Foundation, October 29, 2020, https://glmcgarvin.com/12.6

NOTES

7. Lee Ohanian, "Why San Francisco Is Nearly The Most Crime-Ridden City In The US", Hoover Institute, November 9, 2021, https://glmcgarvin.com/12.7
8. Gayle Ong, "Car break-ins increased 750% in San Francisco's tourist spots", KRON Channel 4 News, San Francisco, CA, Jun 27, 2021, https://glmcgarvin.com/12.8
9. Summer Lin, "Elon Musk, others claim San Francisco crime out of control. But the numbers tell a different story", Los Angeles Times, April 7, 2023, https://glmcgarvin.com/12.9
10. Al Yoon, "Flagship hotels are becoming collateral damage in San Francisco's office mess", Business Insider, Jun 6, 2023, https://glmcgarvin.com/12.10
11. San Francisco Chamber of Commerce, "New Polling Shows That 8 Out of 10 Residents Believe Crime Has Gotten Worse in San Francisco; Vast Majority Support Increasing Police Officers and Expanding Police Work", June 23, 2021, https://glmcgarvin.com/12.11
12. The University of California, San Francisco Benioff Homelessness and Housing Initiative (BHHI), "California Statewide Study Investigates Causes and Impacts of Homelessness", June 20, 2023, https://glmcgarvin.com/12.12
13. Bureau of Economic Analysis, "Gross Domestic Product, Fourth Quarter 2022 and Year 2022 (Advance Estimate)", January 26, 2023, https://glmcgarvin.com/12.13
14. Federal Reserve Economic Data (FRED), "Federal government current tax receipts (W006RC1A027NBEA)", updated September 28, 2023, https://glmcgarvin.com/12.16
15. Federal Reserve Economic Data (FRED), "Federal Government Current Expenditures (AFEXPND)", accessed January 27, 2024, https://glmcgarvin.com/12.17
16. US Debt Clock, UsDebtClock.org, https://glmcgarvin.com/12.14
17. Thomas Grennes, Mehmet Caner, and Fritzi Koehler-Geib, "Finding The Tipping Point -- When Sovereign Debt Turns Bad", World Bank Group, June 22, 2013, https://glmcgarvin.com/12.15
18. Federal Reserve Economic Data (FRED), "Federal Debt: Total Public Debt as Percent of Gross Domestic Product (GFDEGDQ188S)", accessed January 27, 2024, https://glmcgarvin.com/12.18

13. Carefully Orchestrated Chaos

1. Jack Davis, "'Black Lives Matter' Co-Founder Resigns Amid Scandal", The Western Journal, May 28, 2021, https://glmcgarvin.com/13.1

14. Influential People Know the Game

1. Wikipedia, "List of largest companies in the United States by revenue", Accessed November 2023, https://glmcgarvin.com/14.1
2. Committee on the Judiciary and the Select Subcommittee on the Weaponization of the Federal Government U.S. House of Representatives, "FBI WHISTLEBLOWER TESTIMONY HIGHLIGHTS GOVERNMENT ABUSE, MISALLOCATION OF RESOURCES, AND RETALIATION", May 18, 2023, https://glmcgarvin.com/14.2
3. Douglas Blair, "12 People Canceled by the Left After Expressing Conservative Views", The Heritage Foundation, Sep 20, 2021, https://glmcgarvin.com/14.3
4. Briana Bierschbach and Brooks Johnson, "MyPillow is auctioning off equipment after retailers pull its products", Star Tribune Minneapolis, MN, July 10, 2023, https://glmcgarvin.com/14.4
5. Jack Phillips, "Goya CEO Says He Won't Apologize After His Praise for Trump Sparks Boycott", The Epoch Times, July 10, 2020, https://glmcgarvin.com/14.5
6. Andrea Peyser, "Mumford & Sons banjo player and others stand up to cancel culture", New York Post, June 25, 2021, https://glmcgarvin.com/14.6

15. Big Tech: Both Maestro and Tool

1. Wikipedia, "Big Tech", Accessed November 2023, https://glmcgarvin.com/15.1
2. Emma-Jo Morris and Gabrielle Fonrouge, "Smoking-gun email reveals how Hunter Biden introduced Ukrainian businessman to VP dad", New York Post, October 14, 2020, https://glmcgarvin.com/15.2
3. Sohrab Ahmari, "Media disgraceful in trying to suppress Post's Hunter Biden reporting", New York Post, December 10, 2020, https://glmcgarvin.com/15.3
4. David Harsanyi, "How the media covered up the Hunter Biden story — until after the election", New York Post, December 11, 2020, https://glmcgarvin.com/15.4
5. Public Statement on the Hunter Biden Emails, October 19, 2020, https://glmcgarvin.com/15.5
6. Committee on the Judiciary, Select Subcommittee on the Weaponization of the Federal Government, and Permanent Select Committee on Intelligence U.S. House of Representatives, "Republicans Release Report on How Senior Intelligence Community Officials and the Biden Campaign Worked to Mislead American Voters", May 10, 2023, https://glmcgarvin.com/15.6

7. Commission on Presidential Debates, "Presidential Debate at Belmont University in Nashville, Tennessee", October 22, 2020, https://glmcgarvin.com/15.7
8. Johnathan Jones, "Poll: 17% of Biden Voters Would Have Abandoned Him if They Knew About Stories the Media Censored", The Western Journal, November 24, 2020, https://glmcgarvin.com/15.8
9. Paul Sperry, "Shock Poll: 8 in 10 Think Biden Laptop Cover-Up Changed Election", Tipp Insights, August 24, 2022, https://glmcgarvin.com/15.9
10. Matt Taibbi, Capsule Summaries of all Twitter Files Threads to Date, With Links and a Glossary, January 4, 2023, https://glmcgarvin.com/15.10
11. Petr Svab, "The Endgame of Big Tech Is Corporate Socialism, Liberal Studies Scholar Says", The Epoch Times, October 15, 2019, https://glmcgarvin.com/15.11
12. Ari Levy, "The most liberal and conservative tech companies, ranked by employees' political donations", CNBC, July 2, 2020, https://glmcgarvin.com/15.12

16. Censorship Incorporated

1. U.S. Department of Homeland Security, "Statement by Secretary Jeh Johnson on the Designation of Election Infrastructure as a Critical Infrastructure Subsector", January 6, 2017, https://glmcgarvin.com/16.1
2. Maggie Miller, "Cyber agency beefing up disinformation, misinformation team", The Hill, November 10, 2021, https://glmcgarvin.com/16.2
3. U.S. House of Representatives Judiciary Committee and the Select Subcommittee on the Weaponization of the Federal Government, "New Report Reveals CISA Tried to Cover Up Censorship Practices", June 26, 2023, https://glmcgarvin.com/16.3
4. United States District Court Western District of Louisiana Monroe Division, Case No. 3:22-CV-01213, State of Missouri, ET AL. Vs Joseph R. Biden Jr., ET AL., July 4, 2023, https://glmcgarvin.com/16.4
5. Missouri v. Biden Complaint — Document #1, Docket Number: 3:22-cv-01213, May 5th, 2022, https://glmcgarvin.com/16.5
6. Memordandum in Support of Defendants' Motion to Stay Preliminary Injunction Pending Appeal and, Alternatively, for Administrative Stay, Civil Action No. 22-cv-1213, July 6, 2023, https://glmcgarvin.com/16.6
7. Mike Benz, "DHS Censorship Agency Had Strange First Mission: Banning Speech That Casts Doubt On 'Red Mirage, Blue Shift' Election Events", Foundation for Freedom Online, November 9, 2022, https://glmcgarvin.com/16.7
8. Jim Geraghty, "Are You Ready for the DHS 'Disinformation Governance Board'?", National Review, April 28, 2022, https://glmcgarvin.com/16.8

NOTES

9. Caroline Downey, "DHS Secretary Pleads Ignorance on Disinformation Czar's Background", National Review, May 4, 2022, https://glmcgarvin.com/16.9
10. Diana Glebova, "DHS Decides There Is 'No Need' for Disinformation Governance Board", National Review, July 18, 2022, https://glmcgarvin.com/16.10
11. C. Douglas Golden, "Whistleblower Documents Show DHS Secretary Lied About 'Disinformation Board'; Here Was Its True Purpose", The Western Journal, June 21, 2022, https://glmcgarvin.com/16.11
12. Select Subcommittee on the Weaponization of the Federal Government, https://glmcgarvin.com/16.12
13. Chairman Jordan's Opening Statement at the Select Subcommittee on the Weaponization of the Federal Government Hearing, February 9, 2023, https://glmcgarvin.com/16.13
14. House of Representatives Judiciary Committee Reports, https://glmcgarvin.com/16.14
15. Petr Svab, "How NewsGuard Became the Establishment Guard Against Independent Media", The Epoch Times, August 16, 2023, https://glmcgarvin.com/16.15
16. Ben Shapiro, "Meet The Company Trying To Control Your Mind", Daily Wire, Accessed February 17, 2024, https://glmcgarvin.com/16.16
17. Audrey Walden, "CFO Jimmy Patronis: Florida is Prepared to Protect Florida Businesses from NewsGuard", MyFloridaCFO, Sep 20, 2023, https://glmcgarvin.com/16.17
18. Joseph Vazquez, "STUDY: NewsGuard Ratings System STILL Heavily Biased in Favor of Left-Wing Media Outlets", Media Research Center, January 6th, 2023, https://glmcgarvin.com/16.18
19. Bill Pan, "Teachers Union Promotes 'Anti-Misinformation' Tool, Sparking Left-Wing Bias Concerns", The Epoch Times, January 28, 2020, https://glmcgarvin.com/16.19
20. Leif Le Mahieu, "Ben Shapiro Details The Global Entities Working To 'Demonetize And Deplatform' Conservative Voices", Daily Wire, August 1, 2023, https://glmcgarvin.com/16.20
21. U.S. House of Representatives Judiciary Committee, "Chairman Jordan Subpoenas GARM and WFA for Documents and Communications", May 5, 2023, https://glmcgarvin.com/16.21
22. Trusted News Initiative, "What is the TNI", BBC, Accessed February 17, 2024, https://glmcgarvin.com/16.22
23. Roman, Balmakov, "New COVID Vaccine Bombshell Emerges", Facts Matter, Epoch TV, July 25, 2023, https://glmcgarvin.com/16.23

NOTES

17. The Wealth Magnet of Public Office

1. Anna Massoglia, "Clinton Foundation's revenue hit 15-year low after 2016 presidential election", OpenSecrets, December 13, 2018, https://glmcgarvin.com/17.1
2. Stephen Braun, Eileen Sullivan, "Many donors to Clinton Foundation met with her at State", Associated Press, August 23, 2016, https://glmcgarvin.com/17.2
3. Zachary Stieber, "Millions Missing From Top Biden Super PAC in Financial Disclosures", August 23, 2023, https://glmcgarvin.com/17.3
4. Dave Levinthal, "'Conflicted Congress': Key findings from Insider's five-month investigation into federal lawmakers' personal finances", Business Insider, December 17, 2021, https://glmcgarvin.com/17.4
5. OpenSecrets, "Richest Members of Congress, 2018", https://glmcgarvin.com/17.5

18. Never Let a Crisis Go to Waste!

1. Ballotpedia, "Inflation Reduction Act of 2022", https://glmcgarvin.com/18.1
2. Pandemic Oversight, "The Six Laws that Funded Pandemic Relief Programs", November 6, 2023, https://glmcgarvin.com/18.2
3. Congressional Research Service, "American Recovery and Reinvestment Act of 2009 (P.L. 111-5): Summary and Legislative History", April 20, 2009, https://glmcgarvin.com/18.3
4. Tal Axelrod, "Senate Democrats pass climate, tax and health care bill after marathon voting session", ABC News, August 7, 2022, https://glmcgarvin.com/18.4
5. Joe Biden, "Remarks by President Biden on the Anniversary of the Inflation Reduction Act", The White House, August 16, 2022, https://glmcgarvin.com/18.5
6. Micah Morrison, "John Podesta: The Scandal Master Returns", Judicial Watch, October 24, 2022, https://glmcgarvin.com/18.6
7. USA Facts, "How much does the government spend and where does the money go? How does this affect the national debt?", Accessed January 2024, https://glmcgarvin.com/18.7
8. Congressional Budget Office, CBO Report: Supplemental Appropriations Enacted Since Fiscal Year 2000 (as of December 29, 2022), January 25, 2023, https://glmcgarvin.com/18.8
9. Congressional Research Service, "Appropriations Status Table: FY2023", https://glmcgarvin.com/18.9
10. Department of the Treasury, "Historical Debt Outstanding", accessed January 28, 2024, https://glmcgarvin.com/18.10

NOTES

19. The Fed: Enabling Outrageous Spending and Unsustainable Debt

1. Fitch Ratings, "Fitch Downgrades the United States' Long-Term Ratings to 'AA+' from 'AAA'; Outlook Stable", August 1, 2023, https://glmcgarvin.com/19.1
2. Peter G. Peterson Foundation, "What is the National Debt Today?", https://glmcgarvin.com/19.2
3. Department of the Treasury, "What is the national debt?", https://glmcgarvin.com/19.3
4. Federal Reserve Economic Data (FRED), "Federal Debt Held by Private Investors", https://glmcgarvin.com/19.4
5. Federal Reserve Economic Data (FRED), "Federal Debt Held by Federal Reserve Banks", https://glmcgarvin.com/19.5
6. Federal Reserve Economic Data (FRED), "Federal Debt Held by Foreign and International Investors", https://glmcgarvin.com/19.6
7. Department of the Treasury, "Major Foreign Holders of Treasury Securities", March 15, 2023, https://glmcgarvin.com/19.7
8. United States Government Accountability Office, "Financial Audit Bureau of The Fiscal Service's FY 2021 and FY 2020 Schedules Of Federal Debt", November 2021, https://glmcgarvin.com/19.8
9. Federal Reserve Economic Data (FRED), "Assets: Total Assets: Total Assets (Less Eliminations from Consolidation)", https://glmcgarvin.com/19.9
10. William J. Luther, "How the Federal Reserve Literally Makes Money", CATO Institute, June 10, 2020, https://glmcgarvin.com/19.10
11. World Bank Group, "Finding The Tipping Point -- When Sovereign Debt Turns Bad", August 2010, https://glmcgarvin.com/19.11
12. EJ Antoni, "This $6 Trillion Problem Threatens To Push Inflation Even Higher", The Heritage Foundation, April 12, 2023, https://glmcgarvin.com/19.12
13. Federal Reserve Economic Data (FRED), "Money Supply", Accessed January 28, 2024, https://glmcgarvin.com/19.14
14. Federal Reserve Economic Data (FRED), "Gross Domestic Product (GDP)", Accessed January 27, 2024, https://glmcgarvin.com/19.15
15. Federal Reserve Economic Data (FRED), "Consumer Price Index for All Urban Consumers: All Items in U.S. City Average (CPIAUCNS)", Accessed January 28, 2024, https://glmcgarvin.com/19.16
16. Truth in Accounting, "Too much money chasing too few goods (and services)?", July 7, 2021, https://glmcgarvin.com/19.13
17. Federal Reserve Economic Data (FRED), "Money Supply", Accessed January 28, 2024, https://glmcgarvin.com/19.17
18. Federal Reserve Economic Data (FRED), "Consumer Price Index for All Urban Consumers: All Items in U.S. City Average (CPIAUCNS)", Accessed

NOTES

January 28, 2024, https://glmcgarvin.com/19.18

24. The Kings of Astroturfing: Fake Grassroots Movements

1. David Boaz, "California's High-Speed Train Has Done a Lot More Good for Big Consultants than for Taxpayers or Riders", CATO Institute, April 29, 2019, https://glmcgarvin.com/24.1
2. Jack Elbaum, "California's imaginary solar-powered bullet train", Washington Examiner, June 16, 2023, https://glmcgarvin.com/24.2
3. Pierre Kory, "How to Create a Fake News Cycle", The Epoch Times, July, 12, 2023, https://glmcgarvin.com/24.3
4. Matt McGregor and Jan Jekielek, "IN-DEPTH: Online Censorship Corrupts the American Spirit of Individual, Free Thought: Journalist Matt Taibbi", July 19, 2023, https://glmcgarvin.com/24.4

25. COVID Response – Epic Power Consolidation

1. Centers for Disease Control and Prevention (CDC), "United States COVID-19 Hospitalizations, Deaths, Emergency Department (ED) Visits, and Test Positivity by Geographic Area", https://glmcgarvin.com/25.1
2. Centers for Disease Control and Prevention (CDC), "Deaths by Select Demographic and Geographic Characteristics Provisional Death Counts for COVID-19", https://glmcgarvin.com/25.2
3. Shannon Pettypiece, Heidi Przybyla and Lauren Egan, "Biden announces sweeping vaccine mandates affecting millions of workers",NBC News, September 9, 2021, https://glmcgarvin.com/25.3
4. McKenzie Beard, "Covid is no longer mainly a pandemic of the unvaccinated. Here's why.", The Washington Post, November 23, 2022, https://glmcgarvin.com/25.4
5. Nicole Napoli, "Which COVID Vaccine You Get Can Impact Myocarditis Risk", American College of Cardiology, November 7, 2022, https://glmcgarvin.com/25.5
6. Adam Andrzejewski, "BREAKING: Fauci's Net Worth Soared To $12.6+ Million During Pandemic – Up $5 Million (2019-2021)", OpenTheBooks Substack, September 28, 2022, https://glmcgarvin.com/25.6
7. Andrew Follett, "Why U.S. Scientists Lied about the Possibility of a Covid Lab Leak", National Review, July 27, 2023, https://glmcgarvin.com/25.7
8. Gabrielle M. Etzel, "House pandemic panel subpoenas author of COVID-19 origins paper 'prompted by' Fauci", Washington Examiner, June 23, 2023, https://glmcgarvin.com/25.8
9. Roman, Balmakov, "Exposing the FDA's Orwellian Lie About Ivermectin", Facts Matter, Epoch TV, June 5, 2023, https://glmcgarvin.com/25.9

NOTES

10. Mary Margaret Olohan, "Doctors Accuse FDA Of Unlawfully Blocking Their Ability To Treat COVID-19 Patients With Ivermectin", Daily Wire, June 2, 2022, https://glmcgarvin.com/25.10
11. David R. Henderson, Charles L. Hooper, "The FDA's War Against the Truth on Ivermectin", American Institute of Economic Research, October 18, 2021, https://glmcgarvin.com/25.11
12. U.S. Small Business Administration, "COVID-19 Pandemic EIDL and PPP Loan Fraud Landscape", June 27, 2023, https://glmcgarvin.com/25.12
13. U.S. Department of Labor Office of Inspector General, "Potentially Fraudulent Unemployment Insurance Payments in High-Risk Areas Increased to $45.6 Billion Report Number: 19-22-005-03-315", September 21, 2022, https://glmcgarvin.com/25.13
14. Luke Rosiak, "Thousands Of Pandemic Unemployment Claims Listed The Names Of Still-Employed Government Workers, Senator Says", Daily Wire, January 30, 2023, https://glmcgarvin.com/25.14
15. GovTrack.us, "H.R. 6074 (116th): Coronavirus Preparedness and Response Supplemental Appropriations Act, 2020", March 6, 2020, https://glmcgarvin.com/25.15
16. GovTrack.us, "H.R. 6201 (116th): Families First Coronavirus Response Act", May 14, 2020, https://glmcgarvin.com/25.16
17. GovTrack.us, "H.R. 748 (116th): H.R. 748: Coronavirus Aid, Relief, and Economic Security Act", March 26, 2020, https://glmcgarvin.com/25.17
18. GovTrack.us, "H.R. 266 (116th): Paycheck Protection Program and Health Care Enhancement Act", April 24, 2020, https://glmcgarvin.com/25.18
19. GovTrack.us, "H.R. 133 (116th): H.R. 133: Consolidated Appropriations Act, 2021 [Including Coronavirus Stimulus & Relief]", December 22, 2020, https://glmcgarvin.com/25.19
20. Ballotpedia, "American Rescue Plan Act of 2021", March 11, 2021, https://glmcgarvin.com/25.20
21. U.S. Bureau of Labor Statistics, "Unemployment rate rises to record high 14.7 percent in April 2020", May 13, 2020, https://glmcgarvin.com/25.21
22. World Economic Forum, "34% of America's small businesses are still closed due to COVID-19. Here's why it matters", May 5, 2021, https://glmcgarvin.com/25.22
23. Bureau of Economic Analysis (BEA), Personal Saving Rate, Accessed March 16, 2024, https://glmcgarvin.com/25.23
24. Jeff Frantz, "New research finds that pandemic learning loss impacted whole communities, regardless of student race or income", Harvard University Center for Education Policy, May 11, 2023, https://glmcgarvin.com/25.24
25. National Center for Education Statistics (NCES), "Reading and mathematics scores decline during COVID-19 pandemic", September 1, 2022, https://glmcgarvin.com/25.25

NOTES

26. Centers for Disease Control and Prevention (CDC), "New CDC data illuminate youth mental health threats during the COVID-19 pandemic", March 31, 2022, https://glmcgarvin.com/25.26
27. National Center for Education Statistics (NCES), "More than 80 Percent of U.S. Public Schools Report Pandemic Has Negatively Impacted Student Behavior and Socio-Emotional Development", July 6, 2022, https://glmcgarvin.com/25.27
28. Brian D. Ray, Ph.D., "Homeschooling: The Research" National Home Education Research Institute (NHERI), February 9, 2024, https://glmcgarvin.com/25.28
29. National Student Clearinghouse Research Center, "Fall 2021 Enrollment #2 (10.21)", November 10, 2021, https://glmcgarvin.com/25.29
30. Reyes-Portillo, J. A., Masia Warner, C., Kline, E. A., Bixter, M. T., Chu, B. C., Miranda, R., Nadeem, E., Nickerson, A., Ortin Peralta, A., Reigada, L., Rizvi, S. L., Roy, A. K., Shatkin, J., Kalver, E., Rette, D., Denton, E., & Jeglic, E. L. (2022). "The Psychological, Academic, and Economic Impact of COVID-19 on College Students in the Epicenter of the Pandemic. Emerging Adulthood, 10(2), 473-490.", February 8, 2022, https://glmcgarvin.com/25.30
31. Centers for Disease Control and Prevention (CDC), "U.S. Overdose Deaths In 2021 Increased Half as Much as in 2020 – But Are Still Up 15%", May 11, 2022, https://glmcgarvin.com/25.31
32. Eran Bendavid, Bianca Mulaney, Neeraj Sood, Soleil Shah, Emilia Ling, Rebecca Bromley-Dulfano, Cara Lai, Zoe Weissberg, Rodrigo Saavedra-Walker, Jim Tedrow, Dona Tversky, Andrew Bogan, Thomas Kupiec, Daniel Eichner, Ribhav Gupta, John P.A. Ioannidis, Jay Bhattacharya, "COVID-19 Antibody Seroprevalence in Santa Clara County, California", April 17, 2020, https://glmcgarvin.com/25.32
33. Dr. Jay Bhattacharya, Dr. Sunetra Gupta and Dr. Martin Kulldorff, "Great Barrington Declaration", October 4, 2020, https://glmcgarvin.com/25.33
34. "The Man Who Talked Back: Jay Bhattacharya On the Fight against COVID Lockdowns", Interview of Jay Bhattacharya. Conducted by Peter Robinson, May 18, 2023, https://glmcgarvin.com/25.34

26. Donald Trump Disruptor-in-Chief

1. "Trump Administration Accomplishments As of January 2021", The White House, January 2021, https://glmcgarvin.com/26.1
2. David Corn, "A Veteran Spy Has Given the FBI Information Alleging a Russian Operation to Cultivate Donald Trump", Mother Jones and the Foundation for National Progress, October 31, 2016, https://glmcgarvin.com/26.2

NOTES

3. U.S. Senate Committee on the Judiciary, "Chairman Graham Releases Newly Declassified Summary Indicating FBI Knew Steele Dossier Source Was Likely a Russian Agent, Had Been Under U.S. Counterintelligence Investigation.", September 24, 2020, https://glmcgarvin.com/26.3
4. Editorial Board, "Eyes turn to Hillary Clinton, not Trump in the Russiagate scandal", New York Post, February 13, 2022, https://glmcgarvin.com/26.4
5. Special Counsel John Durham's 316-page report on the origins of the FBI's Crossfire Hurricane investigation can be accessed on the National Review website, https://glmcgarvin.com/26.5
6. Jerry Dunleavy, "Final Trump declassification request to DOJ blocked after he left White House", Washington Examiner, July 20, 2022, https://glmcgarvin.com/26.6
7. U.S. House of Representatives Committee on the Judiciary and the Select Subcommittee on the Weaponization of the Federal Government, "FBI Whistleblower Testimony Highlights Government Abuse, Misallocation of Resources, and Retaliation", May 18, 2023, https://glmcgarvin.com/26.7
8. Ian Haworth, "Where's the outrage over Biden's quid pro quo?", Washington Examiner, October 17, 2022, https://glmcgarvin.com/26.8
9. C. Douglas Golden, "Top Trump Enemy Has Staggering Assessment After Indictment Is Unsealed, Leaves CNN Viewers Stunned", The Western Journal, April 5, 2023, https://glmcgarvin.com/26.9
10. Victor Davis Hanson, "Trumpology", The Epoch Times, June 2 2022, https://glmcgarvin.com/26.10

27. The January 6 "Insurrection"

1. Steven Kovac, "Voter Fraud Convictions Challenge Narrative of Secure Elections", The Epoch Times, January 13, 2024, https://glmcgarvin.com/27.1
2. John R. Lott Jr., "America the Outlier: Voter Photo IDs Are the Rule in Europe and Elsewhere", Real Clear Investigations, June 1, 2021, https://glmcgarvin.com/27.2
3. Nathaniel Rakich, Jasmine Mithani, "What Absentee Voting Looked Like In All 50 States", FiveThirtyEight ABC News Internet Ventures, February 9, 2021, https://glmcgarvin.com/27.3
4. Crime Prevention Research Center, "Rasmussen Reports Survey: Most voters think that cheating affected the outcome of the 2020 presidential election", March 15, 2022, https://glmcgarvin.com/27.4
5. John McCormack, "Sorry, Trump Lost", National Review, May 25, 2023, https://glmcgarvin.com/27.5
6. Domenico Montanaro, "President-Elect Joe Biden Hits 80 Million Votes In Year Of Record Turnout", National Public Radio (NPR), November 25, 2020, https://glmcgarvin.com/27.6

NOTES

7. John R. Lott Jr., New Peer-Reviewed Research Finds Evidence of 2020 Voter Fraud, Real Clear Politics, March 28, 2022, https://glmcgarvin.com/27.7
8. Senate Committee on Homeland Security and Government Affairs and the Senate Committee on Rules and Administration, "Security Failures at the United States Capitol on January 6, 2021", June 8, 2021, https://glmcgarvin.com/27.8
9. "Jan. 6 Timeline: Riot at the Capitol", The Wall Street Journal, June 9, 2022, https://glmcgarvin.com/27.9
10. Joseph M. Hanneman, "EXCLUSIVE: Jan. 6 Police Radio Tapes Reveal Orders to Use Force on Early Crowd", The Epoch Times, August 16, 2023, https://glmcgarvin.com/27.10
11. Joseph M. Hanneman, "Use of Grenades, Projectiles, Tear Gas on Jan. 6 Only Enraged Crowd: Police Officer", The Epoch Times, January 26, 2023, https://glmcgarvin.com/27.11
12. Joseph M. Hanneman, "Prosecutor Admits DC Police Officers Acted as Provocateurs at US Capitol on Jan. 6", The Epoch Times, March 24, 2023, https://glmcgarvin.com/27.12
13. Joseph M. Hanneman, "At Least 50 Undercover Officers and Informants Monitored Proud Boys, Jan. 6 Crowds, New Court Filing Says", The Epoch Times, April 10, 2023, https://glmcgarvin.com/27.13

28. January 6 Scorched Earth Aftermath

1. NPR Staff, "The Jan. 6 attack: The cases behind the biggest criminal investigation in U.S. history", National Public Radio (NPR), Updated March 15, 2024, https://glmcgarvin.com/28.1
2. Joseph D. Mcbride, "EMERGENCY REQUEST TO INVESTIGATE MISTREATMENT OF PRE-TRIAL DETAINEES FROM THE JANUARY 6, 2021 U.S. CAPITOL PROTEST", August 3, 2021, https://glmcgarvin.com/28.2
3. Office of Congresswoman Marjorie Taylor Greene, "Unusually Cruel – an Eyewitness Report from Inside the DC Jail", December 2021, https://glmcgarvin.com/28.3
4. Daniel Chaitin, "FBI, Capitol Police Shrugged Off 'Credible Threats' Before Jan. 6, Says Watchdog", Daily Wire, February 28 2023, https://glmcgarvin.com/28.4
5. Ken Dilanian, Ryan J. Reilly, "Top Jan. 6 investigator says FBI, other agencies could have done more to repel Capitol mob had they acted on intel", NBC News, January 31, 2023, https://glmcgarvin.com/28.5
6. Ryan Saavedra, "Top January 6 Investigator: FBI, Other Federal Agencies Could Have Stopped Riot If They Did Their Jobs", Daily Wire, January 31, 2023, https://glmcgarvin.com/28.6

NOTES

7. Senate Committee on Homeland Security and Government Affairs and the Senate Committee on Rules and Administration, "Security Failures at the United States Capitol on January 6, 2021", June 8, 2021, https://glmcgarvin.com/28.7
8. Lorri Wickenhauser, "Tucker Carlson Releases Redo of Explosive Jan. 6 Interview with Former Capitol Police Chief That Fox Never Aired", The Western Journal, August 11, 2023, https://glmcgarvin.com/28.8

29. Trump Indictments—Punishing the Resistance

1. Janice Hisle, "Trump Indicted Over Efforts to Challenge 2020 Election Results", The Epoch Times, August 2, 2023, https://glmcgarvin.com/29.1
2. John R. Lott Jr., "New Peer-Reviewed Research Finds Evidence of 2020 Voter Fraud", Real Clear Politics, March 28, 2022, https://glmcgarvin.com/29.2
3. Brittany Bernstein, "Communications Show Trump Team Was Involved in Georgia Voting-System Breach: Report", National Review, August 13, 2023, https://glmcgarvin.com/29.3

Made in the USA
Monee, IL
17 May 2024